Superbrands

AN INSIGHT INTO 65 OF THE WORLD'S SUPERBRANDS
VOLUME III

This book is dedicated to Daniel and Rachel

creative & COMMERCIAL

Editor-in-Chief
Marcel Knobil

Managing Editor
Julie Apfel

Designer
Adam Selwyn

© 1998 Creative & Commercial Communications Ltd

Published by Creative & Commercial Communications Ltd
14 Kendall Place
London W1H 3AH

Tel: 0171 935 4343
Fax: 0171 486 9704

Printed in Hong Kong

ISBN 0-9528153-3-8

Marcel Knobil

**Chairperson, Creative & Commercial Communications
Chairperson, Superbrands Council**

Research conducted by Infratest Burke on behalf of **SUPERBRANDS** in past years has demonstrated the power of Superbrands. The following are examples of just some of the results.

Consumers will clearly pay a significant premium for branded products. Shoppers claim they will pay a 32% premium, on average, for typical branded goods. Significant cuts in the price of own label are needed to motivate a switch away from brands, yet around 40% claim they wouldn't switch, whatever the price.

Respondents were more than twice as likely to buy Sony than the next most popular competitive brand, and almost three times as likely to purchase McVitie's chocolate biscuits than its main competitor.

All Superbrands researched were felt to be more caring, trustworthy and reliable than the Conservative Party, the Labour Party and the Royal Family.

Respondents were asked to to rank well known personalities (including Eric Cantona, Liam Gallagher, Pamela Anderson, Prince Charles and Tony Blair) in order of preference as guests at their own wedding. The Andrex puppy was added to the list in order to establish the strength of appeal of a Superbrand. The Andrex puppy was top choice!

Superbrands do not sustain their status through chance. Inspiration, consistency, skillful strategy, and exceptional creativity are key ingredients. In the years which I have interrogated brands, these ingredients are most commonly found in Superbrands.

The brands featured in this book are selected from a list of brands formulated by the Superbrands Council. The Council is made up of eminent figures working in advertising, design, market research and PR who together evaluate hundreds of established brands. Every member obviously has a deep appreciation of what makes a great brand.

The following definition of a Superbrand has been developed: "A Superbrand offers consumers significant emotional and/or physical advantages over its competitors which (consciously or subconsciously) consumers want, recognise, and are willing to pay a premium for."

SUPERBRANDS explores the history of these brands, observing how they have developed over the years and highlights their marketing, advertising and design achievements.

There is no simple formula for becoming and remaining a Superbrand. But, through evaluating many of the greatest brands in the world, numerous lessons can be learned.

Why consumers are so loyal to Superbrands according to members of the Superbrands Council

John Ballington

Corporate & Consumer Affairs Director
Lever Brothers Ltd

Consumer loyalty is the most precious commodity in the currency of brands: carefully built, vigorously defended, and yet easily eroded by the complacent.

Some brands that have invested year after year in delivering excellent consumer value, consistent quality and reliable service still do not generate high loyalty.

So what is the added ingredient in a Superbrand that brings consumers back time and time again? I believe it is a unique combination of trust, affection and real consumer benefits that are delivered time and time again, that generates lasting loyalty.

Look at the record of Superbrands, look at their consistent and relentless pursuit of consumer satisfaction, constantly listening, constantly learning, constantly improving, never allowing their offering to stagnate.

So why do Superbrands command higher loyalty? Because they provide us with real benefits and emotional satisfaction, that's why we love them!

Quentin Bell

Chairman
The Quentin Bell Organisation

Fickle Fiona we called her. The beautiful convent schoolgirl would always accept dates from my classmates and I - and, in fact, anyone who cared to ask her. But that was as far as it ever went. She was loyal to no one. She nurtured no enduring relationships.

Superbrands aren't like Fiona. They engage our heads (for their practicality and quality) and capture our hearts (for their charm and allure).

Only rarely are we disloyal to brands we love. They have to commit a major faux pas - like bad service - to earn such a pro-actively negative response. But it happens - and they deserve our disdain.

Why are we so loyal to Superbrands? Because we can forgive them for their occasional flaw. They have earned our support; built up a "deposit account" of trust. So we don't desert them for competitors.

They have passed the fickle test.

Drayton Bird

Managing Director
The Drayton Bird Partnership

James Webb Young was Creative Director and later a consultant to J Walter Thompson in New York for nearly fifty years early in this century. He defined five ways in which advertising works. The fifth was: "By adding a value not in the product."

That is what a brand does. It offers consumers benefits that exist not just in the product, but in the mind.

A myriad of impressions, large and small, determine how each customer feels about your brand. Your advertising - yes; but also how people answer the phone; the quality of your direct mail; how you handle customer complaints; the nature of your PR; the look of your stationery; the language of your recruitment ads; the design of your logo; how fast you reply to advertising enquiries; and how easy it is to understand and respond to what you send out.

Superbrands, quite simply, manage more of these things better.

Alison Canning

Managing Director
First&42nd Ltd

A brand is a set of cues, symbols or experiences which provoke a rational or emotional response in a consumer and combine to create an overall perception which drives behaviour.

By contrast, a Superbrand has accumulated so much equity with the consumer, that their response transcends rationale or emotional evaluation and becomes almost instinctive. Therefore, even if the brand is not significantly differentiated from a competitor product (eg Coca-Cola, PG Tips) or if the price/value equation defies rational justification (eg Stella Artois, Gordon's Gin), the consumer nevertheless remains loyal. In this way, 'Superbrand' status confers considerable trading advantage, as well as a platform of trust and credibility which mitigates in the event of a negative issue or crisis.

This loyalty is both difficult to build and difficult to destroy, but it can be lost, if the key platforms of brand strength - differentiation, relevance, esteem or familiarity - are not maintained over time.

Winston Fletcher

Chairman
Bozell UK Group

Brands are successful because consumers want them. (If consumers didn't want them, nobody would produce them).

Consumers want brands because they offer a guarantee of consistency, of quality, and sometimes - in fashion, for example - of style. Sometimes, naturally, consumers want to experiment. But most of the time they want to be as sure as they can be about what they are getting for their money. And even when they experiment, they want to know roughly what to expect. That's what brands offer.

By definition, Superbrands offer consumers all the above benefits - in trumps. They would not be Superbrands if they didn't. They offer more consumers more quality, more value and - sometimes - more style than other brands. That, in the end, is why consumers are so loyal to them.

Wally Olins

Founder
Wolff Olins

Surprisingly perhaps, and in spite of first appearances, Glenmorangie and IrnBru have a lot in common. Both are drinks: both come from Scotland and both complement the age, social aspirations, wealth and education of the people who buy and drink them. They are social accessories which underline the individual's present status and future ambition. And that's what makes them so powerful.

That's why Burberry is so successful in Japan. While a Japanese executive may not look like Sherlock Holmes from the outside, deep inside himself, just a little bit of some kind of fantasy of a never-never land aristocratic foggy Victorian London may flicker as he puts on his £500 Burberry. Superbrands aren't only about status they're also about internal satisfaction.

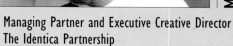
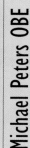

Michael Peters OBE

Managing Partner and Executive Creative Director
The Identica Partnership

There are some Superbrands that are solid and reliable,
some that are honest and trustworthy,
and there are some that have real integrity.

Some are fun,
some are exciting,
and some make us feel good.

Some Superbrands mean increased share value, and some give great dividends.

Whatever the reason, we are loyal to Superbrands because, like people,
they exhibit essential characteristics that appeal to our sensibilities.

Chris Powell

Chief Executive
BMP DDB

Lethargy is the unsung asset of Superbrands.

Careful to provide the best quality at an accessible price, Superbrands define their sectors.

Life is quicker and easier with Superbrands. No one wants to waste time and effort sorting through the claims of rival biscuits or burgers, just go for the main one. You want a TV? Get a Sony. A crisp? Get Walkers.

Superbrands are careful to keep satisfying their customers, there's no need to look for an alternative while you're still comfortable.

For Superbrand owners, the benefit is that your consumers will allow you to buy time. If a competitor beats you to a product improvement - as inevitably they must from time to time - they'll remain loyal while you catch up.

How else could the queues to go up the Empire State building remain so long, when the World Trade Centre and five other buildings are higher.

Tim Sutton

Chief Executive
Charles Barker BSMG

"Forsake not an old friend; for the new is not comparable to him." So says Ecclesiasticus in the good book. The Superbrand as an old friend? A little fanciful perhaps, but a kernel of truth too. In the sometimes confusing and bewildering world of consumer choice with all its claims and counter claims, we can succumb to uncertainty and insecurity. Add the shifting sands of new technology, and it's no wonder we often want to hold the hand of what's known and trusted.

What's impressive about so many Superbrands is their sheer longevity - they span generations. Friendship has to be earned and constantly re-earned too. Friendships are lost when friends let each other down, or when they find they no longer have much in common. Superbrands remember that friendship requires positive effort and it is wise, of course, never to take friends for granted.

Will Whitehorn

Corporate Affairs Director
Virgin Group

Why do brands attract loyalty? The cynic will say that it's because the likes of Coca-Cola invest hundreds of millions of dollars in promoting their brands. However, to really understand what makes a Superbrand we have to go back into the history of brands themselves, because ultimately they are about trust and reputation.

By the late 19th century brands such as Hovis, Liptons, and HP Sauce had become household names because the owners had staked their reputation on producing safe products in an era when the government did not have any legal safety standards. Hovis bread did not kill you, unlike some of its competitors!

It is interesting that many of those 19th century brands are indeed now the Superbrands of today. Bell's, Brooke Bond PG Tips, Heinz and McVitie's all date back to those glory days when you chose the product that wouldn't fail. In a psychological sense, despite living in a modern welfare state with every protection for the consumer, the same holds true for a Superbrand today.

ABBEY NATIONAL®

Because life's complicated enough.

The Market

There are 540 different banks in the UK, six of which are major clearing banks. These are Abbey National, Halifax, National Westminster, Midland Bank (now part of HSBC), Lloyds Bank and Barclays. There are now also a number of former building societies in the sector including Halifax, Woolwich and Northern Rock, and there is the merged Lloyds TSB.

Achievements

In 1989, Abbey National became the first building society to convert to banking status with the intention of becoming the outstanding financial services provider in the UK. In terms of assets, it has already become the fifth largest banking group in the UK and is ranked within the top 50 of the world's largest banks. Abbey National is currently the second largest mortgage lender in the country, helping more than two million people to buy their homes, and has relationships with one in three UK households.

Since it was founded in 1944, Abbey National has enabled thousands of British families to own their own homes and save for the future. One of Abbey National's chief achievements has been to combine the best of its building society heritage with its banking status.

Ian Harley, the Chief Executive of Abbey National plc, says: "Abbey National exists to help millions of people achieve financial security. Since conversion we have diversified away from our original role as a provider of mortgages and savings, to the extent that nearly 50% of income comes from non-traditional businesses such as life assurance, general insurance, unsecured lending and Treasury".

Since conversion in 1989, Abbey National has acquired major operations in life assurance and personal finance among others, and has developed a strong wholesale banking arm.

Abbey National also has a broad base of international operations, with subsidiary companies in Jersey, Gibraltar, Italy and France.

Abbey National's traditional businesses of mortgages and savings are still of prime importance, and it has enhanced this traditional business through the development of telemarketing. The business has evolved to provide a full range of personal financial services and products to meet all its customers' needs, including savings accounts, interest bearing cheque accounts, personal investment planning, pensions, life assurance and general insurance policies, healthcare and personal loans.

Chairman Lord Tugendhat says: "We continue to use the Abbey National brand to develop personal financial services as well as to grow our other brands rapidly. This means we are far less dependent on our traditional mortgages and savings businesses than most of our competitors and better placed in other more rapidly expanding and higher margin sectors.

"We also place a strong emphasis on retaining customers and on building their relationships with the Company. Currently, over 2.6 million customers hold three or more accounts with us."

History

Abbey National was formed in 1944 following a merger between the London-based Abbey Road Building Society (founded in 1874) and the National Building Society (established in 1849). There was large-scale public demand for housing in post-war Britain - which Abbey National helped to meet with the provision of mortgages.

At first, Abbey National focused on savings accounts and mortgages, but throughout the 1960s and 1970s, a wider range of financial services was gradually introduced. By 1989, when Abbey National was officially recognised as a bank by the Bank of England, it had 681 branches nation-wide - a huge leap from 1960 when the building society had just 60 branches.

Abbey National's transition to plc status in 1989 was strongly supported by its members. Up to five million voted their approval in a secret ballot. Almost overnight, the total number of private shareholders in the UK rose from six million to nine and a half million. Today, Abbey National has just under 2.5 million shareholders, of whom a large number have held shares since 1989. Abbey National's

change to bank status also resulted in the formation of its wholesale banking arm, Abbey National Treasury Services plc.

Every leading brand has its legend and Abbey National is no exception - it enjoys a strong association with the fictional detective Sherlock Holmes. The company's London headquarters occupy 221b Baker Street - the home of Sherlock Holmes. Abbey House, as the head office is known, has received thousands of letters over the years from fans all over the world, addressed to Sherlock Holmes.

Abbey National employs a secretary on behalf of the great detective, informing interested parties that Sherlock Holmes has retired from the strains of detective work and now keeps bees in Surrey.

The Product

Abbey National offers a whole range of financial services, from banking services and mortgages to insurance and financial planning and acts as a 'one-stop-shop' for all its customers' financial needs.

Mortgages have always been the backbone of Abbey National's business. It is the second largest mortgage lender in the UK, assisting more than two million people to buy their homes. It offers an extensive range of different mortgages including fixed and capped rates which give customers the security of knowing what their mortgage payments will be even when the base rate rises. Advice on mortgages is available from Abbey National's financial planning advisors who are on hand to guide customers through a lifetime of financial needs.

Abbey National acquired Scottish Mutual in 1992. Although it continues to operate independently, it has helped Abbey National set up its own life assurance operation, Abbey National Life plc, which provides protection products, mortgage related products, savings and investments and pension plans using the Abbey National brand.

Abbey National also offers a full range of banking services, including a bank account, credit card, savings accounts and a variety of loans to reflect different needs. Abbey National's bank account is user-friendly and pays out interest on accounts with balances of as little as £1.

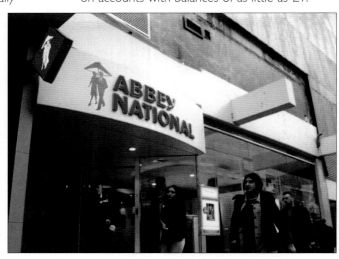

The account also comes with an overdraft facility - an ideal way to bridge a gap or cover unexpected expenses. Other features include a 24-hour telephone banking service and AbbeyLink Automatic Teller Machines (ATMs) linked to over 17,100 cash machines.

Abbey National has added to its range of saving and investment accounts for people with anything from £1 to £2 million to invest. These accounts range from instant access through a range of fixed rate bonds to PEPs and other stockmarket-linked products. In fact the company is one of the top ten unit trust providers and one of the top 20 biggest unit trust management groups.

Recent Developments

The last few years have seen Abbey National use its banking status to further develop its business.

In 1992 the acquisition of Glasgow-based Scottish Mutual led to the formation of Scottish Mutual Assurance plc, followed by the setting-up of Abbey National Life plc in 1993.

1994 saw two further acquisitions, that of the UK residential mortgage operation of the Canadian Imperial Bank of Commerce, renamed Abbey National Mortgage Finance, and

HMC Group plc, an independent centralised lending company.

The acquisition in February 1995 of UK health insurance provider, Pegasus Assurance Group Ltd, took Scottish Mutual into the growth markets of health care and critical illness insurance. In July 1995 a joint venture with Commercial Union created Abbey National General Insurance, the company's insurance wing. In August, Abbey National acquired the UK's largest finance house for consumer credit, First National Finance Corporation, strengthening its share of the personal loan market.

In August 1996, Abbey National successfully acquired the National and Provincial Building Society. Abbey National retained 2.7 million customers from a base of 3.3 million.

Promotion

Abbey National repositioned its brand in December 1997 following extensive consumer and staff research.

The core proposition is to create straightforward, flexible partnerships with customers, summarised as 'because life's complicated enough'. The tangible demonstration of this is fair banking, tailored mortgages, use of jargon-free plain English and a policy of staff not taking their lunch breaks at the busiest time to help shorten queues. At the heart of the repositioning was a determination to make customers' lives easier and to communicate with them in adult-to-adult fashion.

This was promoted through a major TV advertising campaign featuring comedian Alan Davies in a number of humorous situations. The TV ads were supported with a radio and press campaign.

1997 saw the launch of Abbeyvision, a satellite TV station in larger branches as well as a new look across all the bank's marketing material including press ads, posters, literature and direct mail. An additional satellite channel was also launched to improve communications with branch staff.

Abbey National was one of the first banks to establish an Internet site in April 1996 and most of its product groups have their own page with interactive material.

Abbey National supports charitable organisations and projects focusing on housing issues, families in crisis and equal opportunities for disabled members of the community through the Abbey National Charitable Trust. Total donations and community support now exceeds £1 million annually. The company and staff also actively support the BBC Children in Need appeal, raising over £250,000 in 1997. The company has also sponsored the RADAR People of the Year awards since 1996.

Brand Values

Abbey National's positioning in the financial services market is typified by its mission statement which reflects the company's desire to blend the old with the new. Its intention is to "achieve above average growth in shareholder value over the long term, which can only be achieved if we meet the needs of our customers, our staff, and all the other stakeholders in the business".

This approach, combined with listening to and understanding their customers and staff is what 'Because life's complicated enough' is all about.

Things you didn't know about Abbey National

About one in seven mortgages in Britain is provided by Abbey National, making it the second largest mortgage lender in the UK.

Branch staff carry out around 250 million transactions for customers every year.

Abbey National owns several channel tunnel trains and a cruise liner through its Treasury subsidiary.

In November 1984, Abbey National became the first building society to offer a £100 cheque guarantee card.

In 1989, Abbey National became the first UK company to sell mortgages over the telephone.

During the 1989 ballot to decide Abbey's conversion to plc status, there were three flights a day to Germany to pick up ballot boxes billeted at the British army bases.

The 2000th ATM was installed at Abbey National's Baker Street branch in 1997.

The Market

The UK sporting goods industry has grown significantly over the past five years as sportswear has become increasingly fashionable and has stretched beyond sport to become an aspirational product for the nation's youth. The market is driven by two or three authentic sports brands plus a number of niche players, although competition has grown as traditionally fashion-focused brands have entered the business, further fuelling the market growth.

Within the UK, authentic sportswear commanded annual retail sales of more than £2 billion in 1997. Annual retail expenditure for the whole market breaks down into a number of sectors: Footwear (£880 million); Apparel (£1,300 million) and Sports Accessories (£140 million, excluding sports equipment).

Further sales growth is expected to continue into the new millennium although at a more moderate rate as the market approaches a saturation level.

Achievements

After a period of declining sales in the late Eighties, the Nineties have seen adidas successfully rejuvenate its brand image, production efficiency and turnover. adidas is now market leader in Sportswear Apparel, and the clear number two in Sports Footwear. The brand's resurgence both globally and within the UK has coincided with the take-over and leadership of Robert Louis-Dreyfus and a refocusing on consumer marketing, with new strategies put in place targeting both sports participants and the wider youth markets.

Supporting a 'performance positioning' the brand prides itself on signing athletes who represent the best in their field which successfully emphasises adidas' marketing positioning as the 'authentic' sports brand. With names like David Beckham, Naseem

Hamed, Denise Lewis, Tim Henman, Donovan Bailey, Alessandro Del Piero, Patric Kleivert, Kobe Bryant and Anna Kournikova on its books, adidas' reputation is based on results.

adidas has had a long association with FIFA and the World Cup Tournament. It has supplied every match ball since 1974 and in 1998 made history as the first ever official sponsor and licensee of France 98. This provided the brand with a unique platform from which to communicate leadership in Soccer. adidas has also been the official kit supplier to the British Olympic Association since the Los Angeles Olympics in 1984 and has once again been chosen to supply the kit for British athletes competing in the Sydney Olympics in 2000.

History

Adi Dassler, a cobbler from the small village of Herzogenaurach, Bavaria, created the very first adidas sports shoe in 1920. From humble beginnings the adidas operation expanded into a global company that has become synonymous with world sport. Many of the fundamental principles that the first shoes were built upon remain firmly rooted in the company philosophy today.

Dassler was an athlete as well as a shoemaker and applied his understanding to produce products for athletes to improve performance at the highest level of sport. Dassler's efforts in the service of sport earned him more than 700 patents and other industrial property rights, many of them revolutionary new products.

The company was, and remains today, committed to acting on athletes' requirements and learning from them to develop better performance Footwear and Apparel. Today, the phrase "listen, modify, test" which was first used by Dassler himself, remains the key to the company's Research and Development operation.

Technical innovations included the world's first soccer shoes with screw-in studs, and the first screw-in spikes for track and field shoes. Since adidas equipped the first athletes at the Olympic Games in Amsterdam in 1928, over 800 world records and medals have been won by athletes using adidas Footwear and Apparel at Olympic Games and World Championships

The company's obsession for making the best performance products for athletes remains central to the brand's philosophy today.

The Product

Since the introduction of Dassler's first sports shoe in the Twenties, the adidas brand has expanded to such an extent that products are now available for almost every sport.

adidas designs its ranges for the athlete with athletes' functional needs in mind. Design concepts begin with the athlete. Top athletes of yesterday and today confirm that adidas equipment always takes into account latest developments in modern technology.

During the 1996 Atlanta Olympics, adidas put its Apparel through 18 months of athlete track testing to ensure the best possible performance under extremes of heat and humidity. This resulted in record-breaking achievements from athletes such as Steve Redgrave and Haile Gebreslassie, and the improved performance of hundreds of other athletes.

successful launch, which saw stocks sell through within weeks of the consumer launch, adidas has not rested on its laurels. Constant research and development has allowed the Predator football boot to grow from strength to strength.

This research resulted in the launch of the Equipment Predator Accelerator - in time for the 1998 World Cup. The Predator Accelerator features a unique sole unit incorporating Traxion innovation, and is the latest edition to the family of 'Feet You Wear' shoes.

Promotion

The arrival of Robert Louis-Dreyfus as group CEO in 1992 led to a completely new marketing philosophy. For the first time, Communications were acknowledged to be crucial to the overall health of the brand.

Today, adidas is a company that relies not only on a heritage of successful sports promotion but an integrated marketing approach. The biggest component of the brand's marketing activities is high profile, above the line advertising - recent campaigns have featured Prince Naseem, Tim Henman and David Beckham. PR has also played an important role expanding, explaining, and justifying the brands key messages. Major campaigns have been executed to drive awareness of the company's endorsed athletes and technological innovations.

Sponsorship and support of some of the world's top athletes has also helped adidas successfully position itself as the brand the best athletes choose. Meanwhile, grass roots Sports Marketing activity supports local athletes. adidas is committed to reinvesting heavily within a wide range of sports. Integrated Communications plans within soccer, running, tennis, training, workout, basketball, swimming, golf and rugby serving to authenticate adidas as the leading UK Sports brand with athletes of all levels.

adidas works not only with athletes and coaches, but also with the world's top research facilities to improve design and materials and to assure supreme performance and reliability. Additionally, adidas supports sport at all levels and is committed to extensive 'grass roots' programmes across all major sports.

Recent Developments

The latest in a long line of innovations has been 'Feet You Wear' . This brings a new and unique approach to footwear design based on the observation that the foot in its natural state is the athlete's optimal 'footwear' whether bending, pushing or gripping the ground. 'Feet You Wear' marks a new approach to footwear design which enhances and replicates the foot's natural movement.

Initially launched in four categories - Running, Adventure, Basketball and Tennis, the 'Feet You Wear' range is now also available in Women's Workout and Trail running models.

The Predator Soccer shoe created a revolution in Soccer boots when it was launched in 1994. Yet despite its hugely

Brand Values

adidas' brand positioning is clear and distinct. Only adidas has a genuine respect for sport, the company claims, and this is manifested in its obsession for making the best performance products for athletes.

The brand mission is quite simply to become the 'Best sports brand in the world' and the leading performance brand in all competing categories of Footwear and Apparel. This is to be achieved by producing the highest quality performance products at marketplace prices. Products are designed or developed to enhance the performance of all sports participants.

Things you didn't know about adidas

Following the First World War, Adi Dassler trained as a baker but unable to find work, he set up a small shoemaking operation at the back of a local laundry.

The first workshop machine he installed was an ingenious man-powered trimmer made out of a bicycle and some leftover wood.

Black American athlete Jesse Owen won four gold medals in a pair of Dassler track spikes during the 1936 Berlin Olympics - ironic, considering that year's event was intended as a nationalistic showcase for Hitler's Aryan master race.

Adi Dassler's brother, Rudolf, set up Puma in direct competition to adidas.

David Beckham's 60 metre, halfway line goal during the 1997/8 season was scored in Predator Traxion shoes.

The Market

To millions the world over, American Express means 'plastic money'. Although many other financial institutions issue credit cards, American Express undoubtedly boasts the most prestigious brand.

Today, 'plastic money' - both credit cards and charge cards - are fast replacing hard cash as more and more consumers around the world recognise the convenience of carrying a card rather than large amounts of cash. In 1994, the value of transactions using plastic rose by 11% in 1994 to £37.3 billion, according to the Euromonitor International Market Survey. Today, around 42.7 million cards are in circulation worldwide.

American Express, the original 'charge card', now provides a full range of products and financial services to its customers around the world - ranging from its credit cards to travellers cheques, financial planning and investment advice.

Achievements

Since its launch almost 150 years ago, American Express has developed a world-wide financial services system. And, as the world's largest travel company, it has made international travel much easier.

American Express is a truly global brand. The classic green American Express Card, first launched in 1958 and introduced to Britain in 1963, is the most widely recognised charge card in the world. There are currently over 42.7 million cards in use. In 1997 alone, around $209 billion was spent using American Express cards.

As well as dealing with individual members, American Express also has a high number of corporate customers. It currently provides a service to 89 of Fortune magazine's Fortune 100 companies.

The company offers a wide range of additional benefits to its members. These include a travel hot line and purchase protection - where purchases made using the card are insured against theft or damage for 90 days. American Express' Membership Rewards brand loyalty programme, which was launched in 1991, operates in over 27 countries and over five million members have signed up. To deal with such a large number of customers,

American Express has established a truly global presence and now employs 71,000 people around the world.

History

American Express began life as an express freight company with links, through founder Henry Wells, with both Wells Fargo and the Pony Express. The company was established in 1850 with the merger of Wells & Co and fellow express carriers Livingston & Fargo and Butterfield, Wasson & Co. Its origins therefore date back to the opening up of the American Wild West and its business was driven by the need for safe and speedy transportation of goods, valuables, bullion and bank remittances. American Express first operated under the slogan 'Safety & Dispatch' accompanied by a bull dog logo.

During the American Civil War in the 1860s, American Express transported vital supplies to Union army depots and undertook the high risk task of delivering election ballots to troops in the field. In 1882 it first began to underwrite money orders because this was far safer than shipping cash. This type of transaction became increasingly common practice from the mid-1880s onwards.

In 1886, American Express established relationships with banks across Europe - particularly in Ireland and Italy - to allow immigrants to the US to transfer money to their families back home. The company then began setting up offices and agents in Europe to collect accounts, sell consignments and deliver goods for merchants. It also started to pay money by telegraph and to sell small drafts or money orders which could be cashed at 15,000 places.

In 1891, American Express introduced the American Express Travellers Cheque - the first of its kind - which guaranteed that dollar cheques could be converted into a variety of currencies. It was automatically refundable if lost or stolen. American Express freight offices in England, Germany and France also began selling tickets for railroads and trans-Atlantic ships and offered travel information and itineraries.

The company's move into Europe started with American Express paying a British firm, Meadows & Co, to set up a one man office at Liverpool Docks. Before long, American Express had a growing portfolio of European agents

providing services such as collecting accounts, selling consignments, purchasing goods for patrons, delivering goods to merchants and transferring money on Telegraphic Order between cities often thousands of miles apart.

One of the company's most famous offices was set up in 1900 at 11, Rue Scribe, Paris, France. This became a focal point for many tourists travelling in Europe. At the outbreak of the First World War, American Express' European offices helped 150,000 American tourists who were trapped in Europe to get home safely. At the Paris branch, people queued six deep to get funds. In the areas worst effected by war, locals traded in American Express cheques rather than their own currency.

After the war, American Express expanded its travel organisation and extended its international financial operations in Latin America, Europe and the Far East. This side of the business grew rapidly after the Second World War, too, with the expansion of the international tourism business.

The famous green American Express charge card was first launched in 1958 and proved an immediate success. The card conferred an immediate status on its holders - a mark of exclusivity that continues today. The company moved into the corporate credit card market in 1970. Since then, it has broadened both its financial and travel services and in 1996, American Express introduced its first credit card in the UK.

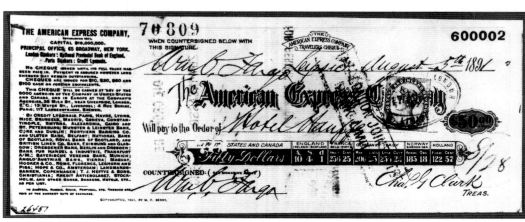

The Product

The American Express Company operates in three core areas: travel, finance and communication. The company's main businesses are American Express Financial Advisors, American Express Bank and American Express Travel Related Services.

American Express Financial Advisors offer financial planning and investment advisory services to individuals and businesses in the US. The banking division has three parts - correspondent, commercial and private banking and consumer financial services.

American Express Travel Related Services is by far the largest of the three, generating around half of all American Express profits. It operates American Express Card products as well as a world-wide network of American Express Travel Service and Representative Offices.

Although most famous for its charge card - which has no pre-set spending limit and is available in green, gold and platinum designs - American Express offers a broad range of products including credit cards, insurance and travellers cheques. Both credit and charge card members can benefit from the award-winning American Express Membership Reward Scheme.

The company has boosted its share of the US card market over the past ten years by offering plastic in a variety of forms, including travel and entertainment, credit, and affinity and airline tie-ins. Today, American Express offers 35 different consumer and business cards, many of them co-branded with other companies. It has also grown sales by increasing the number of places the card can be used. American Express proudly claims consumers can use its cards at 92% of the places where they want to shop.

Recent Developments

Throughout the nineties, American Express has continued to lead the market, offering consumers innovative products designed to suit their individual needs. Building on the success of its charge cards, American Express now also leads the credit card sector with its green and gold credit cards. A new American

Express Blue Card, targeting a younger market, has been introduced in the UK, Taiwan, Australia, Germany, Canada and Brazil and is set for further success as it is introduced across the globe.

American Express continues to build its presence as a global player by forming partnerships with a host of issuers including major banks in over 19 countries.

American Express is the world's largest business travel agent following the acquisition of Thomas Cook in 1993. In the same year, it was awarded the US Federal Government contract for travel and transportation payment - the biggest corporate card account in the world. Under the deal around 900,000 employees became American Express Card members.

The company has also focused on developing a more personal relationship with its customers and has introduced an easier-to-read format for monthly bills providing more comprehensive information on their expenditure.

Promotion

American Express's 'blue box' logo made its debut in 1974. It has since become one of the world's most familiar corporate identities. This is, in part, down to the company's commitment to supporting its products with high profile advertising. High profile campaigns have included the 'American Express? That'll do nicely' series of advertisements as well as the 'Don't leave home without it' campaign.

The benefits of owning an American Express Card were emphasised in the 'Membership has its privileges' campaign which began in 1987. The approach was underlined more recently by the 'Quality People' campaign, launched in 1993. This included testimonies from successful business people such as Terence Conran, Anita Roddick and Rocco Forte.

In 1997, American Express ran a major marketing campaign to target high spending Americans and encourage them to visit Europe. The company has also been involved in a number of sponsorship deals. Among its most recent is the sponsorship of leading designer Alexander McQueen's catwalk show at London Fashion Week in 1997 and 1998.

In early 1998, American Express launched a new series of 'Do More' TV ads starring US comedian Jerry Seinfeld. The campaign was designed by Ogilvy & Mather to reflect the major growth in the number of merchant locations that now accept the American Express Card, particularly supermarket and petrol service stations. The ads, adapted from the US, feature Seinfeld as the 'perfect shopper' and promote UK supermarkets and petrol stations which accept the card - Asda, Sainsbury's, Safeway, Tesco, Waitrose, BP, Esso, Shell and Texaco.

Brand Values

American Express enjoys an international reputation for prestige and excellence. The innovative spirit that pioneered the original charge card in 1963 has seen American Express consistently develop ground-breaking products to suit consumer spending needs. Despite many

imitators, American Express distinguishes itself in a competitive market place by combining first class products with superior customer service.

Things you didn't know about
American Express

American Express invented the travellers cheque in 1891.

An Air Zimbabwe Boeing 707 flying from Harare to London was spared an embarrassing wait at Marseilles by a passenger carrying an American Express card. Before leaving France, the pilot asked the passengers if they had £2,000 to pay for Marseilles Airport's landing fee. Following a stunned silence, one of the passengers offered to pay with his card.

Four survivors of a plane crash were saved from certain death, in shark-infested waters, when one of them flashed his American Express card into the sun to attract a coast guard plane.

American Express helped a naked businessman locked out of his hotel room save face. Finding himself trapped in the hotel corridor, the businessman noticed a rack of American Express application forms. He used one to shield himself as best he could whilst making his way to a pay-phone to ask for help.

A property developer picked up more than 2.4 million air miles with his American Express card after purchasing a £2,477,500 painting at a Sotheby's auction.

American Express card holders earn twice as much as other consumers and spend more on their cards than Mastercard or Visa card holders.

American Express arranged the first around-the-world leisure cruise in 1922.

The Market

Toilet tissue may not seem a particularly glamorous product but it is undoubtedly an essential household purchase. UK consumers spend £748 million on toilet tissue each year, much more than any other North European country (AC Nielsen: 1997). It is often used for 'secondary' functions, such as make-up removal and nose-blowing because UK tissue is generally softer than anywhere else. In fact, some 98% of the UK market is for soft toilet tissue (with 50% for coloured) - a huge increase on 1957, when it accounted for just 25% of the total market. In the 1950s the product was sold mainly through chemists however today it achieves nearly 90% of its sales through major grocery multiples with over 60% for premium quality tissue (AC Nielsen: 1997).

Achievements

Andrex® has been the undisputed market leader for over 35 years and has consequently become a household name due mainly to its high-profile advertising. The Andrex® puppy has won the hearts of the nation since 1972 and is famous as the longest running consistent TV advertising campaign in the UK. The puppy has appeared in over 100 commercials and recently celebrated its 25th anniversary.

Andrex® recently achieved the No.4 position in AC Nielsen's top 10 UK grocery brand list. Andrex® is now ahead of such brands as Ariel, Persil, Pampers, Kellogg's and Heinz and is currently valued at £209 million, a figure which is beaten only by Coca-Cola, Walkers Snacks and Nescafé (AC Nielsen: 52 w/e March 1998).

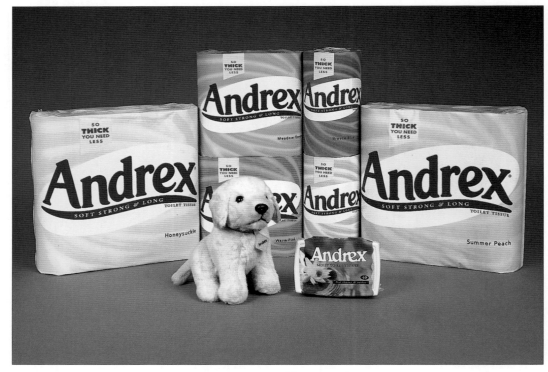

the market consisted of much harsher products often known as 'shinnies', which were sold mainly through chemists. By 1961 the brand achieved market leadership, a position it has retained ever since.

Today Andrex® toilet tissue can be purchased in a range of colours and pack sizes, which have been continually developed since 1957 when Andrex® launched its first colour variant, Magnolia.

The famous Andrex® puppy commercials were first screened in 1972. The original concept included a little girl running through her house trailing a roll of Andrex®. However this was blocked by television regulators who believed it would encourage children to be wasteful. So the little girl was replaced with a playful Labrador puppy and the campaign went on to be one of the most well-known throughout the country.

In 1991 Andrex® saw there was a gap in the market for a moist toilet tissue and so launched Andrex® Moist. Positioned as the perfect complement to dry toilet tissue, Andrex® Moist currently enjoys an impressive 67% value share within its sector (AC Nielsen: 1997).

The Product

Kimberly-Clark Ltd, the manufacturers of Andrex® toilet tissue are committed to maintaining its No1 position in the marketplace. They work continuously to improve product quality which is a priority due to the rising competition from retailer-own and other named brands. The brand was strengthened considerably by the "New Feel" relaunch in 1996 when over 1.5 million consumers were re-introduced to the product and its value rose by 7% (AC Nielsen: 4 w/e 26/10/96). Andrex® now boasts even more soft tissue fibre in every sheet than ever before.

Andrex® has maintained its reputation as one of the highest quality products on the market. Not only is it soft, strong and long, it is also thicker than ordinary toilet tissue making it excellent value for money as it lasts much longer.

Recent Developments

1998 has seen some important developments for Andrex® toilet tissue. As well as becoming the 4th biggest grocery brand in the UK, Andrex® has also updated its packaging and relaunched its advertising. The revamping of the Andrex® logo and packaging has modernised the brand image and helped increase its shelf standout, whilst maintaining the brand's core values of softness, strength and length.

After 25 years of successful puppy advertising it was felt a new approach was needed in order to re-establish the brand icon. The Andrex® puppy remains central of course, but now features as part of the Andrex® Puppy Patrol, whose mission is to ensure that every home has Andrex® toilet tissue. This campaign has proven to be so successful for Andrex® it has now been exported to Europe to be used on its sister brand, Scottex®.

History

Andrex® was developed from a design for gentlemen's disposable handkerchiefs that were sold exclusively in Harrods, London's famous department store. The tissue however took its name from St. Andrew's Mill in Walthamstow where it was first produced in 1942. Before soft toilet tissue such as Andrex® was introduced,

Promotion

Few advertising icons have come to embody their brands core values as perfectly as the Andrex® puppy. It has become inextricably linked with the brand itself, symbolising perfectly the qualities of softness and strength that keep Andrex® ahead of the market.

The puppy has featured in 117 commercials to date, generally appearing in the family home but also with various other animals including an elephant and a giraffe! However it wasn't until 1991 that the product was actually shown in the bathroom. The 'Little Boy' execution was one of the most successful in the history of Andrex® advertising. It is even recalled by consumers today, despite the fact it hasn't been televised for over 7 years! 1998 saw the launch of the Andrex® Puppy Patrol, which was developed to give the puppy a more active role in the advertising.

As brand icon the puppy is also used in a variety of other marketing and promotional devices. This has included calendars, a joint activity with Disney's film, 101 Dalmatians, and several soft toy promotions. Indeed, over the years at least 800,000 Andrex® toy puppies have been dispatched to consumers! Recently to celebrate the 25th year of puppy advertising, Andrex® sponsored an appeal for the Guide Dogs for the Blind Association. Consumers collected over 1.3 million on-pack tokens which amounted to a donation of £270,000 for the charity.

Brand Values

Despite an uninspiring and low-profile product category, Andrex® has achieved a remarkable position as the 4th largest grocery brand in the UK, and market leader for over 35 years. Andrex® has always developed high quality products that provide the best value for families due to its key attributes: softness, strength and length. The renowned puppy advertising has been running successfully for over 25 years and ensures the brand is instantly recognisable. Andrex® is not only a category leader, but also a household name, having established itself within the hearts of the nation.

Andrex®, the Andrex® puppy and Scottex® are registered trademarks of Kimberly-Clark.

Things you didn't know about Andrex®

UK households use over 10.5 million miles of Andrex® per year - enough to make over 80,000 trips around the M25. (Travelling at the speed limit this would take a motorist around 17 years, not counting tailbacks!)

The first press adverts for Andrex® appeared in the early sixties and featured the James Bond star, George Lazenby...holding a baby!

By 1961 Andrex® was the leading toilet tissue brand and in 1972 it became the first toilet tissue brand to gain permission to advertise on television.

The success of the Andrex® puppy has inspired numerous imitations, including a spoof campaign by Hamlet Cigars.

Around 1.5 million rolls of Andrex® are sold in the UK each day which works out as enough tissue to encircle the world one and a half times.

The Andrex® commercial "Little Boy" was the first of its kind to show the product in-situ. It has also been the most successful puppy commercial in the history of Andrex® advertising.

The Market

The UK car market is dominated by volume car manufacturers like Ford and Vauxhall, who account for 19.49% and 13.62% of sales respectively. The prestige car sector - occupied by Audi, Mercedes, BMW, Volvo, Jaguar and Saab - accounted for just 8.9% of the 2 million units sold in 1996.

Yet within this sector, Audi has carved out a lucrative niche through product innovation, astute marketing and advanced design. In 1997, the company enjoyed its fourth successive year of record-breaking sales, selling a total of 35,721 cars, or 1.64% of the total car market. In a market which has grown by 7% during 1997, Audi has seen growth of 15%.

Achievements

At the heart of the Audi brand lies its tradition of technological and product innovation.

During 1995 and 1996, Audi phased the introduction of a range of unique 20 and 30 valve engines across all models, technology which means smaller engines can run more efficiently. The quattro system is unique, independently monitoring each wheel and automatically distributing power where there is most traction. Audi has also developed the Aluminium Space Frame and the company is widely regarded for making among the best diesel engines in the world.

As impressive has been Audi's recent ability to turn around its fortunes. By 1992, sales and turnover had stagnated, yet the Audi brand is now in better shape than ever. The number of car drivers who agreed with the statement "I can see myself driving an Audi" jumped from 49% to 57% between 1995 and 1996 and the percentage of those likely to make an Audi their next purchase more than doubled from 8% to

17% over the same period. In 1997, Audi achieved its fourth successive year of record-breaking sales, selling 35,721 cars - an increase of 82% over the total sales for 1992.

Audi's success in the last five years has been built on the twin pillars of its product excellence and widely admired brand. Both elements were recently recognised when Audi won the Autocar award for Best Manufacturer at the 1996 Birmingham Motor Show and the Marketing Society's Brand of the Year award in the Durables Sector, beating off stiff competition from Dyson, deBeers and Sony Playstation as well as other car manufacturers.

The A3 was recently voted the Design Museum's 101st statement of design.

"It was the sheer completeness of the Audi A3 that led us to conclude that BMW no longer builds the most desirable small hatch in the world. Or the best range of cars," commented Autocar in December 1996.

History

When car manufacturer August Horch was dismissed from his job in the car company that bore his name (it was claimed that he spent too much time driving cars), he immediately set about establishing another company, called Audi. After mergers and name changes during the '30s, the Audi brand name was resurrected in 1965. It wasn't until the late 1970s that export to the UK of prestige car models began in earnest.

During the 1980s, Audi developed a clear positioning in the UK as a technologically advanced, prestige German car manufacturer. This was built around engineering innovations such as the world-beating Audi quattro rally car, and it was supported by the long-running 'Vorsprung durch Technik' advertising campaign. Market share throughout the period was just over 1%.

Tough economic conditions and the discontinuation of the original Audi quattro, however, made 1989-92 difficult years for the brand. Declining sales and a lack of brand clarity proved a handicap, especially in the face of rival BMW's more successful products. But a strategic overhaul in 1993 led to a marked change in Audi's fortunes.

Today, Audi is positioned as the premium marque in the Volkswagen Group.

The Product

The first model in Audi's new 'A' series was the high-technology aluminium-bodied A8, Audi's top end luxury car. The bodyshell of the A8 is 40% lighter than if it were conventional steel construction, giving the car greater performance with lower fuel consumption, shorter braking distances and more responsive handling. The car is also some 30% stronger, due to its Aluminium Space Frame Construction.

The Audi A4 is positioned as the ultimate executive sports saloon. It boasts high levels of specification and offers an extensive range of engines. The A4 Avant is an estate version of the A4, whose driving experience justifies its positioning as "more than a load-carrier".

When the Audi A3 was launched, it was heralded as the world's first prestige sports hatch - so called because it boasted unprecedented levels of standard equipment for its class. In terms of comfort and safety, the A3 is closer to an executive saloon. Features include twin airbags, ABS, electric front windows, alloy wheels, engine immobiliser and an anti-theft system.

In 1997, the new A6 was launched into the prestige executive saloon car sector, currently dominated by the BMW 5-series and Mercedes E-class. The A6 has shaken up the sector with its

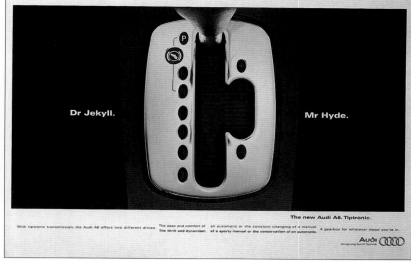

breathtaking design, excellent handling and refinement. The A6 Avant - the estate version of the A6 - was launched in Spring 1998.

The Audi Cabriolet is acclaimed as one of the most stylish cars in its class, and has recently been joined by a removable hard-top version, the Audi Convertible.

Finally, Audi has recently launched the S8 quattro, a high performance luxury sports version of the A8 and flagship of the Audi range. This is to be joined by the S4 quattro, and the S3 quattro will also be available in due course.

Recent Developments

In the 1990s, Audi has undergone little short of a renaissance under the eye of Ferdinand Piech, chairman of its parent group, Volkswagen. New product plans - the launch of the 'A' series of cars - were confirmed. And the first moves were made towards brand separation, when the VW Group decided to separate the operations of its brands (Seat, VW and Audi - Skoda was added later). This gave Audi the opportunity to define its own marketing positioning for the first time.

Audi took steps to define clearly its marketing focus, injecting dynamism, passion and humanity into its marketing activities to balance Audi's historical technology base. The brand was poorly known outside Europe, and in the UK profile was relatively low. Awareness was positive although the Audi brand was not widely understood.

Promotion

Audi's advertising has consistently tried to balance product innovation - as conveyed by its slogan "Vorsprung durch Technik" - with the consumer benefits of this innovation.

Audi's advertising consistently illustrates the superiority of understated class over flashiness and the virtues of progressiveness over staid

tradition. Audi's target consumers are clearly defined as individuals who demand singular solutions, understand that satisfaction comes from refinement not ostentation and know that technological excellence can make a difference and is worth seeking out.

Working closely with its London-based advertising and direct marketing agencies, Bartle Bogle Hegarty and Limbo, Audi has created stylish and impactful integrated marketing campaigns. These have spanned brand and direct response press ads and fulfilment packs.

TV and press work performs a brand-building function, concentrating on injecting dynamism and passion into the brand. Direct response campaigns have been lauded for their recognition of what different types of advertising communication can achieve. Hard working, enquiry generating small space direct response ads, for example, leave TV to do the dedicated brand-building.

Close attention has been paid to fulfilment materials ranging from product or service information to test drive invitations. The end results often extend the campaign rather than merely convey clinical information. Product placement is also an important part of the brand's marketing activities, with Sir Terence Conran and Richard Branson both driving an A8 in 1996.

Audi is also investing in updating its network of Audi dealerships, now called Audi Centres. These are, in effect, three dimensional manifestations of the Audi corporate identity, and represent a major move away from the previous joint VW-Audi showrooms.

Audi participates in the British Touring Car Championship, which the company believes is second only in popularity to Formula One, as well as sponsoring other events which relate closely to its core brand values. These include Laser 5000 sailing, the BBC Design Awards and more recently the Audi Foundation, a charitable

trust established to help young people in the fields of design and engineering bring their ideas to fruition.

Audi claims that its policy of progress through innovation, of finding new and original solutions to age-old engineering problems, of creating new precedents instead of following accepted norms while continually questioning the conventional, has changed general attitudes to cars and the way manufacturers think when designing them.

Brand Values

At the heart of the Audi brand lie three core brand values - modern, innovative, individual. These values apply equally to the cars, the drivers, and the company itself, and provide a 'brand blueprint' against which all marketing activity can be evaluated. Audi has no doubts about its identity and makes a virtue of its unconventionality.

We try harder.

The Market

Vehicle rental has become an increasingly important part of the global travel and transportation business. In Europe, the business is fragmented and characterised by a small number of major international companies - including Avis, Hertz, Budget, Sixt and Europcar - which operate through a combination of wholly-owned and franchised operations.

The industry is split into two: business and leisure. The business sector, which accounts for 46% of the total market, is dominated by Avis Europe and its main competitors. They all have agreements with major companies to provide contracted vehicle rental programmes. The key requirements needed to serve these customers are a wide-ranging selection of competitive products, speed, quality of service and geographical coverage. Avis has all of these and operates programmes with 75% of Europe's top 500 companies. It is located in every European country, including the Ukraine - the most recent addition to its network - and is currently in the process of developing a new loyalty scheme tailored to the needs of its customers worldwide.

The leisure sector is much more fragmented. It includes both customers who pre-book a car prior to departure for their holiday and those who rent a car while at their leisure destination. While the business sector displays a relatively even pattern of demand throughout the year, the leisure market is more seasonal with demand peaking in the summer months.

In Europe's five largest markets - Britain, France, Germany, Spain and Italy - the total business is estimated to be worth over £3 billion. Avis is the leading brand in these countries with a 16% share of the market. In the UK, Avis is market leader with a 15% share of total car rentals.

Achievements

Avis has grown from a three car operation at Detroit Airport to a multi-million dollar brand operating in over 160 countries and 5,000 locations with a fleet of more than 400,000 cars. Avis Europe Plc is the leading car rental company in Europe, Africa and the Middle East. It has the largest rental fleet with the widest choice of cars including models from over 17 manufacturers across Europe.

A significant growth area for Avis is its partnerships. It enjoys more of these than any other car rental company and for example, is in the unique position of having the three main UK airlines - British Airways, British Midland and KLM uk - among numerous partners from all travel sectors.

History

Warren Avis founded Avis Airlines Rent a Car at Detroit Airport in 1946 - it was the world's first car rental operation at an airport. Avis dreamt up the idea while he was flying bombers in south east Asia during the Second World War. He was renowned for taking a motorbike on missions so that on his return he could ride straight from the airbase into town without waiting for a taxi. He decided that he could set up a similar operation at airports using rental cars.

The business began with three cars, a $75,000 loan and a conviction that the post-war era would change the face of travel. Within seven years, Avis was the second largest car rental company in the US. By 1953, Avis had expanded and franchise operations were launched in Europe, Canada and Mexico.

But while the business was expanding it was spending money that it didn't have and by 1963 the firm was in trouble. Although it was the second largest car rental company in the US, its market share was only 10% compared with 75% for Hertz. It decided to launch a bold new advertising campaign which openly admitted that it was losing money, was short of customers and that it was the number two in the market. It was a clever ploy. The 'We're only number two. We try harder' campaign worked because of its emphasis on the company's honesty and its commitment to customer service. Avis made a virtue out of being number two in the market. The campaign is still widely recognised as one of the 'greats' of advertising history.

By 1965 Avis began expanding internationally in Europe, Africa and the Middle East and established its core vision: to be "the best and fastest growing company with the highest profit margins in the car rental business".

Technology is key to Avis' success and over the last 25 years the company has developed

Avis is only No. 2 in rent a cars. So why go with us?

We try harder.
(When you're not the biggest, you have to.)
We just can't afford dirty ashtrays. Or half-empty gas tanks. Or worn wipers. Or unwashed cars. Or low tires. Or anything less than seat-adjusters that adjust. Heaters that heat. Defrosters that defrost.
Obviously, the thing we try hardest for is just to be nice. To start you out right with a new car, like a lively, super-torque Ford, and a pleasant smile. To know, say, where you get a good pastrami sandwich in Duluth. Why?
Because we can't afford to take you for granted. Go with us next time.
The line at our counter is shorter.

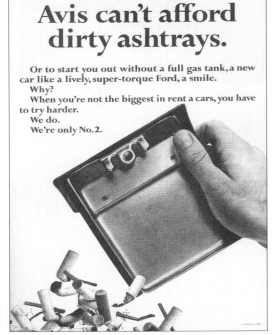

Avis can't afford dirty ashtrays.

Or to start you out without a full gas tank, a new car like a lively, super-torque Ford, a smile.
Why?
When you're not the biggest in rent a cars, you have to try harder.
We do.
We're only No. 2.

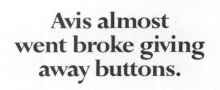

Avis almost went broke giving away buttons.

We try harder. We try harder.
Good old button. Cheap new button.

5 million so far.
At 2½¢ apiece, that amounts to $125,000. And that's a lot of money when you're only No. 2.
So our man in charge of buttons came up with a cheaper version. We're sure it'll work as well for everyone. (Like the Bishop in Africa who got 300 to inspire good works in his district.)
If all it took were buttons, though, the world would be on its way to being a better place.
But it takes more.
We don't just hang a button on a girl and expect miracles. Avis has a will to win and it rubs off. On her. And on the men who whisk the last cigar band out of the Ford.
Avis buttons are yours for the asking. But the button only works as hard as the people who wear it.

Avis can't afford not to be nice.

Or not give you a new car like a lively, super-torque Ford, or not know a pastrami-on-rye place in Duluth.
Why?
When you're not the biggest in rent a cars, you have to try harder.
We do. We're only No. 2.

the most extensive global computer network and information processing system in the vehicle rental industry: the 'Wizard' computer system. The industry's first on-line real time reservation, rental and management information system, 'Wizard' processes 97% of Avis transactions - that's over 30 million incoming customer calls to Avis reservation centres in addition to millions of enquiries and reservations through travel industry partners and the Avis world wide internet site. It was 'Wizard' which allowed the company to expand into the fleet leasing market and in 1979, the company signed a marketing and advertising agreement with General Motors which features GM cars in its worldwide fleet. An improved 'Wizard' system was introduced in Europe in 1985. 'Wizard' now operates in 32 countries.

As the Berlin Wall came down, Avis was the first car rental firm to establish operations in East Germany. Today it is the market leader in Central Europe and has 50 airline partners worldwide. In 1997, Avis Europe successfully floated on the London Stock Exchange and the Avis brand extended to a further 27 territories in Asia, giving the group access to a vast new market.

The Product

The Avis name is recognised the world over and the company serves millions of customers annually. Rental locations are chosen for their convenience with particular importance attached to representation at airports and other major travel points.

The company offers a range of different products and services designed to meet the different needs of every customer. 'Avis Express Service' is a constantly updated, high speed rental system which offers a virtually paperless service. Express allows reservations to be booked over the phone with all documentation ready to sign on collection. Meanwhile 'Avis Express Preferred Service' is for those customers who want to sign only one master rental agreement and need only show their driving licence to collect a car, without having to sign for it each time.

In addition, Avis now offers the UK's first meeting product, 'Avis Conference Connections', a service designed for conference organisers, giving them a flexible, tailor-made product for their ultimate convenience. 'Avis Conference Connections' complements its equivalent US counterpart, 'Meetings Services'. The combination of these services is a unique offering within the European car rental industry.

'Avis Advance' is specifically tailored to the needs of smaller business renters offering special rates, the option to rent cars on the company's own insurance and loyalty bonuses offering free rental days.

'Avis Maxi-rent' is a flexible programme for long-term car rental, specially designed to enable easy and cost effective fleet management.

A chauffeur-driven service is available from Heathrow Airport and operates direct services to the Home Counties.

Avis regularly tracks customer satisfaction. Every year, 160,000 customers are sent a personalised questionnaire asking how satisfied they were with Avis's services, products and staff. This customer feedback is used to help Avis continuously improve its standards.

Recent Developments

Avis recently unveiled a yield-management strategy designed to increase fleet utility and therefore profitability. Its central role is to identify spare fleet and then match it with strictly limited 'Red hot Offers'. These real value offers are marketed to both the trade and consumers direct, mainly focused on

driving rentals in Europe and the USA. 'Red hot Offers', the theme, is designed to enliven the brand, increase awareness and secure a larger slice of the leisure car hire market.

Avis' partnership strength is particularly visible in the domestic railway sector where, following privatisation, it has been successful in winning rail-drive partnerships with GNER, Virgin and Great Western from its competitors. Avis has drawn on its experience of rail partner status with SNCF in France and has extended its UK partnership with Eurostar to feature an all-inclusive rail-drive product which allows customers to pay one price to travel to Eurostar destinations (or stations to which it has a direct connection) on the French or Belgian network, and then pick up an Avis left hand drive car.

Avis is now looking for new opportunities to grow, investing in new markets and expanding in existing ones. It plans to maximise its business relationships with airlines and hotel chains and will investigate opportunities for mutual profit growth which will enhance the Avis brand. In the hotel sector, existing UK partners include Forte, Best Western Hotels and Golden Tulip Hotels whilst Avis's airline partners include British Midland, KLM uk and most recently, British Airways.

This global deal with British Airways aims to provide customers with a seamless travel service, succinctly summed up by the new partnership philosophy: 'Getting together to make travel easier'.

As the new preferred car rental partner for British Airways, Avis has access to the airline's 38 million business and leisure passengers across BA's 175-destination network.

All these partnerships offer customers tailor-made benefits such as exclusive rates, specialised services and unique products. The dominant philosophy pervading Avis' partnership activities, is the guiding principle it applies to its entire operation: 'to meet and exceed customer demands'.

Promotion

Avis is the most promotionally active company within its sector and with its 'Red hot Offers', this pre-eminence now extends across all areas, providing added value offers, upgrades and prizes, all enhanced by creative execution.

To date, Avis has run three national promotions in the UK. The first offered customers the chance to win a Vauxhall Tigra, a Porsche for a month or a Ferrari for a week in a free prize draw, plus a guaranteed reward of £5 petrol cash back.

In a subsequent promotion, Avis brought the indomitable James Bond to its customers, offering them a pair of cinema tickets to see his latest box office block-buster, 'Tomorrow Never Dies' and the chance to win a luxury Bond style holiday.

Through its Soccer Hot Shots promotion, Avis is also the only car rental company to offer the premier prize of a free official World Cup 98 football with every rental of two days or more and the chance to win World Cup tickets or a penalty shoot-out against former England goalkeeper Peter Shilton. The five penalty shoot-out winners tested

their sharp-shooting skills against Shilton and the person who scored the most goals won £5,000 while the runners up received £1,250 each.

Brand Values

Avis' brand values are embodied in its "We try harder" culture which was introduced in the 1960s. Its business philosophy is based on honesty, integrity and empathy with the real needs of customers. The philosophy is apparent in Avis' consistently high standards of service and is tangible throughout the organisation from station staff to the Central Reservations agents and Head Office.

BBC

The Market

For years, the UK broadcasting market has been dominated by established terrestrial television players.

In the beginning there was BBC Radio - the nation's publicly-funded broadcasting service. Next came BBC Television and then ITV, a national advertiser-supported channel made up of regional franchisees - the BBC's first commercial broadcasting rival. In 1982, Channel 4 was launched; it was followed 15 years later by the youngest terrestrial player, Channel 5, which started broadcasting in March 1997.

New technology, however, will revolutionise the broadcast market in coming years. Cable and satellite viewers already can choose between a growing array of niche and broad-based entertainment channels broadcast via satellite - the UK market is dominated by BSkyB - and cable. And the arrival in 1998 of digital broadcasting - which allows hundreds of new channels to be broadcast in the bandwidth previously able to support only a handful - promises up to 200 new additional services.

The effects of all this change are already visible in the market. Established broadcast players are battling for audiences and face unprecedented competition. Channels are being forced to reassess their positioning and more clearly identify themselves, their products and their target market. Marketing and branding are more important than ever before.

competitive broadcast environment, it continues to retain a major share of the broadcast ratings. An estimated 17.5 million people watched the England v Germany match on BBC Television during the Euro 96 football championships; 19.3 million people turned to the BBC for television coverage of the funeral of the Princess of Wales in 1997.

The BBC's pioneering attitude and expertise in broadcasting and production - not just television and radio programming, but films too - has earned it numerous accolades. As a commissioner and broadcaster of new music, drama and literature, the BBC is also a notable arts patron.

It has also gained respect overseas - BBC World Service Radio, BBC World, the BBC's international 24-hour television news service and BBC Prime, the entertainment channel for Europe help to ensure that there is a major British voice in the increasingly global media market.

During 1997, BBC Television programmes won prizes at major industry awards events around the world. Its many awards included two international Emmys, two Prix Italia Awards and 15 Royal Television Society programme awards. BBC Radio was also successful in picking up 79 Sony Awards and two Prix Italias.

The BBC remains part of the UK's social fabric and is also respected and loved by audiences the world over.

a site it still occupies today.

The first major live outside broadcast was transmitted in 1937 for George VI's coronation. The forerunner of the BBC World Service, originally known as the Empire Service, was launched in 1932.

Throughout the Second World War, the BBC was the voice of the nation and of resistance in Europe. It marked many key historical moments including the declaration of war from Prime Minister Neville Chamberlain and King George VI and Winston Churchill's speeches to the nation. Meanwhile, its radio comedians boosted the war-torn nation's spirits.

BBC television broadcasts began in 1939 but closed down during the war to resume in 1946. In 1953, the BBC transmitted pictures of Queen Elizabeth II's coronation live from Westminster Cathedral. Other important landmarks marked by live BBC Television broadcasts include man's first steps on the moon in 1966.

In 1964, the BBC launched a second television channel, BBC2. Full colour television transmissions, again pioneered by BBC Television, began in 1967 together with the launch of Radio 1 and local radio. Other major developments include the introduction of the Ceefax information service in 1974, breakfast television in 1983 and Nicam stereo during the 1980s. BBC World Service Television began in 1991.

Meanwhile, the BBC continues to develop its national and local radio services against growing commercial radio competition from new advertiser-funded national, regional and local services. In 1994, live national sports and news station Radio 5 Live joined Radios 1, 2, 3 and 4.

In the Nineties, the BBC has had to formulate a strategy to deal with the rapidly changing media landscape. It pioneered digital audio broadcasting and is developing a number of new added value services including BBC services on cable, on satellite and on the Internet.

Achievements

The BBC is not just a public institution. It is the nation's memory bank - a repository of collective emotional responses.

Its comprehensive and highly acclaimed news coverage has involved viewers at key junctures in history-making. In times of trouble, it is the broadcast voice the people turn to. BBC commentary is renowned for its impartiality and independence. Its high-class journalism is praised for its objective, intelligent analysis of the issues that matter for all of us.

The BBC has delivered a wide and varied range of entertainment and educational programming on radio and television for more than 75 years. And even in today's highly

History

The 'British Broadcasting Company' was formed in October 1922. Five years later, it was awarded a Royal Charter to provide public broadcasting services in the UK. In its early days, the BBC was a radio broadcaster. It subsequently pioneered television in the UK.

A number of innovations from its early years have become enduring institutions - such as the 'pips' time signal which has been used on the hour, every hour by BBC Radio since 1924. *The Week in Westminster*, meanwhile, began in 1930 and continues to be broadcast on Radio 4. In 1933, the BBC began broadcasting services to the regions - a year after moving into central London headquarters at Broadcasting House,

IN NOVEMBER 1922, THERE WAS AN
INCREDIBLE STORY
ON THE
BBC RADIO NEWS.
THE BBC RADIO NEWS.

Its trailers for programmes and corporate messages have become more sophisticated and entertaining. Perhaps its most successful promotional project for the brand to date has been its 'Perfect Day' film, reminding viewers of the value of the licence fee and leaving a sense of "only the BBC could have done this".

The film featured top musical artists including Lou Reed, Bono, Lesley Garrett and Elton John performing a new version of the classic Lou Reed ballad, 'Perfect Day'. It generated vast amounts of publicity and was so successful that the BBC launched the re-worked song as a single. The single raised almost £2 million for the BBC's own charity, Children in Need.

In recent years, the BBC has become more adventurous in its use of external media. Posters, press and cinema have been used to promote programmes and services in addition to the considerable promotion on the BBC's own airwaves. The Radio Times has also acted as an invaluable promotional tool.

The Product

Today the BBC reaches 95 percent of all homes in the UK. It has two national television stations, BBC One and BBC Two, five national radio stations, Radios 1, 2, 3, 4 and 5 Live and 39 local radio stations together with dedicated services for listeners in Scotland, Wales and Northern Ireland. In addition, the BBC's World Service broadcasts in 44 languages to over 140 million listeners. Billed as the BBC's third service after television and radio, BBC Online features a wealth of information from news and education to children's programmes and popular features. In November 1997, the BBC launched BBC News 24 - a rolling television news service for cable which is also carried by BBC One overnight. This was the first of a package of services developed for digital television, for which widescreen television, additional programmes and information services are also planned.

From the outset the BBC aimed to provide distinct and diverse quality programming. It went out into the world to achieve this, setting in motion a universal recognition of the brand. It established regional centres throughout the UK, placed correspondents across the globe, launched overseas national and regional programming, school broadcasts and outside broadcasts of major events from State occasions to sporting events. The BBC remains committed to providing unparalleled programming including drama, factual, education and children's which will continue to be the envy of the world.

Recent Developments

The BBC must comply with its Royal Charter which lays down certain requirements - notably, its public service remit. It is funded not by advertising but by the licence fee.

However, the BBC is also encouraged to generate additional revenue by exploiting the asset created by the licence fee, through programme sales, joint ventures and publishing activities linked to programmes. These commercial activities have to be carried out

at arm's length, with no cross subsidy from the licence fee; and the revenue from them is re-invested in core services for licence payers.

In addition to its principal funding from a universal licence fee, the BBC also earns revenue from its international and commercial arm, BBC Worldwide. Its joint venture, UKTV, offers four domestic cable and satellite subscription services and it is also responsible for the distribution of two international cable and satellite channels, BBC World (broadcast to more than 50 million homes) and BBC Prime (with 6 million subscribers in Europe) and an extensive magazine, video, book and audio cassette and character merchandise business. It has also launched, with ICL, a commercial online-service - Beeb@theBBC. The BBC's most recent international development is its alliance with Discovery in America. This includes a major joint production agreement and the establishment of joint venture channels around the world as well as paving the way for the launch of BBC America, offering the best of BBC programming to American viewers.

Promotion

Three letters - B, B and C - have come to stand for a broadcast legend and a worldwide brand. The BBC has grown astute in its management of its famous trademark both to promote itself and protect its interests. Its recently re-designed corporate logo is a clear example of this.

In October 1997 the BBC unveiled a new corporate identity designed to carry it into the next millennium. The new BBC logo has helped simplify the Corporation's identity across its broad range of products and services. The lettering of the new logo is simpler and less cluttered; the on-screen visual image on BBC One is accompanied by a hot air balloon sporting a bright map of the globe.

The BBC logo is used extensively and creatively - from television channels to station literature, flags, microphones, cameras, vehicles, merchandising, buildings, books, videos, magazines, CDs and CD Roms around the world.

Brand Values

The BBC still lives by the challenge set by its first Director General, John Reith: "To Educate, Entertain and Inform". This is part and parcel of the BBC's public service tradition, which is deep-seated throughout the organisation. Top quality programming, unbiased and responsible news-reporting, a common ground drawing the British nation together as a whole, excellence and fairness - these are the BBC's values.

The BBC is a heritage brand. It has also become something of a legend.

BELL'S®

AGED 8 YEARS

water of life

The Market

Bell's is the UK's best selling Scotch whisky; it is the number two alcoholic drinks brand in the off-trade and has the highest level of brand awareness for any spirit in the UK. In a highly competitive market Bell's has consistently held its position as the brand leader, in the blended whisky sector. There are over 15 million whisky drinkers in the UK - 7 million of them drink Bell's.

Whisky drinkers in the UK are generally middle-aged and male, Bell's faces the constant challenge of trying to attract new drinkers in today's price sensitive market. The growth of cheaper own label blends has led to a low degree of brand loyalty and difficulty among consumers to differentiate between brands. Despite this Bell's is still the UK's best selling whisky.

By law whisky must be matured for a minimum of three years, Bell's, unlike most other blends, is matured for a minimum of eight years. Bell's is a blend of superior quality - an authentic blend whose roots go back to 1825. Made from only the finest malt and grain whiskies, Bell's offers its consumers a richer flavour, greater depth of character, and a more distinctive taste.

History

In 1825 Thomas Sandeman and James Roy opened a small shop in Perth, Scotland selling whisky, wines, teas and beer. Twenty years later Arthur J Bell joined the business - one of the first whisky merchants to identify the potential of blending malt and grain whiskies. He believed "several fine whiskies blended together please the palates of a greater number of people than one whisky unmixed."

In 1851 Bell became a partner and the company changed names to become Roy & Bell. Twelve years on, Bell introduced his two sons Arthur Kinmond and Robert into the business to take responsibility for expanding the company's domestic and overseas whisky markets.

The name Bell's appeared on the label of blended whisky for the first time in 1904 and in 1925 the phrase 'Afore Ye Go' was registered as the official company slogan.

Arthur Bell and Sons purchased the Blair Athol distillery and the Dufftown-Glenlivet Distilleries in 1933 for £5,600. Nine years later Arthur and Robert died and with them went the last link with the Bell family.

Bell's went public after the Second World War. In 1985 Guinness Plc acquired Arthur Bell & Son and later the Distillers company to form the UK's largest spirits company - United Distillers. Bell's Scotch whisky was re-launched in 1994 as an eight year old blend offering consumers a superior quality blended whisky. It is now the only major brand of its type which

has been matured for a minimum eight year period. In 1997 Bell's adopted a new strapline, coming from the Gaelic 'usige beatha' - from which the word 'whisky' is derived and which can be literally translated as 'Water of Life'.

Guinness Plc and Grand Metropolitan Plc recently merged to form Diageo Plc. Diageo's spirits arm, United Distillers and Vintners, was formed through the integration of UD and Grand Met's spirits division, IDV. Now called UDV, the spirits business portfolio includes 19 of the world's top 100 premium spirits brands.

The Product

Bell's is a blended whisky made up from only the finest malt and grain whiskies, each chosen from the whisky producing regions of Scotland - Highlands, Lowlands, Islands and Speyside for its distinctive regional characteristics. Bell's contains approximately 40% malt, a far higher percentage than the majority of its competitor blends which are made up from an average 25% to 30% malt content; another reason why Bell's is considered to be a superior blend.

Each of its constituent parts has been matured for eight years, five years longer than the legal requirement. This eight-year maturation process gives the individual whiskies time to develop greater contrast, texture and depth and many of them are stored in oak sherry casks to give a rich, deep colour to the blend.

Recent Developments

Bell's introduced its new packaging design in 1997 along with a new TV advertising campaign. The new label design emphasised Bell's rounded smooth flavour with a new curved label and Bell's eight year-old maturation statement. The latest TV advertising campaign was unveiled to over 50,000 football spectators at the Ibrox stadium, home of Bell's league Champions - Glasgow Rangers. A new TV advertising campaign is currently being developed.

1998 was the year for combining modern marketing with history and heritage. Along with new packaging and new advertising the spiritual home of Bell's - Blair Athol, situated in the heart of Perthshire by Pitlochry, celebrated its bi-centenary in 1998. Bell's hosted a number of events throughout the year to commemorate Blair Athol Distillery being 200 years old.

Promotion

United Distillers invested £14 million in the Bell's brand in 1998, targeting its core drinkers. In addition to TV advertising, Bell's is the title sponsor of the Bell's League Championships - Scotland's largest sports sponsorship. A four year sponsorship completed in 1998 injected over £8 million into Scottish football.

Achievements

Bell's has been the UK's leading whisky brand for over 15 years and has a 16.4% volume share of the market. It is also one of the top ten biggest selling brands ranking alongside Mars and Persil (AC Nielsen), with a retail value of £290 million.

In 1994 Bell's officially launched itself as an eight year old blend, the only major blended whisky brand to be matured for this long.

Bell's took the innovative step in 1995 to become the first whisky to advertise on television.

A third TV commercial was recently completed and was part of a £4 million above-the-line campaign which portrays Bell's 8 Year Old Scotch whisky, Uisge-Beatha, 'The Water of Life.'

Wide-ranging promotions have been implemented throughout the UK to link Bell's with football and increase consumer awareness. In Scotland the brand has achieved 67 % brand awareness - the highest level of any spirit brand.

The 1997 advertising campaign captured the urban enlivening spirit of the brand, and underpinned the eight year old proposition. The commercial is set at an urban Scottish wedding - the ideal setting to reinforce the pleasures of drinking together. The wedding imagery underlines the integrity and quality of the product and the eight year age statement was conveyed by images of eight.

This advertisement achieved another milestone as the first screening of the new television commercial was beamed out live on 35 ft. sq. Jumbotrons in front of 50,000 spectators at one of Bell's League Championship football matches in Scotland.

The TV ads were supported by press advertising, to reinforce Bell's core message and emphasise its competitive edge. These ads are evolving to communicate the product benefits to the consumer, to educate them about the importance of maturity in a blended whisky and to justify the brand's price positioning - crucial for Bell's to resist the growth of own label and cheapest brands.

Bell's has been taking the product story to pubs and clubs to educate consumers about what makes a good blend and the benefits of ageing. These 'product appreciation' events are a major part of the Bell's campaign and have been held the length and breadth of the UK, highlighting the superior qualities of Bell's through product tasting.

These events have been expanded to press and radio with United Distillers Brand Ambassador and Master Blender, Gordon Bell. The aim of the media interviews is to conduct tutored tastings on air to reveal the secrets and qualities of the product and information on the history and art of blending.

Brand Values

Bell's is the modern blend with traditional roots tracing back to 1825. Its eight year old maturity underlies Bell's commitment of quality, ensuring a stimulating, powerful drink. Associated with the urban lifestyle, Bell's appeals primarily to male drinkers, giving it a gritty, populist character. Bell's has become synonymous with the sociability and warmth of the shared whisky-drinking occasion.

In personality, the heritage of Bell's reflects urban Scottish masculinity in contrast to Scotch whisky's traditional association with rural, highland locations. Bell's is a blend with great depth of character offering a richer more distinctive taste.

The Market

UK new car sales rose to 2.17 million units in 1997 - a healthy increase but still short of the all time high of 2.3 million units in 1989. Industry estimates suggest that sales will remain at around two million units over the next five years. Today, company cars remain the dominating influence on the market accounting for possibly around half of all cars sold. Imported cars now take a share of over 60% of all UK car sales.

There has been some change in the structure of the market since 1993 with increases in company car taxation causing more people to consider buying their own car. In addition, the increase in the availability of new finance schemes for private and business buyers has stimulated sales.

Achievements

BMW is one of the most famous car companies in the world - one in eight new cars sold in the UK's prestige car market today bears the famous blue and white roundel.

BMW has an enviable reputation for leading edge design, technology and engineering which together with skilful marketing and a strong and loyal dealer network has contributed to sales in the UK increasing over four-fold since 1980. If BMW's sales had grown at the same rate as the rest of the UK car market, around 300,000 BMWs would have been sold between 1980 and 1997. In fact, BMW outperformed the market and sold over 675,000 cars. The UK is BMW's third largest market after Germany and the US.

The brand has benefited from eighteen years of consistent advertising. Brand communication has focused on understatement and exclusivity derived from the car itself - BMW does not rely on borrowed values. And this advertising approach has consistently won awards - most recently, the IPA Advertising Effectiveness Grand Prix Award in 1994 which indicates that strong creative advertising can sell cars as well as build an image.

History

Bayerische Motoren Werke (BMW) was founded in the early 1900s as an aircraft engine manufacturer. Its origins were the inspiration for the 'spinning propeller' logo. The company is now best known for its motorcars and motorcycles, although through a link with Rolls Royce, it is also responsible for the manufacture of aircraft engines once again.

During the 1920s and 1930s BMW had a number of notable successes including the classic BMW 328 which started production in 1936 and in 1940 won the famous Mille Miglia, a 1,000 mile road race around Italy. In 1955, BMW motorcycles won an incredible 57 world records. In 1983 the company developed a power unit for Brabham which helped Nelson Piquet to win the Formula One motor racing championship.

The company's post-war renaissance began in 1968 when the BMW 2002 was introduced. This car is largely credited with introducing the concept of the sports saloon.

In 1980, when BMW established its wholly-owned subsidiary, BMW (GB) Ltd, some 13,000 BMWs were sold in Great Britain. By 1997, this had grown to a new record total of 63,000 sales. The product range has been considerably expanded in the intervening period, and BMW enjoys the support of probably the strongest and most profitable dealer network in the UK automotive industry.

The Product

BMW cars epitomise the finest design, engineering and quality available in motoring today.

Quality, technology, performance and exclusivity are the cornerstones of BMW's reputation. Research and development is an absolute priority for the company. BMW is thought to spend a higher percentage of its turnover on R&D than any other company. Its research and development centre in Munich is home to over 5,000 designers and engineers.

From this strong base, BMW designs cars that follow a well-established theme: its cars are always at the vanguard of automotive design and engineering.

'Style' is often used to characterise the appeal of BMW. By maintaining key motifs such as the classic 'kidney grille', a BMW is recognised anywhere in the world. The clear differentiation between the model Series 3, 5, 7 and 8 also provides a simple route map for consumers. Many other manufacturers have sought to emulate this concept of house style but precious few have succeeded.

Innovation and technology go hand in hand at BMW. The company is renowned as an engine company and so many of its advances have been in the area of driveline technology, i.e. engine and gearbox innovations.

BMW is obsessed with the dynamic performance of its vehicles. This is more than mere straight-line acceleration or an ability to go around corners quickly. It is founded on a belief that a car should be balanced and harmonious in all of its areas of operation. The feel of a switch, the positioning of the steering wheel, the lighting of the instrument panel - all are important factors, along with the feel of the suspension and the engine. This is what makes one BMW feel so similar to the next.

BMW has also continued to build its reputation within the motorcycle industry. The company's motorcycle division has produced over one million bikes since 1923 and half of these are still on the road today. Building on its strengths of quality and reliability, BMW has always been at the forefront of motorcycle technology. BMW has claimed many

firsts by introducing technologies on its bikes such as 'ABS', 'Paralever', 'Telelever' and catalytic converters.

The 1997 launch of the K1200RS - the most powerful BMW motorcycle ever built - made the brand a successful player in the performance-oriented sports touring sector. The introduction of the R1200C later in the same year convincingly combined avant-garde styling with cutting-edge technology - it was BMW's first bike in the cruiser sector. The R1200C was also one of James Bond's vehicles in the 1997 Bond movie 'Tomorrow Never Dies'.

With a yearly production of over 50,000 units, BMW motorcycles continue to achieve record sales figures. In 1998, the motorcycle division celebrated its 75th anniversary - 75 years in the pursuit of building bikes for the 'ultimate riding experience'.

Recent Developments

The new BMW 5 Series was launched in 1996 to critical acclaim. As with the majority of Series launches, the car immediately assumed benchmark status in its sector.

The launch of the Z3 roadster early in 1997 saw BMW return to its roots - the car echoed the pure driving exhilaration of its forerunner, the 1950s BMW 507.

During 1998, two Motorsport derivatives of the Z3 - the M roadster and M Coupé - were launched. They were joined, in the autumn, by the launch of the all-new BMW 3 Series Saloon. Other new 3 Series model shapes and a new M5 will soon be launched.

The range of cars that BMW now makes is wider than ever before. It encompasses two-seater sports cars, four-seater convertibles, three-door hatchbacks, four-door saloons, two-door coupés and five-door estates. In terms of engines there are four, six, eight and twelve cylinder petrol engines together with four and six cylinder diesel engines. Such proliferation, however, in no way sways BMW from its rigid adherence to the rear wheel drive format and near 50:50 front to rear weight distribution for all of its cars, two necessary features for the delivery of dynamic handling.

Promotion

Much of BMW's success in Great Britain is attributed to its marketing communications.

BMW's primary communications weapon over the last 19 years has been advertising. The campaign created by agency WCRS has proven extraordinarily effective and, in 1994, won the brand an IPA Grand Prix Award for long term advertising effectiveness. A year later, it was awarded an AME international advertising effectiveness gold award. These awards recognised a tremendous feat achieved by BMW - a trebling of UK sales in just 14 years

between 1980 and 1994 during which time the company also continued to strengthen its exclusive, performance car image.

BMW's advertising avoids using people, situations or stories which detract from the car itself.

Initially, the campaign focussed on double-page colour spread advertising in up market magazines and Sunday colour supplements to the point where readers came to expect that the first advertisement in the magazine would be for BMW. The brand campaign was subsequently moved on to television with innovative 20 second "posters on TV". The media strategy targeted particular programmes and relied on a large number of individual commercials, each one centring on a different aspect of the BMW product.

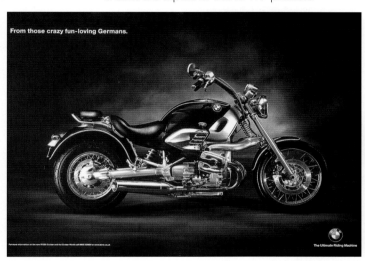

From those crazy fun-loving Germans.

BMW's 1998 advertising campaign focused on the sense of driving exhilaration provided by the range of BMW cars through one of the strongest product differentiators for BMW against competitive manufacturers - driving responsiveness. A fresh photographic style was adopted for the colour press brand campaign communicating the spirited performance and outstanding handling characteristics of the cars. This theme was followed through on TV with a range of commercials communicating the superiority of BMW driving technology.

Recognising the importance of new media, BMW launched a creative, practical and interactive presence on the Internet in January 1996. Like all BMW communications, the site (www.bmw.co.uk) is driven by the goal of creating a consumer experience that promotes the BMW brand. The site is part of a strategy which respects the individual strengths of all media, hence it provides information that is not readily supplied

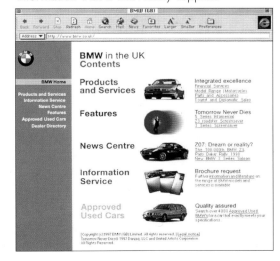

elsewhere. For example, a constantly updated Approved Used Car directory has been developed for the site from which the visitor has up-to-the-minute access to the range of used cars available through the national dealer network.

Brand Values

BMW has used the expression 'The Ultimate Driving Machine' for over 18 years. This line succinctly expresses BMW's brand position and is played back by consumers in research as summarising what they feel about the brand.

BMW sees no need to move away from its four core values of quality, technology, performance and exclusivity. These values permeate every aspect of the BMW brand. From the product itself right through to the customer's experience of the brand when visiting a dealership.

In 1998 and beyond, BMW is expected to show a consolidation of UK volume sales with car volume consistently around the 60,000 level. But BMW does not only measure success in terms of volume and profit. For the future, the company's stated aim is to become the most admired and respected service organisation in the UK.

Things you didn't know about BMW

Each year BMW runs April Fool's Day advertisements featuring almost believable technical innovations, such as a steering wheel which can switch sides for continental driving, 'prescription' windscreens for those with impaired vision, an insect repellent windscreen and a convertible which can keep out the rain, even with its roof down.

One BMW April Fool's ad trumpeted the arrival of WAIL, a Wildlife Acoustic Information Link which used ultrasonic soundwaves to warn hedgehogs of oncoming vehicles!

BMW developed the first European car powered by liquid hydrogen - the 745i, introduced in 1986.

BMW only produces rear wheel drive cars, be they 3, 5, 7, or 8 Series. This traditional sports car set-up ensures the delivery of a dynamic driving experience.

In 1919, Franz Zeno Diemer piloted his Fokker aircraft to a height of 9,760 metres, establishing a new world record. The plane's engine was built by BMW.

BMW is at the leading edge of in-car technology - in the near future you will be able to tell your BMW where you plan to drive to, and it will answer back by suggesting the best route, warning you of traffic jams and even recommending restaurants along the way.

One of the world's fastest and most expensive production cars, the McLaren F1, uses a BMW 6-litre V12 engine, generating 627 bhp. This engine powered the car to many world sports car victories, including outright victory and domination of the podium in 1996, and a class victory in 1997 at Le Mans.

Owners of 7 Series BMWs in Cologne have no trouble parking: thanks to BMWs Global Positioning System, an on-board computer can locate and reserve a parking spot anywhere in the city.

Since 1994, BMW has owned the British Rover Group which includes the famous Land Rover, MG and Mini brands.

The Market

One of the most important sectors of the UK beer market is 'standard bitter' - a beer which is not particularly strong in terms of alcohol content and is predominantly used in prolonged 'session' drinking over the course of an evening. The five major brewers are fighting head to head for dominance of this market because it generates high volume sales.

Whitbread, the owner of the Boddingtons Strangeways brewery in Manchester, historically competed in this sector with Whitbread Trophy and Whitbread Best. But by the late 1980s these brands had begun to lose their appeal with consumers who were turning to cask ales such as John Smiths and Tetley. Whitbread decided to develop a brand of cask bitter. In 1989 it bought the Boddingtons brewery in Manchester to allow it to compete more effectively for a share of the 'session' drinking market.

Achievements

Boddingtons has moved from being a regional brand with its heartland in the north west of England to a truly national brand. Since its national roll out in 1991, it has achieved exceptional levels of growth and is now the UK's fourth largest bitter brand. Boddingtons in cans was also launched in 1991 - at that time only Guinness bitter used a similar in-can 'widget' system to ensure an authentic 'pub taste'. Following the success of Boddingtons in cans, most of the other major beer brands entered the market with similar products using in-can systems.

Both Boddingtons Bitter and Boddingtons in cans have been successful but Boddingtons Bitter accounts for 80% of total volume.

Boddingtons now has retail sales value of £250 million and is the number one 'widget' ale in the take home sector (TGI). It sells over 175 million pints a year and has grown from a brand hardly known outside its home town of Manchester to a multi-million pound award-winning brand enjoyed in over 30 countries around the world.

History

The Strangeway's brewery was founded in 1778. It traded under a number of different names until, in 1853, Henry Boddington, a local corn miller, bought it and re-named it Boddingtons. The company started advertising its ale a year later using the slogan: "Pale Ale brewed especially for private families".

Under the leadership of Henry Boddington, the brewery's output grew steadily. By 1877 it was producing 100,000 barrels a year, making it the largest brewery in Manchester. It also owned 71 pubs and leased 32 others.

During the 1880s the brewery underwent considerable modernisation and the famous chimney which still dominates the site was built. Its product range included Pale Ale, Mild Ale, Bitter, Stout and Extra Stout as well as a wide range of wines and spirits.

When Henry Boddington died in 1886, the brewery was left under the management of his sons Henry, William and Robert. The company continued to grow until the 1929 depression when profits fell by half. The war years also took their toll - in 1940 the brewery was badly damaged during an air raid and production was brought to a halt. After the war a major rebuilding programme began and the brewery steadily expanded.

The company signed a trading agreement in 1962 with Whitbread and Ind Coope Tetley Ansell to sell their products in its 600 pubs. Boddingtons also agreed to brew draught beer for Whitbread.

Throughout the 1970s, further investment resulted in the installation of a modern bottling plant. A new logo was introduced which incorporated the barrel and bees symbols which had been used by Boddingtons since the turn of the century - the bees were taken from the Manchester coat of arms symbolising a hive of industry.

Boddingtons Strangeways brewery was acquired by Whitbread in October 1989 for £50.7 million. Meanwhile the Boddingtons pub empire was retained by Boddingtons Pub Company, the drinks retailing division of Boddington Group Plc.

The Product

Boddingtons is still brewed to the traditional recipe using the finest hops and malted barley and water from a 200 ft well at the Strangeways brewery.

However, there are now a number of different variations. Boddingtons Draught is the traditional keg product with a creamy head, aimed at drinkers aged between 18 and 34 and sold in city centre bars, restaurants and night clubs. Boddingtons Draughtflow is the same product but served extra-chilled for a smoother taste.

The company has also developed a system to give its canned product, Boddingtons Draught in a can, the same quality of taste enjoyed in the pub. This system uses an ingenious 'insert' charged with nitrogen which jets a fine stream of bubbles in to the beer to give it an authentic 'pub' taste.

Boddingtons Bitter is a subtle, fruity bitter with the traditional Boddingtons creamy head and Boddingtons Gold is a hybrid ale which was introduced in 1996 to appeal to lager, ale and stout drinkers. The company also produces Pub Ale which is sold in 30 countries and is known universally as 'The Cream of Manchester, England'.

Recent Developments

Boddingtons introduced Boddingtons Gold in 1996 to appeal to a broader range of drinkers. It offers the traditional creamy characteristics of Boddingtons but has the added kick of a higher alcohol content. Boddingtons Gold is available on draught and in cans and is sold mainly in trendy bars and night clubs; its drinkers tend to be younger than those who drink Boddingtons Bitter.

In the autumn of 1997, Boddingtons launched a special draught 500ml bottle in yellow shrink wrap. The special bottle contained a floating widget to deliver the perfect head. In 1998, Boddingtons introduced an updated logo to give the brand a fresh look across all products and merchandise in the run up to the millennium. The new logo still features the bees and barrels that have been a trademark of the brand for the last 100 years.

Promotion

Boddingtons first used national advertising in 1991. The brand had to appeal to two different groups of drinkers - those from the north west of England, who were familiar with the product, and drinkers across the rest of the country who were not.

THE CREAM OF MANCHESTER.

So, Boddingtons had to work hard to retain its strong sense of heritage and integrity and not appear to be compromised by the takeover of the brand by Whitbread. 'Heartland' drinkers needed to feel that their favourite pint hadn't changed and Boddingtons was keen to ensure that they did not feel disenfranchised. New drinkers had to be presented with a truly authentic regional product.

Advertising for rival bitter brands at the time focused on the drinker rather than the product, so advertising agency Bartle Bogle Hegarty focused on the creaminess of the product and its Manchester heritage. It was the first advertising and marketing campaign for the brand outside its Manchester base in 200 years.

The company used press advertising in weekend newspaper supplements to reach consumers when they were relaxed and before they went out for a lunch time drink.

Specialist titles, such as The Economist and Punch, were used to reinforce the message that the brand was aimed at discerning drinkers. Images such as a blue tit drinking from a can of Boddingtons and a cut throat razor skimming the creamy head off a pint underlined the smooth creaminess of the product in a witty, contemporary way. The outside back covers of magazines - traditionally the preserve of tobacco companies and book clubs - were used so that the advertising was visible but didn't appear to be desperate to be seen.

Television advertising followed two years later featuring humorous images such as the Manchester Ship Canal doubling up for Venice and a pint of Boddingtons used as face cream. All the ads have featured stunning girls with strong Manchester accents and the line: "The Cream of Manchester".

For the national launch of Boddingtons, the company spent £1.8m - only 55% of that spent on rival brand John Smiths. It has now increased its annual advertising budget. The press campaign launched in September 1997 took Boddingtons into an elite club of brands which can afford to leave out conventional brand names or logos. Endorsed by pre-launch consumer research, 84% of the sample recognised the distinctive product imagery combined with the black and yellow styling as Boddingtons advertising.

Boddingtons advertising campaigns have won a string of awards including a silver at the British Television Advertising Awards, a gold award at Cannes and a BAFTA.

To coincide with the World Cup frenzy gripping the nation during France '98, football's best-known anchor man, Desmond Lynam, joined the Boddington's team to launch a £5 million-plus promotion package. Included were a World Cup 'survival kit' stuffed full of beer and goodies to see fans through, match after match.

The Des' Dream Team on-pack promotion gave consumers the chance to win a total of £250,000 in cash prizes by matching players' names printed on gamecards against those of 44 of the World Cup's greatest players drawn on Channel Four every Saturday evening during the tournament. The promotion was backed by the introduction of an extensive range of POS material featuring a picture of Des Lynam, made available to participating outlets.

In addition, Boddington's sponsorship of Skinner and Baddiel's Fantasy World Cup Live show broadcast on ITV every night of the World Cup, as well as its series of football-themed 'Cream of Manchester' ads on the back covers of national press supplements and listings magazines, ensured that the brand stayed in the media focus during the summer of 1998.

WATCH THE CREAM OF WORLD FOOTBALL WITH BODDINGTONS

NO.1 IN THE BODDINGTONS WORLD CUP VIEWING PACK. CALL 0891 191 191* FOR YOUR COMPLETE PACK AND FREE BODDINGTONS DREAM TEAM DRAW CARD FOR A CHANCE TO WIN £100,000. SEE PROMOTIONAL PACKS AND PARTICIPATING OUTLETS FOR DETAILS.

Brand Values

Boddingtons' brand values are built around a product that is creamy-looking when poured and settles into a clear, golden coloured pint with a thick white head. It is smooth and refreshing with a distinctive taste and is ideal for 'long haul' drinking. It is also essentially Mancunian in character - solid, straight-talking, irreverent, urban and contemporary.

BODDINGTONS. THE CREAM OF MANCHESTER.
Boddingtons Draught Bitter. Brewed at the Strangeways Brewery since 1778.

Photo: Tiff Hunter

Photo: Tiff Hunter

Things you didn't know about
Boddingtons

Boddingtons is sold from Australia to Zimbabwe with over 175 million pints produced in Manchester each year.

The brand enjoys sales of £250 million a year.

The water used in Boddingtons comes from a well 200 feet below the Strangeways brewery.

The bees and barrels logo was introduced at the turn of the century. The bees were taken from the city of Manchester's coat of arms and symbolise a hive of industry. It was also intended as a pun on the two 'Bs' of Boddingtons Beers.

The Market

The worldwide telecommunications business is rapidly changing. Although its origins lie in telephony, it has become a communications industry worth around $670 billion - a figure set to exceed one trillion dollars by the year 2000. By then, it is predicted that worldwide, 95 billion minutes a year will be spent on international communications - talking on the phone, faxing, sending data and surfing the Internet.

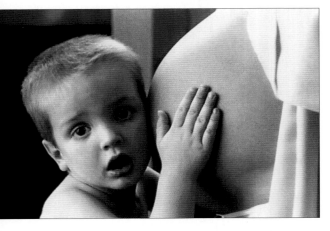

The big challenge for BT will be meeting demand on such a scale. The market in which it operates is already changing fast. Rapid technological change, worldwide deregulation and convergence of the communications, IT and entertainment industries have changed the rules. Video conferencing, ISDN and the Internet - virtually unknown a decade ago - are now commonplace. And the future will bring more new technology to change and improve people's lives.

Meanwhile, telecommunications markets around the world are opening up to competition. Britain has lead the way since 1984 when telecoms moved out of state control and into the free market. Once a monopoly, the UK market is now the most open market in the world with over 200 operators.

Achievements

BT aims to become the most successful worldwide telecommunications group. The company's central purpose is to provide world class telecommunications products and services. It is also committed to developing its networks at home and overseas to meet the requirements of its customers, sustain growth on behalf of shareholders and contribute to the communities in which it operates.

To keep abreast of rapid regulatory change and technological advancement, BT and a number of telecoms companies around the world have formed joint ventures, alliances and partnerships. BT is concentrating on three key areas to achieve its global ambitions - Europe, Asia Pacific and the Americas. Strategic partnerships offer the scale, reach, resources and expertise necessary for survival in the fast-moving communications marketplace of the 21st century.

BT's network is one of the world's most technologically advanced. The company has spent over £27 billion on its development since privatisation in 1984. Every year BT spends around £2 billion on modernising and expanding its network to meet the needs of its customers at home and abroad.

At the heart of the UK network are more than 7,500 local exchanges, 69 switching exchanges, four special switching units in London and a further seven units dedicated to international calls. All these run on digital or modern electronic technology. Digital technology enables all types of information to be transmitted in pulse form over the network at great speed. It is the foundation for BT's Integrated Services Digital Network (ISDN), which provides the high-speed transmission of voice, data, image and text throughout the UK and to a growing number of countries worldwide.

BT has completely changed its pricing structure since privatisation. Call prices have reduced significantly - locally, nationally and internationally - discounting and value plans have been introduced, itemised billing is now available and charging has been simplified.

In the financial year to March 31 1997, BT's turnover was £14,935 million - up from £14,446 the previous year. Pre-tax profits were £3,203 million - up from £3,019 million in 1995/6.

In the 1997 UK Quality Awards, BT won two prizes - for its Business Division and for BT Northern Ireland. BT has a worldwide reputation for innovative research and development and has won six Queen's Awards for Industry.

History

For many years, the UK's telephone service was provided by the General Post Office. In 1969, the Post Office became a state public corporation and was split into two separate entities. The corporation responsible for telecommunications took on the trading name British Telecommunications and in 1984, British Telecom, as it was then popularly known, was privatised.

British Telecommunications plc was the first privatised company of its kind in Europe. It set about introducing extensive changes. For example: mobile telephony - via joint venture company Cellnet - was launched in 1985; the first international optical fibre cable, linking the UK and Belgium, was laid in 1986; an £87 million programme to provide itemised telephone bills for customers was announced in 1987.

In 1991, British Telecom was restructured and relaunched as BT with new branding, a new logo and the introduction of the Customer's Charter.

In 1993, BT announced its intention to form a strategic alliance with US long distance telecommunications company, MCI. This alliance was called Concert. BT acquired 20% of MCI in 1994 and it was intended that the two companies would merge in 1997. Although the merger did not take place, Concert continues today as one of the world's most successful global telecommunications companies.

BT is rapidly becoming a leader in the field of many other communications technologies including the Internet and corporate intranet markets. The launch of BT's Intranet Builder portfolio in 1997, enabling customers to build their own intranets, followed the announcement in late 1996 of an alliance with Microsoft to jointly develop and market a range of intranet services to meet growing demand.

On January 1 1998, the European telecommunications market opened to competition. BT was poised to exploit the new opportunities this represented. The company already had a number of 'distributorship', joint ventures and alliances in France, Germany, Gibraltar, Ireland, Italy, the Netherlands, Portugal, Spain, Sweden and Switzerland.

The Product

BT is one of the world's leading providers of telecommunications services. Its main business is the provision of local, long-distance and international telephone services; private circuits for businesses; the provision and management of private networks, and the supply of mobile communications services.

BT also provides a national and international directory assistance service, public payphones, contacts to the emergency services, and maritime services such as calls to and from ships at sea.

BT provides customers on digital exchanges with a range of Select Services including Call Waiting, Three-Way Calling, Call Diversion, Caller Display and Ring Back When Free. Its most popular digital service is the 1471 service, allowing customers to know which telephone number last called. 1471 is used around 11 million times a day.

BT provides a range of services for customers with special needs including a free

priority fault repair for customers whose telephone is a vital lifeline, free directory assistance for visually-impaired people and others unable to use a phone book, and telephone bills in Braille or large print. BT operates Typetalk which allows deaf or speech-impaired customers to use textphones to make or receive calls from hearing people. Typetalk is run by the Royal National Institute for the Deaf with substantial funding from BT.

BT has a 60% interest in Cellnet, one of the UK's four network providers for mobile telephony. By 1997, over £1 billion had been invested in the Cellnet network, and a further £1 billion is to be invested by the year 2001 - the equivalent of £1 million every working day.

Cellnet and BT Laboratories in Martlesham are working together to develop solutions for business customers' needs. They have developed Network Positioning software, allowing customers to position a mobile handset to within 25-50 metres of themselves and Phone E-mail, the conversion of e-mail text into speech, enabling customers to phone in and hear e-mails.

Recent Developments

Being in constant contact is now an essential requirement for many people. BT is at the centre of the explosive growth in mobile communications through its BT Mobile division and joint venture Cellnet. BT Mobile leads the way in the provision of integrated and innovative mobile telecommunication solutions.

BT has a wide range of communication solutions to turn a home - or anywhere else - into an office, including faxes, answering machines, data/fax modems, audio and video conferencing services, Internet and e-mail connections.

With BT's audio and video conferencing services, customers can hold telephone or video meetings between hundreds of locations anywhere in the world without anyone having to leave their desk. And with BT's Conference Call Presenter, customers can use the power of the Internet to add visual presentations without investing in special equipment.

Touchpoint, BT's interactive multimedia service, is another recent development, bringing the benefits of the 'information society' to everyone. Around 200 Touchpoint kiosks have been located in major shopping and tourist sites in the London area. At the touch of a screen, users access eight channels of information including entertainment listings, news and weather, street guides, offers and competitions.

In autumn 1997, BT announced it is to provide schools across the country with access to the Internet for less than £500 a year. From January 1998, the service allowed unlimited access for schools for up to ten hours a day. BT is also providing low cost, high-speed digital access to the Internet using ISDN lines. Internet connection should help to transform the level of take-up of information and communications technology in schools throughout the UK.

Promotion

BT is among the UK's biggest advertisers. Its main advertising agency, Abbott Mead Vickers BBDO, came up with one of the most famous endlines - and indeed campaigns - in British advertising history: "It's good to talk". Judged by the advertising industry to be the most effective campaign in Britain between 1994 and 1996, it has revolutionised the way British people regard the telephone and it is still running.

In 1994, residential customers were spending an average of just over eight minutes per household, per day on the 'phone. By the end of 1997, this had increased by more than two minutes - an impressive 25% rise in under four years.

In 1998, BT introduced the Talking Direct campaign, featuring ordinary people in everyday situations. The campaign focused on quality of service and what the company can do to improve people's lives.

One of BT's other successful campaigns is "You are always on our mind". This was designed to promote BT's Community Partnership Programme activities and enhance the company's corporate reputation. In the 1996/97 financial year, BT contributed £15 million to community causes; it has donated over £150 million since privatisation. BT is committed to being a good corporate citizen. Research shows that people who see the advertising understand more about the overall range of BT activities with charities and community bodies, and on average, think more positively about BT as a result.

Another campaign targeted business customers. The "Why not change the way we work?" ads were launched in 1997. Press, TV and radio ads featured questions such as: "Why do we fight the traffic at the same time every day when a home PC and a modem could make the journey unnecessary?" and "Why do we fly off around the world for business meetings when we could hold a video conference?". The campaign challenged current working practices and highlighted opportunities generated by the communications technology revolution.

BT's global "Let's Talk" advertising campaign was launched in 1995. It helped to bring the BT brand to the rest of the world - and to promote BT's sponsorship of round the world yacht race, the BT Global Challenge. The campaign won Media & Marketing magazine's Europe Award for the best global press campaign.

BT's identity, introduced in 1991, features a piper - a universal symbol of communication. The piper and the BT brand have been 'going global' in recent years. Joint venture companies in Europe, such as Albacom in Italy, use the piper as their own. And the BT Global Challenge raised awareness in many new countries.

BT's clear and well-executed promotional strategy is endorsed through customer research and increasingly strong brand recognition throughout the world.

Brand Values

At the heart of the BT brand is recognition of the fundamental importance of effective communication in people's personal and business lives. This is expressed as "better communications mean better relationships, a better life, better business and - ultimately - a better world". BT means communications in its widest sense - not just telephony.

BT stresses five key perceptions about the company in all its communications: that it is service orientated, trustworthy, good value, innovative and passionate about communications.

BT was voted fourth most admired company in Britain in 1997 in an annual survey conducted by Management Today magazine.

Things you didn't know about BT

BT operates 27.5 million lines in the UK - 20.4 million residential and 7.1 million business exchange lines. It carries around 105 million calls each day.

In real terms, the cost of inland calls has halved since 1984 and international call prices have been reduced by over 56%. The UK is one of the cheapest countries in the world in which and from which to make a call.

BT had 11 million Friends & Family customers and 3 million PremierLine customers in 1997.

BT customers can dial direct to 99% of the world's 700 million phones.

BT operates around 136,000 public payphones throughout the UK. In 1997, on average, 96% were working at any one time.

BT has laid enough optical fibre to circle the earth more than 80 times. One strand of optical fibre is capable of carrying almost 8,000 simultaneous calls.

Virtually every picture seen on UK television, including live sports coverage, advertisements and popular entertainment programmes, has been carried at some time over video circuits provided by BT Broadcast Services.

KING OF BEERS.

The Market

The alcoholic drinks market is highly competitive, constantly changing and rapidly evolving as brewers fight to increase their share of a relatively fixed volume business by introducing new products and developing different categories.

Throughout the 1990s, there has been increased consumer demand for new and innovative drinks such as 'ice beers', so-called 'alcopops' such as Hooch and most recently spirit mixed drinks such as Moscow Mule.

In the UK, the lager market has traditionally been split into two categories - standard and premium, based on differences in price and alcoholic content. The standard lager sector has remained static in recent years. Premium lager, however, has seen a rapid increase in consumer demand. In revenue terms, it is now the fastest growing alcoholic drinks sector.

Budweiser now leads the field in premium packaged lager having overtaken former brand leaders Becks and Holsten Pils in 1994. It is also the world's best-selling beer brand.

History

Budweiser has been brewed and sold since 1876 and is now the best-known beer in the world.

In 1852, the world's largest beer company was established by George Schneider in St. Louis. Competing with 40 other local breweries at that time, the company soon fell into financial problems and Schneider was forced to turn to the successful businessman Eberhard Anheuser to rescue it from financial ruin. A year later, in 1861, Lilly Anheuser married Adolphus Busch, creating the link that has transformed brewing

history. Anheuser's experience combined with Busch's marketing flair led to revolutionary developments and huge economic success.

Budweiser was first brewed in 1876. By 1878 Anheuser-Busch had won its first legal battle against a rival company producing counterfeit Budweiser and registered it's trademark. The verdict, 'Genuine as Decreed by the Courts' was incorporated onto the label and underlines the marketing strategy today.

By 1901, Anheuser-Busch was producing over 1 million barrels of beer per annum. With growing success, Anheuser-Busch realised the necessity to expand and open new markets whilst continuing their pledge to the delivery of quality beer. Anheuser-Busch was the first brewer to build rail-side ice-houses to keep the brew cool and fresh on its journey across the country. It was the first to use pasteurisation to ensure the product didn't spoil. And it used, before any of its competitors, plant refrigeration rail-cars on a massive scale.

The beginning of the century saw August Busch Sr. take over as president of Anheuser-Busch. During Prohibition Anheuser-Busch turned its energies to other industries, producing over 1 million gallons of ice cream in 1926. Soft drinks, commercial refrigeration and the production of baker's yeast were also subsidiaries of Anheuser-Busch. The repeal of Prohibition was celebrated by a crowd of 25,000 at the brewery doors on midnight of April 6th/7th 1933. Budweiser was freely distributed and Anheuser Busch delivered a case of post-prohibition Budweiser to President Franklin D. Roosevelt in the White House.

Today, production has reached 96.6 million barrels per year world wide. Anheuser-Busch

own 12 breweries and produces over 30 different brands of beer including Budweiser, Bud Light and Michelob. August Busch III is now the 5th generation Anheuser-Busch president. The opening of new markets, the introduction of new technical developments and the modernisation of business functions has led to the expansion of Anheuser-Busch and the creation of 12 subsidiaries within Anheuser-Busch Inc.

Achievements

Budweiser has successfully superseded Becks and Holsten Pils as the leading premium packaged lager. It has managed to combine tradition and quality with innovation and diversification. Budweiser continues to grow despite increasing competition and an over crowded market and has overcome many major problems that face the Premium Packaged Lager market in the 1990s. The introduction of new faddish drinks has increased the potential rejection by a younger generation who are wary of brands associated with and consumed by their parents. At the same time, over familiarity has a potentially negative effect on consumers. Constant brand marketing initiatives have enabled Budweiser to maintain its premium status whilst appearing modern and appealing to new consumers entering the drinks market.

Today Budweiser enjoys over 30% share of premium packaged lagers' sales in pubs and clubs. This has been reinforced by a solid distribution base - the brand enjoyed distribution in 77% of the UK's pubs and bars in 1998.

The Product

Budweiser's unique crisp taste is due to the use of natural ingredients, no artificial additives, the Anheuser-Busch traditional brewing technique and the guarantee of freshness on delivery.

The 5 ingredients, barley malt, hops, rice, yeast and water, are all selected to a high standard. There are 10 different hops variations used to create Budweiser's unique blend.

Anheuser-Busch operates 2 hop farms, one in Hallertau in Germany and one in Idaho which is also the largest hop farm in the world. Barley is the soul of Budweiser beer. Anheuser-Busch experts visit more than 2,500 barley fields a year to assess crops for colour, texture, taste, health and quality. Budweiser's light and crisp taste comes from the use of rice and the yeast used in Budweiser brewing is a direct descendant of the original yeast used to make Budweiser in 19th Century. Even the water is checked for impurities with daily tastings by the brewmasters!

Anheuser Busch boasts 120 years of brewing tradition. Budweiser's brewing technique is a natural process taking up to 30 days and has not changed in over 120 years. The traditional Beechwood aging process naturally carbonates the beer, eliminating the need to add quantities of Carbon Dioxide prior to packaging, and is an example of commitment to tradition and quality.

The Budweiser label states, "We know of no brand produced by any other brewer which costs so much to brew and age. Our exclusive Beechwood Aging produces a taste, a smoothness and a drinkability you will find in no other beer at any price".

Recent Developments

Budweiser has been brewed and sold in the UK since 1984. In 1992, Anheuser-Busch took control of the marketing, sales and distribution of the Budweiser brand that had been controlled by Grand Metropolitan. This move resulted in more focused marketing activity based on the brand's authentic American heritage and brewing quality.

Meanwhile, parent company Anheuser-Busch Incorporated continues to expand its business interests. Busch Entertainment Corporation was established in 1979. Today, it operates 9 theme parks, including four Sea World and two Busch Gardens parks, and has equity investment in Port Aventura in Barcelona, Spain.

Promotion

UK consumers in the highly competitive premium packaged lager sector fall naturally into two groups - young males aged 18-24 who conform with the rest of their peer group and more discerning drinkers, aged 25 and above, who are looking for 'real' product values in their beer.

Budweiser aims to build on its brand leadership by recruiting younger drinkers while maintaining the loyalty of the brand's older consumers.

All subsequent marketing and promotional activity was therefore required to meet the principles - "dynamism", "authenticity" and "stature".

Marketing activity is centred around TV and press advertising, promotions and sponsorship. Two recent commercials, 'Taxi' and 'Poker'

portrayed contemporary American scenarios aimed at 18-24 year old British drinkers. Each centred on the aspirational story of a young American hero representing the "genuine article" - as Budweiser does to beer.

Meanwhile, press advertising was used to build the brand's stature and heritage. Two executions, 'Labels' and 'Cans', demonstrated the consistency of Budweiser through time, (both in its physical label and in its quality and brewing techniques). 'Labels' won both the 1997 Grocer award for best press advertising and the 1998 Drinks Advertising Awards for best press advertising.

Sponsorship deals include top tier sponsorship of the World Cup in 1998 following the successful sponsorship of three previous events. Activities include TV and press advertising as well as Internet sponsorship, all featuring the new strapline 'One World, One Game, One Beer'. The brand is also a sponsor of the Budweiser Basketball League, the Irish Derby and V98.

In 1997 a contemporary youth retail clothing range was introduced. Items include mens' clothing under the Budweiser Clothing label. Product placement is also an important promotional activity for the brand. Exposure in Mission Impossible, Donnie Brasco, The Jackal, GI Jane and Copland in 1997/98 were typical examples.

Anheuser-Busch takes an active part in encouraging responsible drinking. Alcohol abuse and misuse are bad for the product, the company, the industry and society. That's why the company has so far invested more than $160 million worldwide in preventing misuse of its products through a broad range of activities including community programmes, school modules, videos and telephone help-lines.

Brand Values

Budweiser combines the 3 principles,

"dynamism", "authenticity" and "stature" to ensure its continuing growth and popularity amongst it's target market. "Dynamism" ensures the brand is perceived as young and hip, necessary to appeal to the primary target market, 18-25 year olds. "Authenticity" is reinforced by Budweiser's 120 year tradition of brewing and its continuing commitment to quality that appeals to the more discerning older consumers. Budweiser's heritage and roots are a clear differentiation for the brand. And "stature" is reinforced by its number one status in the UK and by being the largest selling beer brand in the world. All three principles are embodied in the product's unique packaging - classic long-necked bottle with distinctive label.

The Market

The UK is Carlsberg's oldest and largest international market but it is a market characterised by stagnating consumption and excess capacity. The ale market has been the most severely affected in recent years, although this decline has been offset by the continual growth of lager. However, even the lager market has experienced changes as the trend towards stronger, 'premium' brands has affected the standard lager market for beers with between 3.4% and 4.2% alcohol by volume (ABV). The premium lager market (4.3% - 7.4% ABV) increased by 9% in 1997, against an increase of only 2% in the standard lager market.

Achievements

The Carlsberg Group is one of the world's major international brewing groups and Carlsberg is among the most widely sold beers in the world - available in over 130 countries. The world-wide success of the brand (family) is exemplified in the UK. Carlsberg Lager was relaunched with new product and packaging in 1996, since when sales have increased by almost 25%. During this time, Carlsberg has overtaken Heineken to become the Number 3 in the UK on-trade standard lager market with sales over 1 million barrels - worth over £530 million.

Carlsberg Export was relaunched in 1998 as consumer preferences shifted further towards premium lagers. Carlsberg Export is currently number three in the draught premium lager market, with a 12.6% share of a market worth £1.5 billion, a position the brand will strengthen during the year. Carlsberg Special Brew is the UK's number one 'super strength' lager (+7.5% ABV) with a market share of 34%. In the off-trade alone 150 cans of Carlsberg Special Brew are sold every minute!

History

Denmark's first lager beer was launched in 1847 by Captain J C Jacobsen in Valby, a small town set on a hill overlooking Copenhagen. Carlsberg was named after his son, Carl - with 'berg' translating as 'on a hill'. His declared aim was: "to develop the art of making beer to the greatest possible degree of perfection".

Carlsberg's popularity in the British market began when Danish sea captains brought personal supplies ashore to share among local friends. Such was the beer's reputation that from 1868, supplies were imported on a regular basis at the Edinburgh port of Leith. During the 1940s and 1950s, Carlsberg's phenomenal success in the UK led to the founding of three separate trading companies, with some fifty brewers and bottling companies becoming distributors for the brand.

This operation was consolidated in 1974 with the inauguration of the Carlsberg Brewery in Northampton. The Northampton Brewery not only provides all of the Carlsberg required for UK consumption, but it also became a showcase for modern brewing methods and innovative industrial technology. Every day 'blind' taste test panels sit and sample lagers in order to assess them for quality. The data from these samplings is sent back daily to Copenhagen so that Carlsberg's internationally renowned standards are always maintained.

In 1992 Carlsberg UK merged with the brewing division of Allied Lyons (later to become Allied Domecq), Allied Breweries to form Carlsberg-Tetley. This joint venture gave Allied Domecq and Carlsberg an equal 50% stake in Carlsberg-Tetley - giving Carlsberg immediate access to existing Allied accounts in its Tied Estate, and their Free-Trade business. Since January 1998, Carlsberg A'S has taken 100% ownership of Carlsberg-Tetley.

The Product

Danish yeast is the most important ingredient in Carlsberg. The yeast, known as Saccharomyces Carlsbergensis, has become the derivative for all modern day lager yeasts. Each on-trade stockist is issued with a detailed set of guidelines to ensure that the product is served to the consumer in peak condition.

Carlsberg has 5 brands within the family: draught, bottled Carlsberg Lager (3.8% ABV); canned Carlsberg Lager (4.2% ABV); draught, canned, bottled Carlsberg Export (5.0% ABV); bottled Carlsberg Ice Beer (5.0% ABV); bottled Carlsberg Elephant Beer (7.2% ABV) and canned, bottled Carlsberg Special Brew (9.0% ABV).

With these brands, Carlsberg has a presence in all the major beer sectors in both the on and off trade. Carlsberg Lager, the third biggest standard lager brand in the UK, is 3.8% ABV in draught and bottled format, and 4.2% ABV in canned format. It accounts for over 65% of total Carlsberg sales.

Carlsberg Export, the third biggest premium lager in the on-trade, was launched in the UK as a premium lager with a rich flavour. This was followed by a relaunch in the spring of 1998.

Carlsberg Elephant Beer is a strong, imported, premium lager with a distinctive image. It was launched in the UK in 1989 and has developed a reputation amongst connoisseurs of imported lagers. Elephant Beer derived its name from the imposing Elephant Gate entrance to the Carlsberg Breweries in Copenhagen.

Carlsberg Special Brew, the superstrength lager market leader, was first produced in 1950 to commemorate the visit of Winston Churchill to Copenhagen. It is a dark, very strong lager which immediately gained a reputation among discerning drinkers - a reputation that has remained ever since. Carlsberg Ice Beer is the latest product to be produced by Carlsberg - launched in 1994. It is brewed with the unique 'Ice Brewing' process which results in a beer with a crisp, mellow taste with extraordinary balance. In May 1998, Carlsberg Ice was relaunched with striking new packaging.

Recent Developments

The most enthusiastic beer drinkers in the UK are aged between 18 and 24. Carlsberg Pilsner, however, was particularly popular with an older audience - 25 to 34 year-olds who traditionally do not drink as much. So in 1996, Carlsberg decided to relaunch the Carlsberg Pilsner brand to make it more attractive to younger, higher volume consumers. The strategy involved a new product with improved taste, texture and body, and the alcohol by volume (ABV) content was increased to 3.8% for the draught and bottled product and 4.2% for the canned product. The Carlsberg Pilsner name was dropped in favour of Carlsberg Lager, because the term "pilsner" had become a commodity term used by cheaper, lower strength brands.

New typography was used on the packaging to give a younger and more upmarket feel to the brand. The aim to attract the younger consumer was also the most important reason for exploiting the association with football and music.

Promotion

"Carlsberg... Probably the best lager in the world" is one of the most famous slogans in British advertising, which is unsurprising given the enduring longevity of the campaign. In fact, in 1998 the "Probably..." campaign enjoyed its twenty fifth anniversary, making it not just the longest running beer campaign, but one of the longest running ad campaigns for any product category.

Over its 25 year history and more than 100 commercials the campaign has had many high points: the long, lingering product close-ups of the early 1970s, the still remembered Carlsberg 'Complaints Department' ad in the mid-Eighties (the department featured in the

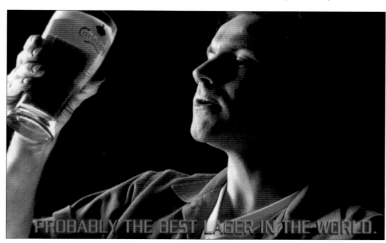

PROBABLY THE BEST LAGER IN THE WORLD.

ad was - of course - never used) and more recently 'United Nations', the science-fiction extravaganza in which the best lager in the world is the only thing to cause aliens to invade. All have been amongst the best commercials of their day.

The campaign has also employed many famous names over its life, most notably Orson Welles but also James Coburn, Ian Botham and more recently, Angus Deayton. However, there is one thing that has remained consistent over these years: the message. For a full 25 years, the focus of the "Probably..." ads remained the quality of ingredients and brewing excellence that make Carlsberg such a fine pint.

Carlsberg's memorable advertising campaigns have been supported by high profile sponsorship arrangements. Since 1992, Carlsberg has been the proud sponsor of Liverpool Football Club, one of the most famous club sides in the world. Not only does Carlsberg receive the benefit through the hundreds of thousands of visitors to Anfield, and the millions watching on TV, but through the replica Liverpool football shirts that are sold in their millions across the world. Carlsberg's connection with football extends

beyond Liverpool, however, as it touches every level of football from grass roots to the international stage. The Carlsberg Pub Cup (a concept invented by Carlsberg-Tetley) and the FA Carlsberg Vase give amateur players the opportunity to play at Wembley, as a fitting climax to the two biggest, and most highly acclaimed competitions in amateur football.

Carlsberg has been sponsor of the European Football Championships since 1982, with particular prominence in Euro 96. In 1998, Carlsberg was also the Official Beer of the FA Cup, European Cup Winners Cup, and UEFA Cup; and for the year of the World Cup '98 - the second biggest sporting event ever to be held - Carlsberg was 'Official Beer of the England Team'. This provided Carlsberg with a promotional hook for the summer of 1998. 'Go all the way with England' is the largest nation-wide promotion ever to be organised by Carlsberg in the UK. It is anticipated that this promotion will help increase annual sales to three million pints in the on-trade and 45 million cans in the off-trade.

Carlsberg has also been associated with a number of music events. Since 1990, Carlsberg has been fully available at the Glastonbury, Phoenix and Reading Music Festivals, attracting a combined total of 250,000 visitors each year. In 1998, the Reading Festival was sponsored by Carlsberg Export. In August 1997, Carlsberg hosted one of the music events of the year.

An audience of 84,000 people filled Wembley stadium to watch the Carlsberg Concert '97 featuring stars like Jon Bon Jovi, Rod Stewart and Seal. The idea was to do something extra special to celebrate Carlsberg's 150th birthday. The concert was screened on BBC 1 and world-wide reaching half a billion viewers. As with the football in 1998, the concert provided a hook for nation-wide promotions in the on and off-trade. Carlsberg also has a two year sponsorship of the MTV Music Awards.

Brand Values

The values of the Carlsberg brand are encapsulated in its legendary line "Carlsberg... Probably the best lager in the world". Quality of ingredients, excellence of production, and a heapful of charm contribute to a heraldic communications platform with humour eclipsing arrogance.

Things you didn't know about
Carlsberg

One million pints of Carlsberg Lager are sold every day in the UK. This is the equivalent of 23 pints every second!

Carlsberg has its own yeast for brewing all its lagers - Saccharomyces Carlsbergensis.

Carlsberg's founder established the Carlsberg Foundation which has the task, amongst other things, of acquiring works of art for Danish museums and institutions. The Foundation is required by its charter to hold a minimum 51% of the share capital of Carlsberg A'S.

Carlsberg is sold in over 130 countries world-wide.

Carlsberg is the second largest brewer in the world in terms of sales outside the home market.

Club Med®

The very first Club Med village was opened in 1954 and comprised army surplus tents in Alcudia on the Balearic island of Majorca. The first of Club Med's straw hut villages - modelled on a Polynesian village with beads as currency for use at the bar - opened the same year on the island of Corfu. This village, Ipsos, still features strongly in the Club Med programme. Not much has changed since the early days, although huts now have concrete floors and electric light. The company opened a mountain village in Switzerland in 1956. The first Club Med village-hotel opened in Agadir, Morocco nine years later. Subsequent years saw the business spread around the world with Club Med resorts opening in Brazil (1979), Colorado (1980) and Sahoro, Japan (1987), Cuba (1998). Club Med's sailing cruiser, Club Med 1, was launched in 1990. The second largest sailing cruiser in the world, Club Med 2, was introduced the following year.

Club Med became a limited company in 1957. In 1966, Club Med shares were first traded on the French Bourse. Club Med was rated on the New York stock exchange in 1984. In 1994, Club Med celebrated its 20 millionth customer.

The Market

In a holiday market dominated by cut-throat price promotions, greater standardisation of the holiday package and ever increasing competition, it is becoming more and more difficult to please discerning consumers.

In the past, the world seemed a much bigger place full of undiscovered corners, but with the advent of mass-market travel, exotic and exclusive spots have become more of a rarity. Consumers are now more sophisticated than ever and demand value for money, new experiences, beautiful surroundings and good food - in short, a quality escape from the realities of everyday life.

Social demographic changes such as the increasing number of single parents, lone travellers and the rise of affluent mature travellers have had a huge impact on the travel industry. This coupled with a growing trend towards late booking means that holiday companies have to be more adaptable if they are to target relatively well-travelled, increasingly sophisticated consumers.

Achievements

Club Med is a global organisation, dedicated to giving consumers an escape from reality. Its unique philosophy makes it more than just another tour operator or hotel organisation. It offers more than just a holiday - it proposes a way of life. It is the original, the largest and most comprehensive, all-inclusive holiday organisation in the world.

In 1997 Club Med was ranked as the world's 13th largest hotel chain. It employed over 25,000 people worldwide, of which 9,000 work as 'Gentil Organisateurs', also known as 'GOs', in Club Med village resorts. In 1997, Club Med organised holidays for over 1.6 million people of which over 250,000 were children.

History

Club Med was conceived in 1950 when Gerard Blitz, a Belgian diamond cutter, water polo champion and ex-resistance fighter set up in business to offer the public an escape from the dreary realities of post-war Europe. Following a camping holiday with a group of friends he decided to place small advertisements in newspapers offering the first ever all-inclusive holidays. Over 2,000 people responded and Club Méditerranée was launched. Blitz was soon joined by Gilbert Trigano whose vision and commercial acumen drove subsequent development of the Club Med business.

The Product

The beads, huts and lotus-eaters are still part of the Club Med image, but today they exist alongside smart-cards, luxury accommodation and a clientele varying in age from infants to pensioners. The average Club Med member is aged between 35 and 40 and around 65% of guests come as part of a family. A high proportion of club members - around 60% - return year after year to soak up the sun, meet like-minded people and indulge in some golf, tennis or watersports.

Club Med is also one of the world's oldest ski-tour operators. Its first village was launched

in Leysin, Switzerland in 1956 and today its programme features 27 winter sports destinations in Switzerland, France, Japan and the USA.

To be able to go on a Club Med holiday, you have to become a 'Gentil Membre', or 'GM', and pay a minimal joining fee and annual subscription fee. Holidays are then all-inclusive and the price covers: return flights & transfers, full board (including wine with lunch and dinner), sports facilities, qualified instruction, children's clubs (for children aged four or more), evening entertainment as well as comprehensive travel insurance.

The winter sports holidays also include an area lift pass and ski and optional snowboard lessons. The only extras are special courses, green fees, scuba diving, excursions, telephone calls, bar drinks and special health and beauty treatments.

completion by 1999); a refocusing on business, services and marketing; a rationalisation of operating procedures and management and the implementation of a "fair price strategy" clarifying and streamlining pricing.

Med's brochure is now translated into ten languages and has a circulation in Europe of around 3 million. The Club Med brochure can be found on the Internet (www.clubmed.com) as well as on CD-Rom.

The company's present communications strategy is designed not only to attract new consumers to the brand, but also to provide existing clients with a clearer picture of the benefits of travelling with Club Med. The aim is to provide a consistent brand message to differentiate it from competitors by re-affirming the inimitable essence of Club Med.

Club Med has invested over £50 million in a world-wide reservation and information system to handle the projected increase in members, home shopping facilities and other new developments. This allows sales staff to respond immediately to customers' requests, as well as integrate marketing data with cost analysis and to track sales trends.

Brand Values

Club Med is committed to ensuring its customers' experience of a Club Med resort is happy, relaxing and enriching. This pledge goes right to the very core of Club Med's philosophy. However, the company wants to attract a broader range of customers as well and plans to do so by reinforcing the brand's youthfulness.

Partez avec un sac sous le bras, revenez avec deux valises sous les yeux.

Club Med Ψ
PRIX APPEL LOCAL N° Azur **0 801 802 803**
Club Med Voyages. Havas voyages et agences agréées.

Club Med's main point of difference is the 'GO' system. 'GOs' are multi-lingual, multi-talented and multi-national hosts and hostesses who are responsible for everything that happens in the village, from the food to accommodation, sports to entertainment. The teams of 'GOs' headed by a 'Chef de Village', participate in all aspects of village life and might be sports instructors by day, table companions at meal times and entertainers in evening shows.

Recent Developments

Philippe Bourguignon, Club Med's President since 1997, unveiled a 'Refoundation Strategy' for the business in 1998. This initiative comprises five key components: The creation of a premium around the single flagship brand - Club Med - expressing strong values; improvements to the product through renovation of villages (due for

The Club hopes this fresh approach will attract and retain a broader range of customers and reinforce the brand's youthfulness and strength.

Club Méditerranée will also enlarge its leisure and recreational service business. It aims to turn from a company whose sole asset is the management of resorts to one whose primary asset is its brand. The unique image expressed by the Club Med name could be applied to a wide array of activities or products with high growth potential.

The Club is now undertaking the first phase of its 'Refoundation' programme. Aquarius villages were merged into the Club Méditerranée product line in April 1998 to allow the promotion of a single brand. Selected prices will be significantly reduced - particularly early and late in the season and in the most affordable villages. And the segmentation of Club Med villages will be simplified by 'comfort category' and 'type of clientele', for example recommended for people with or without children.

Promotion

A major advertising and promotional campaign for the Winter 1998/1999 is in progress devised by the recently appointed worldwide agency Publicis, to inform a wide public about recent improvements to service and pricing introduced by the Club. Meanwhile, the company's policy of globalisation will continue. Club

---

Prenez enfin des photos de famille où vos enfants vous ressemblent.

Club Med Ψ
PRIX APPEL LOCAL N° Azur **0 801 802 803**
Club Med Voyages. Havas voyages et agences agréées.

The Market

The importance of the soft drink market can never be underestimated. Already a huge business, it still has enormous potential to grow. In the Nineties, most adults have grown up with soft drinks. For many, a soft drink is as common a form of liquid refreshment as a traditional hot beverage. Children, meanwhile, take today's soft drink culture for granted. As a result, their expectations of manufacturers and their brands are even greater.

Carbonates currently make up over half of the UK's £6.7 billion soft drinks market. Cola-flavoured carbonates account for a large proportion of the carbonates sector.

Achievements

Coca-Cola® is the most valuable and powerful brand in the world - a grand claim but one that has been repeatedly endorsed by brand audits and valuation surveys such as Financial Review's annual valuation of the World's Top Brand Names. In the autumn of 1997, Financial World found Coca-Cola marginally ahead of Marlboro. Both the Coca-Cola and Marlboro brands were worth more than twice the value of the IBM brand in third position.

The Coca-Cola Company and its bottling system sells half of all soft drinks consumed throughout the world. In 1997, Coca-Cola's estimated share of the world-wide soft drink industry's sales stood at approximately 50%. Coca-Cola is distributed to more than 200 countries. It is market leader in many and often takes second position as well, either with its diet Coke formula or with Fanta, the company's orange carbonate drink.

Coca-Cola achieves and maintains this position of pre-eminence through powerful branding. It is the best-recognised commercial

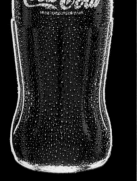

trademark in the world today, according to a number of surveys conducted by design and branding consultancy Landor Associates.

The company has also cultivated a highly successful business strategy. It has built up an extensive and well-organised distribution network, so guaranteeing the ubiquity of its products. This has been supported by powerful global advertising. Its approach is founded on a belief that Coca-Cola must try to quench the thirst of everyone in the world - all 5.6 billion of them!

The dedication of Coca-Cola sellers is quite remarkable and bears testimony to the company's determination to provide a "pause for refreshment" any time, anywhere.

Distributors are supplied by a comprehensive network of bottlers who ensure that Coca-Cola maintains a world-wide presence. Coca-Cola's bottling system is the largest and most widespread production and distribution network in the world. As a result, it has been able to establish a firm foothold in new and emerging markets. Today, you can buy a Coke almost anywhere from Beijing to Delhi, from Moscow to Mexico City.

Not only is Coca-Cola the best-selling soft drink the world has ever known, its powerful brand personality has become a vehicle for promotion in its own right. Today, Coca-Cola has provided a platform for a number of highly successful artistic and sporting events, including the Olympics. The brand has also proven to be strong enough to support a wide range of branded merchandise - bought not only for its quality but because it's fashionable.

History

Atlanta pharmacist Dr John Styth Pemberton first brewed the syrup that would eventually become Coca-Cola in a three-legged brass pot in his backyard in 1886. So good was the end result that Dr Pemberton took his new product to a local pharmacy where it was sold at five cents a glass. The syrup was mixed with carbonated water and hailed by all who tasted it as both delicious and refreshing - two product claims Coca-Cola has carefully cultivated ever since.

Dr Pemberton and his partner, Frank M Robinson, decided to go into business. Their early marketing of the drink was simple and straight forward: 'Drink Coca-Cola', the first shop signs declared. Yet the pair failed to fully realise the potential of Dr Pemberton's creation. Shortly before his death in 1888, the doctor sold his interest in Coca-Cola to Atlanta businessman, Asa G Candler.

Candler secured sole ownership in 1891. A confirmed believer in the power of advertising, he enthusiastically embraced the world of mass-merchandising, ensuring the Coca-Cola trademark was depicted on countless novelty products such as fans, calendars, clocks, ornate leaded glass chandeliers and urns. He distributed thousands of coupons for free glasses of Coke. Colourful signs promoting the brand were displayed on trolley cars and in shop windows. Just three years after the official incorporation of The Coca-Cola Company in 1892, Coca-Cola was drunk in every state and territory in the United States.

As business grew, the company had to address the growth of copycat soft drinks eager to cash in on the increasingly famous brand's success. Marketing was developed to underline the Coca-Cola brand's superiority - both in terms of product quality and market positioning as the original cola product. Advertising boards urged consumers to: 'Demand the genuine' and 'Accept no substitutes'.

As important for the development of the brand, however, was distribution. Today's vast Coca-Cola bottling system dates back to 1894 when a local shopkeeper installed a bottling device at the rear of his store and proceeded to trade crates of Coke up and down the Mississippi River. The first major bottling plant was inaugurated soon after.

In recent years, a number of very large bottlers have been formed. The world's largest is Coca-Cola Enterprises which holds franchises for much of the USA, Netherlands, Belgium, Luxembourg, Great Britain and most of France. Coca-Cola Enterprises has owned Coca-Cola Schweppes Beverages Ltd (which has held the GB franchise for the past ten years) since early 1997.

From 1926 onwards, bottling operations were opened abroad by Coca-Cola's foreign department, renamed The Coca-Cola Export Corporation in 1930. By the outbreak of the Second World War, Coca-Cola was being bottled in 44 countries including some of those countries soon to be considered to be the enemy.

War favoured rather than hindered Coca-Cola's development as a world brand. US soldiers posted abroad demanded huge quantities of their favourite drink - which boosted international distribution. Coca-Cola was therefore well-placed to seize opportunities when the war ended. Its post-war message contrasted strongly with the preceding conflict. It was based on global friendship and harmony - timeless concepts that the brand still uses today.

Coca-Cola subsequently introduced other branded products and wider choices in size and styles of packaging. Taking full advantage of staggering advances in communications technology, Coca-Cola has launched highly-successful advertising campaigns. Different campaigns in different markets may vary in style, but they never fail to relay Coca-Cola's essential brand values.

In 1982, diet Coke was introduced - the first extension of the Coca-Cola and Coke trademarks. It was a stunning success. By 1984, diet Coke had become the top low-calorie soft drink in the world.

The Product

Coca-Cola is a drink which needs no introduction. Diet Coke is its sister - a low-calorie format developed to satisfy growing demands for a diet alternative. Subsequent variations have included caffeine-free diet Coke and Cherry Coke.

A key part of the Coca-Cola legend, however, is the secrecy that shrouds the product's recipe. Coke's taste certainly enjoys emotional resonance amongst its many long-time consumers. For proof, look no further than the hue and cry surrounding attempts to change the Coca-Cola formula in 1985. The company duly responded with the re-introduction of its original product under the title 'Coca-Cola Classic'.

Recent Developments

Coca-Cola has expanded its world-wide share of global soft drink sales. World-wide unit case volume continues to grow - volume was up 9% in 1997. By the first quarter of 1998 around one billion drinks per day were consumed.

Over the last two years, The Coca-Cola Company has continued to increase market value beyond $93 billion. By 1997, it had achieved a market value of $164.8 billion, making it the second largest US-based company behind General Electric. (Source: Bloomberg)

The Minute Maid Company, a division of The Coca-Cola Company, is the largest marketer of juice and juice drink products in the world. Minute Maid has become a leading fruit beverage trademark.

Promotion

Coca-Cola's TV advertising campaigns have produced a number of famous slogans and jingles. These include: 'Things go better with Coke' (1963), 'It's the real thing' (1942 and 1969), 'Coke adds life' (1976), 'Have a Coke and a smile' (1979), 'Coke is it!' (1982), 'Can't beat the feeling' in the 1980s, and the 'Always' campaign introduced in 1993.

Radio and television have provided Coca-Cola with endless valuable opportunities to spread the Coca-Cola theme. Coca-Cola sponsors major events as well as radio and TV programmes. The Coca-Cola trademark is a crucially important marketing tool, inspiring recognition wherever it is positioned, whether it be on a billboard, bottle or T-shirt.

The brand's main UK marketing activity in recent years has focused on its football sponsorship. The successful 'Eat football. Sleep football. Drink football' campaign features real fans in real circumstances including Crystal Palace supporter Pete the Eagle and, in another ad, a blind fan who regularly attends West Ham matches. Coca-Cola built on its Euro 96 campaign with a wide range of activities based around the 1998 World Cup.

Coca-Cola has always been associated with high-quality packaging. The graceful curves of the Coke bottle have been admired since 1916 when the contour bottle replaced the straight-sided design, thereby distinguishing Coke from its competitors.

Acknowledging its importance to the heritage and authenticity of the brand, the design of the Coca-Cola 'contour bottle' was eventually registered as a trademark by the US Patent Office in 1977 - an honour bestowed upon only a handful of packaged products at the time. It was a shrewd move. Coca-Cola's own research has uncovered a consumer preference for the contour bottle over the straight-sided variety by a margin of 5-to-1. Following a change in legislation, the famous contour bottle became the first 3D depiction of a trademark to be registered in the UK in 1995.

The distinctive shape of the Coca-Cola contour bottle has recently been introduced for plastic bottles. In 1997, the company brought back the famous glass bottle in a 330 ml size unique to the UK.

Meanwhile, the famous signature flourish of 'Coca-Cola' was registered back in 1893 while the short but sweet 'Coke' won trademark registration in 1945.

Brand Values

Coca-Cola's brand values are encapsulated in its marketing messages. Slogans like 'It's the real thing' and 'Coke is it!' articulate perfectly the core elements of Coca-Cola - the first authentic, truly genuine article.

Coke is still portrayed as a life-giving force. Not only does it quench your thirst but it rejuvenates, inspires, instils youth and vitality.

It's fun. It's youthful. Wholesome. And, of course, global.

Coca-Cola's famous 1971 TV advertisement united young people from various nationalities to sing: 'I'd like to buy the world a Coke'. Even today, this single image typifies the Coke approach - to satisfy, inspire and unite in a global marketplace without frontiers.

Things you didn't know about
Coca-Cola

When the United States entered the Second World War in 1941, Coca-Cola's president Robert Woodruff decreed: "That every man in uniform get a bottle of Coca-Cola for 5 cents, wherever he is and whatever it costs the company".

In 1943, General Dwight Eisenhower urgently telegrammed Coca-Cola from his headquarters in North Africa requesting an instant shipment of three million bottles of Coke as well as materials and equipment for ten bottling plants. Throughout the war more than five million bottles of Coke were consumed by American soldiers, not forgetting the countless servings dispensed through mobile, self-contained units in war-torn areas.

Coca-Cola was first introduced to Britain in 1900 by Charles Howard Candler, the son of the company's founder. Whilst on holiday, he took a jug of Coca-Cola syrup to Britain and as a consequence an order for five gallons of Coca-Cola was sent to Atlanta.

Coca-Cola has been a sponsor of every World Cup football tournament since 1978 and also sponsored the Euro 96 football championships held in England. Coca-Cola was also an official sponsor of the 1996 Olympic Games, maintaining an unbroken presence at the Games since 1928.

Coca-Cola is second only to 'OK' as the best-known word in the world.

Smash hit pop songs have topped the charts as a direct result of having been been featured in Coca-Cola ads. The famous "I'd like to teach the world to sing" was derived from the Coca-Cola song "I'd like to give the world a Coke".

The famous red and white costume of Santa Claus was actually based on an idea from Coca-Cola! Before Coke, pictures of Santa (St Nicholas) portrayed him in flowing robes.

The Market

As new technology transforms the world of global communications, so the demand for high speed dispatch of packages and original documents grows. The European air express market is now estimated to amount to more than 360,000 shipments every day.

What was once seen as an emergency measure has evolved into an essential business tool, helping companies to retain their competitive edge. DHL's growth has reflected this evolution. Its network of hubs, gateways and logistics centres now covers 227 countries and 635,000 cities and towns, carrying over 85 million packages a year.

Achievements

DHL was the first international air express company. Through its commitment to service and reliability, it remains the market leader in international air express with a 40% share of the global market. DHL has consistently led the industry into new countries and territories. The company successfully pioneered air express services in Asia, Europe, the Middle East, Latin America, Africa, Eastern Europe, the People's Republic of China and the CIS. The first ever express shipments to North Korea and Bosnia by an air express operator were both aid packages carried by DHL, and the company continues to service both destinations.

Many of the customers who began doing business with DHL almost 30 years ago are still customers today, although their shipments and destinations may have changed significantly. This is testimony to DHL's commitment to developing long term relationships with customers and to the company's willingness to reconfigure its operations to meet customers' evolving needs.

As customers have expanded their horizons, so the DHL network has responded and the number of employees has risen rapidly. DHL now employs more than 55,000 people - over 30,000 of whom have joined within the last ten years. Some 2.5% of annual revenue is reinvested in the training and development of staff, rising to 8% in some developing markets.

In spite of its economic and physical growth, DHL has embraced the challenge of defining best environmental practice. In several European cities the company is testing electric vehicles. Mobile service centres, such as a high tech bus in Ireland and a canal boat in Amsterdam, help take traffic off the streets. In the air, all DHL aircraft are fitted with 'hush' kits to meet the Civil Aviation Authority's stringent noise emission targets, far in advance of the 2002 deadline.

History

DHL was set up in 1969 by Adrian Dalsey, Larry Hillblom and Robert Lynn - whose last names form the letters DHL. Their first service delivered shipping documents by air from San Francisco to Honolulu so that they reached the customs office before a ship was scheduled to arrive. This eliminated the expense and time delay of ships standing idle in port while they waited for customs clearance.

Since then, growth has been rapid. The company began operations in the UK in 1974 and moved into the Middle East three years later. In 1990, DHL formed an alliance with Japanese airline JAL, Lufthansa and Nissho Iwai.

Over the past 30 years, DHL has evolved from carrying mainly documents. Today, it carries everything from contracts to vital medical supplies and even aircraft engines.

Annual express deliveries have mushroomed from 50,000 deliveries per day worldwide in 1969 to more than 8.8 million from the UK alone in 1997.

The Product

DHL takes pride in being first with the post. It offers a range of services which enable customers to send almost anything, anywhere in the world at any time and its 'nothing is too much' approach ensures a high degree of customer focus. Only one phone call is required to make a booking, only one price is quoted up front - there are no hidden charges. One company picks up and delivers door to door, and the customer receives one invoice.

DHL's aim is to help companies conduct their international business affairs as effectively as possible. In delivering documents, parcels and freight all over the world, the company sees itself as a vital part of the global economy - the sending and receiving of goods and documents is an essential part of business that need not be a headache if left to DHL. In fact, through a vast array of services, both standard and bespoke, DHL can accommodate the entire range of distribution needs.

To meet the new mandates for improved customer service and quick response, which are superceding product innovation and differentiation as the means by which companies gain competitive advantage, DHL has created a wide range of logistics services on a global scale. DHL's Express Logistics Centres and Strategic Parts Centres are vital resources for many of its global customers. They enable companies to hold optimum stocks of spares and near-finished products close to important markets, without the cost of owning and operating depots, reducing their lead times and improving their customer responsiveness.

minute by tapping their account number and pick up time directly into a touch tone phone.

DHL's success looks set to continue as the market continues to grow. Despite recession in the late Eighties and early Nineties, the communications revolution has significantly increased businesses' expectations and demands for high speed, quality delivery services. Over the past six years, DHL's business has grown ahead of the rest of the express delivery market.

Growing competition from other service providers has kept the business on its toes. Building loyalty is now a central part of DHL's relationship with its customers. At the same time, DHL continues to make significant inroads into the consignment categories that were once the domain of traditional freight carriers.

Recent Developments

DHL has recently introduced a number of innovations designed to make its service even more accessible and easy to use. It now has an Internet site called DHL Red Planet, at dhl.co.uk, which enables customers to look up prices and track and trace their shipments, as well as offering information about the company's sponsorship activity. It recently introduced an automated 'SpeedBooking' service which allows customers to order a shipment in under a

Promotion

As a global company, DHL has established many strong local markets. DHL management sees itself as a worldwide team and allows local market decisions to be made at a local market level. While there is consistent brand positioning across each continent, individual countries are free to dictate their own product and tactical advertising.

For example, the UK airs a pan-European corporate TV campaign, positioning DHL as a reliable international business partner, backed by radio and press which inform people about product and service offerings. Familiar imagery in the TV ads includes red laser lines and the song 'Ain't No Mountain High Enough'. These elements act as instant identifiers of DHL and represent valuable brand equity. The long-running radio campaign, featuring comedian Bob Mortimer, reflects the confidence and humour which also characterise the UK brand. Press advertisements are also big, bold and contemporary - the 1998 SpeedBooking ad, featuring England footballer, Ian Wright, is archetypal.

DHL also conducts a wealth of below the line activity, including an extensive relationship marketing programme, 'Cradle to Grave', which guides customers through their entire shipping lifecycle, providing them with information and offers appropriate to their needs at any time.

Recent sponsorship activity includes involvement in the Financial Times' EMU supplements and co-hosting of six regional roadshows on European Monetary Union with the FT. DHL have also supported the British Touring Car Championships - holding race days at Silverstone, Knockhill and Brands Hatch and sponsoring Vauxhall driver,

John Cleland. DHL also conducted the biggest, most adventurous outdoor radio promotion of 1997, taking the Virgin Radio Breakfast Experience round the world in ten days, with live broadcasts from ten worldwide cities, including Bahrain, Sydney, Honolulu and Mexico City. This drove awareness substantially among listeners and communicated DHL's huge international capabilities in a friendly, accessible manner.

AIN'T NO PLANET FAR ENOUGH.

(Visit our Red Planet Web Site: www.dhl.co.uk)

Brand Values

DHL defines its brand values as speed, reliability, confidence and a focus on people. It places a strong emphasis on its corporate identity to communicate the consistent high quality of its service.

Employees are seen as playing a vital role as a living embodiment of the company's core values - they are, after all, the interface between company and customer.

IAN. NOW THERE'S AN EVEN FASTER WAY TO GET A BOOKING.

It's called Speedbooking and it makes booking a collection from DHL so fast and simple, you don't even have to open your mouth.

The latest in a line of brilliant new technical innovations from DHL, Speedbooking is a touch-tone telephone activated system that eliminates the need to wait while someone types in your name, address,

telephone number and collection time every time you need a pick-up.

Now, you simply call us, punch in your account number and the time you wish us to collect and we'll be there before you can say "Oh come off it refl!"

For more information and to register for DHL's new Speedbooking service call us on 0345 100 300 now.

DHL
WORLDWIDE EXPRESS
We keep your promises

DIRECT LINE ™

The Market

There are around 20 million private motorists in the UK and although patterns of car usage show signs of changing, car ownership continues to grow. As a result, motor insurance is big business.

Anyone driving a car on public roads is obliged by law to have insurance which, at the very least, covers them for injury caused to other people, their cars or property. However, the majority of motorists prefer the extra security offered by comprehensive cover, which gives protection against damage to - or theft of - their own car. In the UK, around three quarters of the £8 billion spent annually on motor insurance is for policies offering comprehensive insurance.

There are more than 300 insurance companies authorised by the Department of Trade and Industry to underwrite motor business. In practice, however, only around 65 companies - plus 20 Lloyd's syndicates - actively transact motor insurance business. The largest ten of these companies have a 50% share of the entire market, with the top five taking around one third of the entire market.

Today, motor insurance in the UK is a highly competitive business. The price war which hit the market in the early 1990s helped to push premiums down for millions of motorists but resulted in a bruising battle for business among the growing number of companies in an overcrowded market.

Much of this competition was created by the introduction of 'direct selling' in the mid 1980s. This apparently simple idea helped to change the face of insurance and altered the expectations of millions of consumers. It was pioneered by one organisation which is now the UK's largest private motor insurance company: Direct Line.

Achievements

When Direct Line Insurance was launched in 1985, it was the first insurance company to use the telephone as its primary sales tool. By dealing directly with the public - cutting out middlemen and their commissions - the company was able to use the advantages afforded by its technological efficiency and underwriting precision to reduce premiums for millions of UK drivers. In the process, it started a revolution which has re-shaped the entire general insurance industry.

To begin with, Direct Line offered motor insurance by phone but later added home insurance as its second core product. More recently, it has become a provider of a wide range of financial services including mortgages, pensions and travel insurance.

Today, Direct Line has 3 million customers. It is the UK's largest private motor insurer and the seventh largest insurer of homes and their contents. It employs over 4,000 people in six UK cities and has total assets of more than £2.7 billion.

A striking factor in the early years of the business was the speed of its growth. Direct Line achieved underwriting profit by its third full year of trading despite offering premiums which were typically 20% lower than other players in the market. This helped to fuel growth and by 1989 the company had gained around 300,000 customers, making it a significant player in the market. This, however, was just the beginning.

In the next three years, Direct Line achieved close to 500% growth. By 1993 Direct Line had signed up its one millionth motor policy insurance holder and a year later - less than a decade after its arrival in the market - had doubled this figure once again making Direct Line the largest ever private motor insurance company in the UK.

Aside from its extraordinary growth, however, Direct Line's entry into the market also set new standards of service for the insurance industry. It was the first company to offer extended opening hours, keeping its lines open 8am to 8pm weekdays and 9am to 5pm on Saturdays. It was also the first to provide a service to enable customers to register their claims by telephone and the first to provide 24 hour emergency helplines.

History

Direct Line began in 1984 when four businessmen, led by the company's former chief executive Peter Wood, used their experiences in the insurance and IT industries to take a fresh look at private motor insurance. Their view - that traditional insurers had lapsed into a culture of complacency typified by over-pricing and under-service - provided the stimulus for a new perspective on the industry. They focused on the consumer and developed an idea that brought new standards for simplicity, service and value for money into the industry.

Following a search for companies to back their proposals, an agreement was reached with The Royal Bank of Scotland who provided initial funding of £20 million for Peter Wood's plans and on 2 April 1985, Direct Line opened its telephone lines to the British public. Today, Direct Line Group remains a wholly owned subsidiary of The Royal Bank of Scotland.

In the early days, business was driven by tactical advertising in the national press and marketing to customers of The Royal Bank of Scotland.

The company's first television advertisements appeared during the late 1980s but its branding breakthrough came in 1990 when the first TV commercial featuring the distinctive Direct Line

red phone on wheels appeared on UK screens.

Within three years of its launch, the business extended its product range into home insurance, adopting the same tactics of keen pricing, a straightforward product and a challenge to the status quo - which in the case of home insurance, involved the grip on the market exercised by mortgage lenders.

In 1993, when the company's two flagship products were both the fastest growing in their sectors, Direct Line decided to enter the broader financial services marketplace with the introduction of unsecured personal loans for existing customers. This was followed by a mortgage product in 1994, and then a series of further financial services including life insurance (1995), a tracker PEP and a savings account (1996), travel and pet insurance (1997), and the Direct Line Personal Pension (1998).

The company's most recent product, Direct Line Rescue - a service to challenge traditional motor breakdown companies - was launched in May 1998.

The Product

Each of Direct Line's products is designed with the same basic philosophy: to offer consumers clear, straightforward, good value alternatives to products which are sold through traditional distribution channels - especially where those channels involve a 'middleman' who can be cut out to reduce costs.

As the company carries out the vast majority of its business using the telephone, customer service is at the core of the Direct Line proposition. It introduced new levels of service to the financial services sector, putting consumer needs and considerations first in everything that it does.

To ensure that standards are maintained, the company provides all staff with extensive customer care training and re-engineers sales processes to cut out complicated forms and jargon. In one of its first revolutionary moves,

Direct Line removed the need for 'cover notes' by arranging for all documents such as policy schedules and insurance certificates to be laser printed immediately and forwarded by first class post to customers - usually in time for the following day.

Innovative technology helps Direct Line keep down costs which, in turn, helps to reduce premiums. For example, most Direct Line products are paid for using credit cards or direct debits so that all payments are processed electronically. This keeps staffing levels and overheads to a minimum.

Automated call handling systems also ensure that the company's 15 million customer calls each year are quickly and effortlessly re-routed between Direct Line's six different city centres to ensure the minimum wait for an available operator.

Recent Developments

In addition to product launches, Direct Line has also expanded overseas with a joint venture motor insurance company in Spain - Linea Directa Aseguradora, currently Spain's fastest growing general insurer.

As part of The Royal Bank of Scotland Group's strategic alliance with Scottish Widows, a further joint venture company, Direct Line Life, was established in 1997. Direct Line and Scottish Widows each have a 50% stake in this company which offers life insurance, PEPs and a 'transparent' personal pension plan.

Also in 1997, The Royal Bank of Scotland and Scottish Widows formed a joint venture company with Tesco - Tesco Personal Finance. This company markets a range of financial services - including Direct Line Insurance products - to Tesco customers.

Today, Direct Line continues to improve its services in a number of ways, usually by challenging industry norms and offering innovative consumer benefits. These range from the use of daily interest calculation on mortgages to a 'pet bereavement helpline' for pet insurance customers. The company also takes staff development seriously with initiatives such as cross-training sales and claims staff so that the same people can handle both areas of work. The result is a more interesting role for staff and a faster, more responsive service for customers.

In tough market conditions, Direct Line continues to demonstrate its strength and retain a unique position in the marketplace.

Promotion

Direct Line enjoys huge marketing benefits from its long-running and high impact TV advertising campaigns featuring the Direct Line red phone on wheels. The phone, devised in conjunction with the company's former advertising agency, Davis Wilkins, appears in all advertising and marketing communications as a vivid icon acting as a reminder of Direct Line's brand personality. It evokes feelings of friendliness, fun, innovation and the arrival of a rescuer - emotions

rarely associated with the dry world of insurance business.

This icon, with its associated jingle, rapidly established high levels of recall among consumers helping to push the company's awareness ratings to levels normally only associated with high profile consumer brands. In 1994, Direct Line became the first insurance company ever to win the ITV/Marketing Week Brand of the Year Award.

Direct Line also invests in sponsorship. Since 1995, the company has been the sponsor of the International Ladies Tennis Championships at Eastbourne, the main ladies preparatory event for Wimbledon. Direct Line has also been the main sponsors of the Cliff Richard Tennis Trail, an initiative which introduces the game of tennis to children who might not otherwise get the chance to play.

Brand Values

Challenging convention, making services and products easier to understand, providing excellent customer service and value for money are core elements of the Direct Line brand.

The company positions itself as customer-focused, innovative and pioneering. Thanks to advertising and PR, the level of prompted consumer awareness of Direct Line in the UK reached 95% by 1997 (Millward Brown).

Things you didn't know about Direct Line

Direct Line became the largest private motor insurer ever in the UK less than a decade after its launch.

Direct Line handles more than 15 million calls each year.

Direct Line sells a motor insurance policy every six seconds of every working day.

Direct Line's sophisticated computer and telephone system automatically re-routes hundreds of calls a second around a network spanning six cities so that customers are never kept waiting.

The voice-over on Direct Line's TV commercials from 1990 to 1997 was John Alderton, famous for his TV sitcoms with wife Pauline Collins.

Following a positive appearance on the BBC's Watchdog programme at the beginning of 1998, Direct Line Financial Services received as many calls in one hour as it normally handles in several days.

Pictures of Direct Line's red phone made the pages of the national press when sun reflecting off a model of it stopped play at the Eastbourne Tennis Tournament.

first direct

The Market

Ten years ago, just three per cent of bank customers had access to telephone banking services. First Direct, however, changed all that. Today, personal banking by telephone has become the preferred method of banking for a growing proportion of the UK's 33 million banking customers.

Today's banking market is more crowded and more competitive than ever. However, rewards are still high for those offering the highest levels of banking service and value.

Achievements

First Direct was the first 24 hour person to person telephone bank - it has no branches and all customer transactions are conducted via the telephone.

Despite being one of the youngest of Britain's banks, First Direct has been the most successful of the past decade. Its customers are the happiest and it is the bank most recommended by customers to non-customers, according to an NOP poll conducted in December 1997.

First Direct has raised consumer expectations, service, quality and flexibility. By late 1997, 90% of First Direct consumers claimed to be 'extremely' or 'very satisfied' with their bank compared with 64% of Lloyds' customers, 51% of Nat West's, 50% of TSB's and just 42% of Barclays'.

History

First Direct, the UK's first 24 hour person to person bank, was launched on October 1, 1989. At that time, banks were widely disliked by customers. Banks were seen to complicate rather than simplify their customers' increasingly busy lives.

First Direct was launched as the antidote to the hassles of traditional banking. It was designed to be 'better', built on the principle of all good services industries: that the customer comes first. This was not a principle any other bank could legitimately claim.

Three main initiatives revolutionised First Direct's relationship with its customers. Firstly, the use of technology to simplify the banking process. Secondly, First Direct had no branches. It therefore had no queues, no forms and did not close. Thirdly, the attitude of First Direct's staff.

Telephone operators were a crucial part of this new proposition. So as not to reinforce the 'them and us' ethos of traditional banking, First Direct personnel were selected on the basis of their interpersonal skills. They were trained to treat customers as individuals rather than account numbers.

By the end of 1997, First Direct had 800,000 customers and every other bank had developed its own telephone banking service.

The Product

First Direct provides a full range of banking services. A key difference in its product proposition is free banking, which means no charges for normal banking transactions within the UK irrespective of whether the customer is in credit or overdrawn. Another feature is interest payable on current accounts in credit.

The First Direct Card guarantees cheques up to £100 and lets customers pay by Switch. Account holders can withdraw up to £500 a day from one of the largest cash

machine networks in the UK. An automatic overdraft of £250 is available with no fee. Telephone bill payments are also free.

Other services include savings, loans, credit cards and mortgages by telephone. All calls are charged at local rates from anywhere in the UK. Cheques can be paid in via post or at any Midland branch.

Recent Developments

When First Direct launched, telephone banking was unusual and many consumers had only just come to terms with dealing with the hole in the wall 'automated teller machine'.

As First Direct customers became more comfortable using their telephone for banking, they wanted to use their PCs. First Direct research revealed more than half of them had access to a PC at home. So, the bank developed PC Banking - a fully integrated PC-based addition to the First Direct telephone banking system.

First Direct PC Banking allows customers to view their statements, transfer money between accounts, pay bills, gain information on other services and e-mail First Direct all from their own computer screen.

The company is now considering the potential offered by the imminent launch of digital TV. As the distinction between PC and TV set blurs, there may come a time when First Direct enables customers to bank by using only a remote control to direct instruction via the TV screen.

First Direct has worked hard to associate itself with pioneering technological solutions to its customers' needs.

Promotion

Over the past two years, First Direct has been consistently outspent in terms of marketing investment by its banking rivals. Nat West spent £29 million in 1996/7, Barclays £20 million and Halifax £13 million. In contrast, First Direct's marketing expenditure was just £8 million, according to Register Meal.

Despite this, almost one in three people who moved their bank account between 1996 and 1997 moved to First Direct. This is an impressive achievement made even more remarkable given the bank's short existence. It has been made possible by a

carefully structured and tightly targeted marketing strategy.

All marketing activity is developed according to a model of customer acquisition. This model measures prospective customers on a scale ranging from 'cold' - in other words, happy with their bank and/or don't know much about First Direct to 'hot' - unhappy with their bank and actively interested in First Direct. All consumer communications are designed to move prospects up the scale from 'cold' to 'hot'.

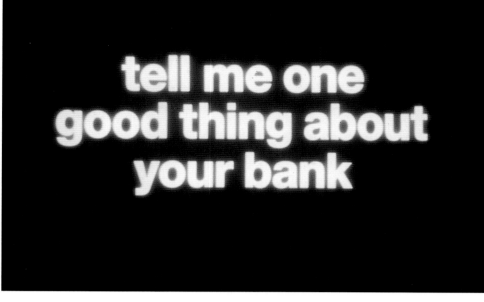

tell me one good thing about your bank

messages. In March 1997, First Direct became the first financial company to use CD-Rom as part of its direct marketing campaign.

Later in the year, First Direct launched 'Project Velcro' - a strategy designed to maximise the marketing budget by strengthening the links between above and below the line activity. The idea was that people should experience a single, consistent and relevant brand image at every point of contact. Carefully co-ordinated executions spanned TV, press, poster and radio ads as well as

Given the limited marketing budget, an integrated approach is essential to ensure all communications across different media work in harmony. So, above-the-line brand awareness advertising is complemented by highly personalised direct marketing messages using one of the most sophisticated consumer databases in the UK.

First Direct's launch advertising campaign, devised by London agency HHCL & Partners, set the trend for its subsequent ads. TV and press ads featured a selection of deliberately irrelevant images - a basket of washing, a bucket of fish and dogs.

The bank was launched through two simultaneous ads on ITV and Channel 4. It was developed more as a fashion brand than as a bank - imagery was accompanied by a prosaic

voice-over detailing rational reasons to join. The campaign achieved its objective - parent company Midland Bank estimated that First Direct needed to sign up 100,000 customers in its first year. It easily exceeded this.

First Direct began 1997 with its 'Tell me one good thing' multimedia campaign. This was designed to get other banks' customers to question the belief that their relationship with their bank was the best it could be.

This initiative was followed by a TV campaign devised by London Agency WCRS featuring the comedian Bob Mortimer which highlights the absurdities of conventional banking. Different TV ads focused on different First Direct propositions, such as 'No queuing' and 'No closing'. Associated media extended this TV theme with more specific and targeted

direct mail and 'ambient' media, including branded car park barriers.

Brand Values

First Direct positions itself as "tomorrow's bank today". Its message to the busy Nineties customer is simple: "The hassle-free alternative". There is, however, a third important part of the branding strategy - the issue of control.

The Nineties consumer demands greater control over his or her life than previous generations. They are no longer preoccupied by location - where then can get a product or service, but access - how they can get it at a time that best suits them.

First Direct therefore also works to ensure people perceive it as a way to take greater, individual control of their own lives.

The Market

The UK beer market has never been more competitive and as consumers become increasingly discerning and marketing literate, only brands which offer a relevant proposition will prosper.

Lager accounts for just over 50% of the total British beer market and commands an estimated retail sales value of more than £8 billion every year. The lager sector continues to centre around big brands which are well-supported by advertising and promotion and which provide drinkers with taste and quality. Indeed, the top five brands today account for more than 75% of the UK standard lager market.

Achievements

Foster's has enjoyed unprecedented success in Britain since the brand was relaunched in October 1993 - a move which promoted Foster's to the number two position in the UK standard lager market. It has an annual retail sales value of more than £1 billion. The brand now commands a 21% market share and is the fastest-growing of the top five standard draught lagers, selling almost two million pints every day.

The 'Amber Nectar' also enjoys the widest distribution of any draught beer in the UK and is available in more than 20,000 pubs and clubs across the country. With these impressive sales and distribution figures - and the fact that more people claim to drink Foster's than any other lager - Foster's can boast that it is the UK's most popular beer brand.

However, Foster's success reaches beyond the shores of its Australian homeland and the UK. Australia's most famous export is sold in more than 130 countries around the globe from Italy to China and Canada to Brazil and over the years, the brand has been the recipient of numerous Brewing Industry Awards.

In 1998, Scottish Courage - who brew and market Foster's in the UK under licence from Australia - unveiled a major brand investment programme which is designed to drive Foster's to overall market leadership by the year 2000. The Foster's success story continues...

History

The Foster brothers - WM and RR - arrived in Melbourne from New York in 1886, bringing with them a German-American brewing expert and a refrigeration engineer. They invested £48,000 to establish the Foster's Lager Brewing Company in nearby Collingwood.

Brewing began in November 1888 and, by the following February, Melbourne drinkers were able to take their first taste of Foster's. The new beer quickly established a trend in Australia - a bottom-fermented lager, brewed in the German style and served ice cold. Up until this time, most Australian beers were brewed in the style of English ales, using imported English malt and hops. Even in those early days, the quality and presentation of the Foster's brand was regarded as crucial and every hotel that served Foster's received a free supply of ice to go with it.

The Foster brothers sold their interest in the

brewery one year later for £45,440 16s 10d and returned to New York, little did they know that they were turning their backs on what was to become one of the most famous beers in the world.

The Foster Lager Brewing Company was purchased by a consortium of Melbourne businessmen who had their first meeting on 12 November 1889. One of their first actions was to mount a marketing campaign: they bought

360 cases of safety matches with "Drink Foster's Lager" on the label and installed beer engines in a number of Melbourne hotels.

Despite the twin challenges of the Australian economic recession and a vociferous temperance movement, Foster's continued to grow in popularity. By 1901, the beer was being exported to South Africa and Samoa. However, company directors began to realise that intense local competition was damaging growth prospects.

In 1903, representatives of the big

metropolitan brewers got together and formed the Society of Melbourne Brewers. By 1906, The Foster Brewing Company, Carlton Brewing Ltd, McCracken's City Brewery Ltd, Shamrock Brewing and the Victoria Brewery decided to form a joint company. The result was the creation of Carlton & United Breweries Proprietary Ltd which was registered on 8 May 1907, with Foster's Lager as one of the joint venture's most important products.

Foster's Lager - The 'Amber Nectar' - is now sold in every major European market and in more than 130 countries worldwide. The international growth of Foster's has been fuelled by a series of high-profile sponsorships that have made Foster's one of the most visible names in sports arenas and race tracks around the world. From Formula One Grand Prix motor racing and the Melbourne Cup - Australia's most famous horse race - to Test cricket and yachting, the Foster's name is associated with some of the most exciting events in international sport.

In 1975, Foster's Export was first sold in Britain - Foster's first appeared on draught in the UK in 1981. In 1993 it was relaunched and today the brand enjoys the No 2 position in the UK standard lager market with its eyes set on market leadership.

Foster's boasts an annual retail sales value in excess of £1 billion and has recently achieved its highest-ever UK market share in both the on and off trade markets and the highest year-on-year growth rate of the top five standard lager brands.

A comprehensive programme of marketing activities for Foster's in 1998 is designed to drive the brand towards market leadership and includes a new national advertising campaign, a new look bar fount and upweighted investment to capitalise on the brand's sponsorship of Formula One motor racing.

The Product

Foster's Lager - at 4% alcohol by volume (ABV) - is brewed to an original recipe using Australia's Pride of Ringwood hops. Outside Australia, Foster's is now brewed under licence in Britain, the USA, Canada, Ireland, Germany, Sweden and China. In the UK, Foster's is brewed by Scottish Courage in Reading, Tadcaster and Manchester.

Foster's is available on draught in either keg or tank in more than 20,000 pubs and clubs throughout the UK and from off-licenses and supermarkets in 440ml cans, four packs and 12-packs.

Foster's Export - at 5% ABV - is a full-strength premium lager which is brewed to the same recipe as the original Foster's lager imported into the UK during the 1970s. It is available in both 330 ml bottles and cans.

Foster's Ice was introduced in July 1994 and widely hailed as the most successful packaged beer launch in the history of UK brewing. It quickly established itself as the UK's number one ice beer and is currently among the top five biggest-selling premium packaged lagers in the country. At 5% ABV, Foster's Ice is available in 330 ml bottles in both on and off trade markets.

Recent Developments

Scottish Courage has undertaken a major brand investment programme which is designed to make Foster's the biggest-selling beer in Britain by the year 2000.

A £25 million brand enhancement programme which began in May 1998 introduced a new-look fount, improved product dispense and a new TV and cinema advertising campaign.

Upweighted investment in Formula One motor racing for 1998 capitalises on Foster's status as 'an Official Sponsor of Grand Prix' and forms a key part of the brand's comprehensive marketing programme.

This package of activity is designed to increase sales and drive Foster's further towards its goal of market leadership.

Promotion

Innovative marketing has been a key driver of Foster's performance for more than 100 years. Its first brand marketing campaign was launched in Australia in 1889 with the slogan "Drink Foster's Lager".

Since then, Foster's has benefited from some of the beer industry's most memorable ad campaigns including the highly-acclaimed 1980s

TV ads featuring Paul Hogan and the award-winning cinema spoof of the Häagen Dazs ice cream ad.

1993 saw the launch of the 'Search for The Amber Nectar' campaign. Directed by Ridley Scott, the commercials starred Slake and Beanbag as comic post-apocalyptic characters roaming the Australian outback in search of refreshment. Then, in 1996, the famous Australian comedy duo Roy and HG urged drinkers to "Tickle It You Wrigglers", reinforcing the brand's laid-back Australian attitude to life.

The laid-back 'No Worries' attitude is central to Foster's proposition and is perhaps best portrayed in the brand's new advertising campaign titled 'Honorary Australians'. The series of ads show Foster's drinkers reacting to problematic, potentially stressful situations in a laid-back 'No Worries' way. Foster's is seen as the hero of the ads because it allows people to tap into the relaxed Australian approach to life. The endline, 'He who Drinks Australian thinks Australian', sums up the message that drinking Foster's and having a 'No Worries' attitude are one and the same.

High-profile advertising for Foster's is matched by the brand's commitment - across all marketing disciplines - to big activity. 'Destination Australia' and 'Fostralia 1000' were Europe's biggest-ever beer promotions and Foster's has built up a high profile at key sporting events worldwide. The brand's status as 'an Official Sponsor of Grand Prix' inextricably links Foster's with one of the world's most exciting and glamorous sports and other key sporting associations include The Melbourne Cup - which represents one of the most important dates in the world horse-racing

calendar, sponsorship of the Foster's Oval cricket ground and signage at all major Test and County cricket grounds in Britain.

Brand Values

Foster's is archetypally Australian in both heritage and attitude. The brand's claim on the Australian 'No Worries' attitude to life - which is aspirational for hundreds of millions of consumers around the globe - forms the cornerstone of the Foster's proposition.

The 'No Worries' proposition - together with the brand's refreshing flavour and quality image as the 'gold standard of lagers' - makes Foster's one of the world's most recognised and best-loved brands. With its sights firmly set on UK market leadership, the Foster's success story is about to enter a new phase...

Gillette

The Market

The male grooming market was worth £445 million in 1997 and has become one of the fastest growing sectors within the toiletries industry with sales now growing at an estimated 6.5% a year. It is the largest sector within the health and beauty category and can be broadly divided into four key product sectors - blades & razors, shave preparations, mass market male fragrances and male anti-perspirants and body sprays.

Over the past ten years, men's attitudes to their personal health and appearance have changed dramatically and many have been persuaded to reconsider their attitudes to personal "grooming". Today, 90% of men use some form of male grooming product of which 75% wet shave. Small wonder, then, that men's bathroom cabinets are increasingly likely to be filled with as many products as women's. As a result an enormous number of new products specifically formulated and designed for men have been launched to cater for this growing demand.

Meanwhile, more men are buying their own toiletries. Ten years ago, two thirds of men said that women bought their toiletries for them. Now, 72% actually purchase their own, meaning companies have been forced not only to alter their products but also their style of advertising. Research shows that men now want to use high performance products such as aftershave conditioners, pre-shave gel's and deodorising body sprays.

The male grooming market is forecast to grow rapidly over the next five years. As it does, it looks set to become increasingly complex and sophisticated.

Achievements

Founded in 1901, The Gillette Company is a world leader in male grooming products - a category that includes blades and razors, shaving preparations, post-shave conditioners and electric shavers.

Gillette also holds the number one position worldwide in selected female grooming products, such as wet shaving products and female shaving preparations. It is also a world-leading supplier of toothbrushes and oral care applications, as well as being one of the leading suppliers of writing instruments and correction products through its Parker & Waterman subsidiaries.

The Company's manufacturing operations are conducted at 57 facilities in 28 countries. Products are distributed through wholesalers, retailers and agents in over 200 countries and territories.

In the UK, Gillette is the only company to enjoy market sector leadership in all three wet shaving categories. The largest of these is blades & razors where Gillette dominates with 64% market share and 72% by value of male shaving systems.

Gillette also enjoys market leadership in the second category, shaving preparations, where it commands a 52% share of the market. The third is the post shave conditioner category in which Gillette is also number one manufacturer with 15% market share.

The Company has long been at the forefront of the shaving market, introducing and patenting many innovations that are now taken for granted by customers. Adjustable razors, a fully contained cartridge, the pivoting head, the Lubrastrip, spring-mounted twin blades and soft, flexible microfins have all contributed to Gillette's powerful market share.

History

In 1895, a prosperous travelling salesman called King C Gillette had an idea that was to revolutionise shaving. His idea? A disposable steel wafer blade. Gillette began work on a prototype and a promotional campaign to interest people in the concept. However, he was initially met with disbelief as everyone believed it was impossible to sharpen a thin piece of metal enough to make a razor blade.

Unperturbed, King C Gillette persisted. He met and recruited William Nickerson, a chemist trained at the Massachusetts Institute of Technology and a highly imaginative thinker and inventor, who once developed a light-bulb manufacturing process that even Thomas Edison had said was impossible. Nickerson believed Gillette's idea was technically feasible, which led to the formation of The American Safety Razor Company in 1901.

New processes for hardening and tempering steel and mass production machinery were subsequently developed. In 1902, the business changed its name to The Gillette Safety Razor Company and, a year later the first razor went into production. In that first year, just 50 razor sets were sold - a far cry from the 300 million a year now sold in Britain alone!

In 1904, the company received its first US patent for the safety razor and sales increased to a staggering 12 million blades. Since then, Gillette has patented many of the major innovations relating to shaving. During the 1960s and 1970s, Gillette engineers were the first to patent a special polymer coating on the blade edge. This was followed by the first system razor, the Techmatic, in 1967. This was a 'continuous band' razor, which meant that the customer no longer had to touch the blade. GII followed in 1971 and brought with it the concept of twin blade shaving. This was followed by the pivoting head Contour razor and then, in 1986, the Lubrastrip.

In 1989, Gillette brought out the world's first razor with spring mounted blades - the Sensor. Five years later the company launched Sensor Excel with flexible microfin guard. 1998 saw the launch of the latest revolutionary razor called Mach3, which with its triple bladed shaving system gives men an even closer shave in fewer strokes with less irritation.

Gillette has also revolutionised the female shaving market. In 1993, the company introduced Gillette Sensor for Women; the first product specifically designed by women to meet women's shaving needs.

By the time Mr Gillette first conceived his razor blade in 1895 he was already well known in radical political circles. The previous year, in a book titled 'The Human Drift', he had proposed a sweeping plan to re-organise the entire world as a gigantic corporation that would be owned and managed by the people. Gillette evidently had hopes that the scheme would usher in an earthly paradise, and went on to spend much of his life promoting his peculiar version of Utopia.

As it turned out, the world was more interested in the clean, close comfortable shaves promised by the Gillette razor than its inventor's philosophy. As a result, his curious economic and political notions have been all but forgotten. King C Gillette had thought he might be remembered as one of history's social and economic reformers. Instead, he is recalled as the inventor of the safety razor with its disposable blade and as the founder of the major American Corporation that still bears his name.

The Product

The Gillette Company has always been famous for its razors and blades, in particular its system razor for men - Sensor Excel. The razor brought a revolutionary new technology to shaving. The Sensor razor was first developed at Gillette's UK R&D Laboratories in 1979 by Dr John Terry. Development continued for a further ten years in the US with an investment of more than £100 million before its launch in 1989. Today, Sensor has secured 26% of systems blade sales.

Sensor Excel followed which set a new benchmark in shaving technology and performance. Its revolutionary spring-mounted twin blades, Lubrastrip technology, five soft flexible microfins, combined with the new Flexgrip handle, offers men a closer, smoother shave. The microfins precede the blades and gently stretch the skin, causing the beard hairs to spring upwards, enabling them to be cut further down the shaft, with greater comfort than ever before.

Recent Developments

However, Gillette continues to seek improvements. In autumn 1998, Gillette launched MACH3, a triple bladed shaving system with progressively aligned blades to give men a closer shave in fewer strokes with less irritation. Gillette MACH3, with its breakthrough technological features, outperforms all other razors, including the current category leader Gillette SensorExcel, making this system the most significant men's shaving product introduced since the world's first twin blade razor, Gillette GII in 1971.

Gillette MACH3 has been supported by significant advertising investment including an Internet site (www.mach3.com), and is expected to add over £27 million to the value of the UK wet shaving category within the first year of launch.

The first Gillette Series male grooming products were launched in 1993 in response to the changing male attitudes. Gillette Series products are now available in three invigorating and fresh fragrances - Cool Wave, Wild Rain and Pacific Light.

The first range, Cool Wave fragrance, took three years to develop and includes 13 high performance products. In 1996 Gillette added Gillette Series Pacific Light fragrance to the range, which incorporated skin benefits and is one of the first new products to bring a light and subtle fragrance to the mass market

For women, Gillette has built on its revolutionary Gillette Sensor for Women with the launch of Sensor Excel for Women - the most advanced women's wet shaving system, which promises softer, smoother legs. The interest created by these launches prompted Gillette to broaden its range with the launch of female grooming product Gillette Satin Care Shave Gel - the first non-soap based moisturising shaving gel for women. This product includes moisturisers and skin conditioners that provides maximum comfort for the customer.

Gillette takes the women's market very seriously indeed. In 1998 it invested £4 million in a multimedia advertising campaign and is further set to build its volume share in blades and razors.

Promotion

Gillette is committed to building its technologically advanced, high performance branded products through consistent and heavyweight marketing investment.

In 1998 Gillette sponsored the World Cup football championships. The company's involvement in the World Cup dates back to 1970, making Gillette the oldest sponsor of this huge event. The reason for this is the clear synergy between the Gillette brand and the World Cup; both are active, aspirational and performance focused and both are all about being "The Best". Gillette's male grooming products are the best performing products in the world - and the World Cup brings together the best in world football.

Disposable Razor   **Gillette SensorExcel**

In 1998 Gillette brought some of the life, excitement and energy of World Cup to the world of male grooming products via a fully integrated marketing campaign. Activities began in February with a national leaflet promotion offering consumers the chance to attend the World Cup finals in Paris. A 'spot the ball' competition offered consumers the chance to win 100 VIP trips. National TV built Gillette brand awareness while radio advertising was used to drive consumers in store where eye-catching displays and point of sale material featured World Cup branding.

Gillette had at least two perimeter advertising boards at every World Cup game - seen by an estimated 13 million UK TV viewers watching at any one time.

Another recent promotion was the SensorExcel Challenge. This was a "no risk" trial offer with a strong built-in incentive for repeat purchase. The strategy was designed to encourage male wet shavers to trade up to use improved technology products offering a superior shave.

Activities began in February 1997 with a multimedia campaign comprising TV and humorous radio ads which spoke directly to disposable users, encouraging them to "Take the Gillette SensorExcel Challenge - One Shave

and We Bet You Won't Go Back to Disposables". Special eye catching promotional packs were sold which included a £1.50 off next purchase coupon. The campaign was a great success with growth in market share and an estimated 400,000 new users recruited to the Sensor brand in the UK alone.

Brand Values

The Gillette Company celebrates world class products, world class brands and world class people. These three factors account for their global achievements. Their world class products are distinguished by their quality, value, safety and effectiveness. Their world class brands are known and trusted by people the world over. Their world class people are the 33,000 employees whose skill and dedication ensure the company's continuing success.

Gillette is a world leader in the production of blades and razors. Its progress and brand values are reflected in its achievements in new technology and innovation. Gillette is renowned for leading edge products, which are technologically advanced and offer consumers superior performance.

The male image is sporty, masculine, clean and immaculately groomed. The female image is modern, energised and an understander of women's needs. Gillette knows what it takes to make men and women look and feel their very best by continually producing technologically advanced grooming products.

The following are registered trademarks of Gillette: MACH3; GILLETTE; LUBRASTRIP, TECHMATIC, GII, CONTOUR, SENSOR, SENSOREXCEL, FLEXGRIP, COOL WAVE, WILD RAIN, PACIFIC LIGHT, SATIN CARE.

Things you didn't know about Gillette

The annual production of Gillette razor blades is enough to go round the world 12.5 times.

The average male will spend 139 days of his life shaving.

Shaving does not remove a tan. Tans are caused by melanin deep within your skin. If anything, shaving enhances a tan by removing flaky skin that hides a tan's glow.

Gillette introduced the first razor for women in 1903 called the Milady Decollete.

In 1918 the United States government decided to issue every soldier and sailor with his own shaving equipment and the Company shipped 3.5 million razors and over 36 million blades to the armed forces.

Gordon's

The Market

The gin market has grown steadily since commercial production began some 200 years ago. By the early twentieth century, worldwide consumption was established and Gordon's Gin enjoyed leading brand status in many markets, particularly in the UK.

More recently, however, gin manufacturers have battled against declining gin consumption. In 1980, for example, 10.3% of British adults regularly drank gin; by 1995 the figure had fallen to 8.6%. Volume consumption similarly declined - from 144,000 h/ltrs pure alcohol to 100,000 h/ltrs over the same period. The problem was an aging customer base as younger drinkers found the drink less relevant to their needs than a host of newer alcoholic drink brands.

By 1995, Gordon's decided a new strategy was required if it was to attract future drinkers and maintain the loyalty of its existing customer base. It had to cast off its conservative and traditional image while not alienating the millions of existing brand loyalists, and did so in a new and exciting way.

Achievements

Gordon's Gin has long been brand leader in many markets and today accounts for seven out of every ten gins sold in UK pubs and bars. In the off licence sector, Gordon's again dominates - accounting for 31.7% of sales, although own label collectively accounts for a greater proportion at 47.8%.

The Gordon's brand enjoys two Royal Warrants (one from the Queen and one from the Queen Mother) and has won many awards including a Bronze in the 1996 International Wine & Spirit Competition Awards and a Gold at the same event in 1995. The brand has also won Gold, Grand Gold and Gold (Trophy) at the Monde Selection for the past three years.

History

The first spirits flavoured with juniper and produced on any significant scale were developed in Holland in the sixteenth century and brought home by English soldiers and merchants. Within two centuries, gin was the English national drink, holding the position whisky had in Scotland.

In the late eighteenth century, much of the gin produced in Britain was poor in quality and made by distillers of dubious reputation. A handful, however, became known for the quality of the product and most of these have survived in business until the present day. Gordon's Gin was one of these.

The brand was founded by Scotsman Alexander Gordon 200 years ago. He established a distillery in Goswell Road, Finsbury in 1796. By 1800, Gordon's Gin had made its name both at home and abroad thanks to the sailors of the British Navy and Merchant Navy who carried it to all corners of the world. By the late nineteenth century, Gordon's was established as a true international brand.

The early twentieth century saw gin gain popularity throughout the US. Expansion in markets closer to home, notably continental Europe, has come more recently as people switched from other products. Today Gordon's Gin, now owned by United Distillers, occupies the leading position in almost every European market and is exported to some 150 countries around the world.

The Product

Gordon's Gin is the world's best known and largest selling London Dry Gin. Recognisable by its distinctive green bottle and logo, it is

consumed at the rate of two bottles a second, day and night.

London Dry Gin is essentially a rectified or redistilled grain alcohol flavoured with juniper berries, coriander seeds and various other aromatic herbs. The production of an authentic dry gin comprises three important and distinct processes: the distillation of the basic spirit, the rectification or redistillation which gives it the required degree of purity and thirdly, a new redistillation with the flavouring ingredients (the exact recipe for which is a closely guarded secret known only by 12 people in the world!).

Unlike whisky or cognac, there is no maturing or aging process required. On the day London Dry Gin is produced it can be drunk. It is the most adaptable of drinks and mixes perfectly with fruit juices, soft drinks and colas. In many countries, however, the most popular accompaniment for Gordon's is tonic which, when mixed together, transform into a uniquely invigorating and uplifting drink.

The recipe for Gordon's Gin has remained pretty much unchanged for many years. The company has, however, developed a number of innovations to extend the Gordon's franchise. These include Gordon's & Schweppes Tonic Pre-Mix, a ready-mixed single drink pack designed to appeal to new and current users of the brand and sold in grocers and specialist off-licence channels and a larger version, sold in a 75cl bottle.

Recent Developments

After a steady decline in the gin market since the late Seventies, Gordon's Gin launched a regeneration strategy in March 1995. Activities were designed to target two groups - upmarket gin drinkers aged 45 and over and 25 to 34 year-olds - with messages of quality and relevance.

Promotion

Gordon's advertising has developed significantly since the still remembered slogan of the Seventies and early Eighties - 'It's got to be Gordon's' - and the 'Versatility' campaign of the early Eighties encouraging the use of several mixers.

In the late Eighties, Gordon's set about presenting a more contemporary image to attract new users with the launch of the 'Green' campaign (1989). This was designed to present Gordon's as being more approachable, humorous and clever than its rivals in an attempt to ditch any perception of the brand as stuffy and traditional. This worked well for Gordon's with younger consumers reassessing how they felt about the brand. However, as the only media used were cinema and print, the campaign was not exposed to the mass market and did not seem to make the audience it did reach want to try a gin.

This all changed in 1995, however, when Gordon's unveiled its new national advertising campaign on TV, ending the voluntary TV ban on spirits advertising in the UK. This new campaign adopted a fresh theme, 'Innervigoration', which focused on the physical, emotional and spiritual refreshment offered by a Gordon's and Tonic.

The new TV advertising was only part of a 'Regineration' initiative comprising a range of marketing activity including a press campaign designed to overcome the belief that all gin is the same, the first ever spirit-scented advertisement and a 'brand ambassadors' roadshow to build brand awareness and a better understanding of the product amongst younger drinkers.

At the same time, Gordon's focused on staff training to improve the presentation of Gordon's in pubs and bars. It developed a 'Perfect Serve' programme which led to a 6% sales increase in participating outlets. This focused on presenting the perfect Gordon's and Tonic in bars: fill a tall, clean, chilled glass 3/4 with ice; pour Gordon's over the ice; top up with a chilled bottle of premium tonic; add a wedge of lime or lemon and stir.

In one commercial, created by advertising agency Leo Burnett, Gordon's demonstrated how to make the perfect gin and tonic accompanied by the smell of juniper berries which was pumped amongst audiences in selected cinemas.

Gordon's spent over £20 million on the brand in 1996/7. The net effect of all this has been that the gin market has now returned to long-term growth, increasing at the rate of 5% a year in pubs and bars.

Brand Values

Gordon's core values are quality, clarity and stature. At it's heart is a recipe which has remained unchanged since 1769.

As a product, Gordon's Gin has always been known for its refreshing, aromatic, clean, crisp and reviving qualities. Under the 'Innervigoration' initiative, the company has attempted to better communicate emotional effects such as 'enlivening', 'invigorating', 'cleansing' and 'awakening'.

Gordon's & Tonic
innervigoration

Things you didn't know about
Gordon's

The origins of gin lie in a twelfth century Italian monastery where monks made medicines from local herbs, including a conifer called juniper. The end result was stimulating, sudorific, diuretic and was thought to be good for arthritis and rheumatism. It was later used as a cure for the Black Death! The monks soon realised the juniper concoction was better mixed with alcohol as they had already perfected the art of distillation.

By the late nineteenth century, export orders for Gordon's Gin were coming from all round the world. One of the first was from a group of Australian settlers who sent their payment in advance - in gold dust.

Gin and tonic was first drunk in India in the 1850s. British troops stationed there suffered terribly from malaria for which the only remedy was quinine. But quinine tasted awful. Until, that is, a resourceful officer started mixing his regular dose with sweetened seltzer, or soda water, and eventually gin, which made the taste even better.

Recently, a huge new complex has been constructed for Gordon's at a site 50 km outside London where all bottling and storage now takes place.

At the Gordon's distillery, the last two processes of the three-step production process take place in large copper stills, the oldest of which - 'Old Tom' - is over 200 years old and survived the destruction of the distillery during the last war.

Ten million cases - or about 100 million bottles of Gordon's Gin - are produced and sold in the course of a year. About half of this comes from the London distillery.

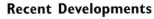

FRESH CREAM *Ice Cream*

The Market

Ice cream was once viewed merely as a treat for kids. Not any more. Since the launch of Häagen-Dazs in the UK in 1989 luxury, premium quality ice cream has become a sophisticated and stylish indulgence for adults. The UK ice cream market is now worth more than £1 billion a year (sales) and Häagen-Dazs has a 24.2% share of the one litre and under dairy ice cream market (Nielsen 23/1/98). In 1997, the ice cream market grew in value by more than 13%; Häagen-Dazs' market value grew by almost double this - at a rate of 24.3% (Nielsen 23/1/98).

Achievements

Häagen-Dazs is the brand leader in the 'super premium' ice cream market. It virtually created the premium ice cream market in the UK which had previously consisted of one or two small regional brands. In its first year alone it took 8% of the market, proving popular with gourmets and the style-conscious alike. Häagen-Dazs is now a global brand which enjoys strong sales in Singapore, Japan, France, Germany, Canada, North America and a host of other countries.

The brand is committed to flavour innovation - there is now even a Green Tea Häagen-Dazs ice cream available in Japan.

History

In the 1930s, New York entrepreneur Reuben Mattus set out to produce the world's finest luxury ice cream. Twenty years later his small family business had grown to be a thriving company selling ice cream under the brand name Ciro's. Mattus was one of the first to recognise the potential for wide scale distribution of ice cream by selling through grocery outlets and supermarkets. To secure his product a place in these new outlets, Mattus was determined to produce the best tasting, highest quality ice cream available and

gave it a Danish sounding name - Häagen-Dazs - to emphasise its creaminess.

In 1961, the first three Häagen-Dazs flavours - vanilla, chocolate and coffee - were sold in New York delis and word soon spread until there was nationwide demand for the product, all without any advertising. By the mid 1970s, Mattus phased out the Ciro brand to concentrate on Häagen-Dazs and his daughter developed a strategy to take the brand one step further. She opened a 'dipping store' in Brooklyn, paving the way for what are now approximately 650 Häagen-Dazs shops around the world.

International distribution of the product took off in 1982 when it first became available in Canada. Häagen-Dazs was then sold to the Pillsbury company and a year later it signed an agreement with Japanese companies Suntory and Takanaski to produce Häagen-Dazs in Japan where it quickly became the best selling premium ice cream brand.

Since 1987, Häagen-Dazs has made in-roads into European countries including Britain, France and Germany.

In January 1989, Pillsbury was acquired by Grand Metropolitan Plc which continues to invest in the brand. Pillsbury UK is now one of the food divisions of Diageo which was formed by the merger of Grand Met and Guinness plc.

The Product

Häagen-Dazs ice cream is manufactured in two high-tech plants in the US, one in France and one in Japan. Only the highest quality natural ingredients are used - fresh cream and milk, sugar, eggs and natural flavourings, with no artificial flavours and colourings.

The rich, creamy texture is created by ensuring that the ratio of cream to air is extremely high, unlike cheaper brands in which substantial quantities of air are pumped into the ice cream.

Häagen-Dazs is available in a wide variety of flavours and the favourites include Vanilla, Strawberry, Belgian Chocolate and Pralines & Cream.

Recent Developments

In March 1998, Häagen-Dazs, committed to flavour leadership and innovation, launched a limited edition line called 'Season's Selection' which changes flavours with the seasons - spring was Häagen-Dazs Toffee Creme and summer, Häagen-Dazs Orange Vanilla. These limited editions will provide retailers with the opportunity to capitalise on the incremental sales that new flavours bring. They are just another example of the company's innovative approach resulting in even greater choice of supreme quality product for the customer.

In May 1998 Häagen-Dazs tempted UK consumers with the taste of summer fruits in the form of its newly introduced range of sorbets. The company claims the range will redefine perceptions of sorbet as a weak and watery dessert by offering stronger flavours and a fresher, smoother texture. The Häagen-Dazs sorbet range includes Raspberry Classic, Mango Tropicale, Margarita - an adult sorbet with tequila and lime - and Pear Choc Fudge. The new range is also intended to give retailers an opportunity to enter a market that is growing strongly. It will be supported by advertising, PR activity and a heavyweight media relations campaign which carries a similar humorous theme to the above-the-line activity. The range enhances the retailer's offering and provides customers with the ultimate fruit indulgence.

Häagen-Dazs has also relaunched its premium ice cream stick bars with its most popular flavours - Pralines and Cream and Cookies and Cream - moving into this format in 1998.

Promotion

The marketing campaign behind Häagen-Dazs has been instrumental in the success of the brand. The company started stealthily and did not advertise, instead it made sure that the product was distributed in upmarket outlets such as Harrods and began a 'whispering campaign' about this new, incredibly creamy ice cream from the US. The campaign then went one step further with PR activity and sampling of the 'Häagen-Dazs experience' in stores, at college freshers' balls, at celebrity parties and film premières.

Full scale press advertising began in 1991 and presented the brand as an adult pleasure through images of couples enjoying the product together. At the time, ice cream was seen as something for children; Häagen-Dazs attempted to challenge this notion by presenting ice cream as sensual and seductive.

As a result of its unique advertising and strong product, Häagen-Dazs soon took over a quarter of the market, and inspired a host of cheaper imitations. It still remains the number one premium ice cream.

In spring 1998 it launched a $30 million European marketing package to take the strategy one step further. The ad campaign was the first time Häagen-Dazs had focused on national TV rather than on cinema or press campaigns and also ran in Germany, France and Spain and was supported by a print and poster campaign in nine European countries.

"AT HÄAGEN-DAZS WE hold WITH THE PRINCIPLE THAT ICE CREAM SHOULD BE THICK AND CREAMY CONSEQUENTLY WE KEEP tight CONTROL ON THE AMOUNT OF AIR BEATEN INTO OUR PRODUCT."

Häagen-Dazs

Dedicated to Pleasure.

The overall theme of the advertising focuses on something that at first glance appears to be perfect but turns out not to be - against the consistent perfection of Häagen-Dazs. The new campaign has a strong sense of humour and irony.

The 40 second commercial features a young couple on a romantic dinner date. All seems perfect and for dessert, the pair feed each other Häagen-Dazs. The end to a perfect evening awaits ... until the bill arrives, upon which the man pulls not a credit card but a calculator from his pocket and starts dividing the cost of each's meal - right down to the last bread roll.

New press advertising picked up on this theme. In one execution, a photo of a glamorous woman above the line: "She's wealthy, she's witty, she's intelligent, she's celibate" was juxtaposed with a photo of a tub of Häagen-Dazs ice cream and the words: "It's fresh cream; it's pure pineapple; it's laced with rum; it's good in bed" and "100% perfect".

Brand Values

Häagen-Dazs has established itself as a leading brand in a relatively short period of time due to its premium quality and effective marketing. The sensual and emotional experience of eating Häagen-Dazs is a prominent feature of the brand's positioning and has transformed ice cream from a children's treat to a stylish indulgence for adults. It is a brand dedicated to innovation and perfection - its ice cream experts took six years to get Häagen-Dazs Strawberry just right! Its dedication to producing the most perfect ice cream in the world is very much a core value.

100% Perfect.™

Häagen-Dazs
PRALINES & CREAM

Things you didn't know about Häagen-Dazs

Despite its strategically placed 'umlaut' and some creative spelling, the Häagen-Dazs name is not even of foreign derivation - the Mattus family simply made it up to sound distinctive and exotic.

It took six years to develop the perfect formula for Häagen-Dazs' Strawberry ice cream.

When the company ran its sexy ad campaign focusing on couples enjoying the product only real couples were used for the shoot to ensure the right chemistry.

Häagen-Dazs uses only the finest ingredients from around the world - the Macadamia nuts come from Hawaii and the vanilla comes from pods grown in Madagascar.

Britain's top three Häagen-Dazs flavours are Pralines & Cream, Baileys and Vanilla.

The Market

The financial services business has enjoyed rapid growth in recent years. In spite of this, however, it is not a market sector renowned for consumer-friendly marketing.

Banks and others involved in consumer lending have traditionally suffered a poor image as a result of weak branding and lack of customer focus. Increased competition, however, now looks set to reverse this trend. The established banks' poor marketing track record has led a number of non-finance businesses - including Sainsbury and Virgin - to identify a clear market opportunity.

Halifax, however, is one of the few traditional players in the high street which has successfully maintained its customer focus and effectively communicated its range of products and services in a distinctive and profile-raising way. The company, which started out as a regional building society, floated on the Stock Exchange in 1997 - resulting in the UK's largest ever increase in share ownership. Today, Halifax is Britain's fourth biggest bank.

Halifax provides mortgages, savings, life and personal insurance products as well as banking, personal lending and estate agency services. With continuing rationalisation and consolidation across the range of its activities, further growth for the company is therefore likely to come from both organic growth and acquisitions. Future success will also depend on Halifax maintaining its clear and personable brand image in the market.

Achievements

Halifax was the world's biggest building society until conversion to plc and remains the UK market leader in mortgages and savings. Halifax began investing heavily in information technology 25 years ago. Its on-line system allows customers to use any branch irrespective of where the account is held, and enables transactions made at branch counters to be immediately updated on the customer's account. It was the first building society to launch a credit card and a combined cheque guarantee, cash machine and debit card with Switch facility on its current account. It has been the best known and best regarded financial services provider since 1992, according to MORI. And its acclaimed 'People' TV advertising campaign has been the most consistently well noticed and popular financial services campaign of the Nineties.

Over 20 million customers trust the Halifax to take care of some part of their personal finances. Some 30,000 staff work to ensure the continuing success of the company whose total assets now exceed a massive £131 billion.

History

The Halifax was established in 1853 in the West Yorkshire town of the same name, where its head office is still based. It was set up as a building society - a concept that originated in the north of England to provide finance for housing through thrift. So successful was this blueprint that the system subsequently spread to other countries, including Australia, the US and South Africa.

The mills and factories which sprang up in the northern towns like Halifax at the time of the industrial revolution attracted workers from surrounding farmland. They flocked to the towns only to find a severe housing shortage. Building Societies were formed by small groups of craftsmen and other white collar workers who regularly saved to build up a fund that was then used to buy land and build houses.

As each house was completed, the group held a ballot to decide which member should occupy it. Each continued to pay his subscriptions until all were housed and the group's activities ceased. These groups were called 'terminating societies'. They were quickly superseded by a modified and more permanent type of organisation - the 'permanent societies'. Permanent societies were backed by people who already owned their homes. Those who had spare money to invest loaned funds to those needing homes in return for interest. This was the model for the present day building society.

Halifax was set up by a group of men who met at the Old Cock Inn, Halifax. The minutes of those early historic meetings were recorded in an ordinary school exercise book. For 85 years, the society was managed successively by Jonas Dearnley Taylor and Enoch Hill, who was later knighted for his work. This stability and the decision to open branches (taken in the first year of the Society's existence) was crucial in securing the society's future.

In 1913, Halifax Permanent was the country's largest building society. In 1928, it merged with the Halifax Equitable, then the second largest building society. As a result of this merger it became five times the size of its nearest rival. Since then, Halifax has continued to grow through a series of mergers and acquisitions. It has also expanded its activities into other countries. It has a Spanish subsidiary, Banco Halifax Hispania, launched in November 1993. And in 1995, it opened its second Spanish branch - in Madrid. Halifax International offers a range of offshore sterling investment accounts from Jersey and the Isle of Man.

The Product

Halifax plc has six business sectors: Mortgages, Liquid Savings, Retail Banking and Consumer Credit, Personal Insurance, Long Term Savings and Protection Products and Treasury. The company's mission is to become the UK's leading provider of financial services. Its corporate objectives are to maintain its lead in mortgage lending and steady diversification into other forms of secured lending; to expand further its current accounts and consumer credit; to develop income from risk investment, life assurance and insurance products and to distribute through a wider variety of channels to suit its many customers' needs.

Halifax provides a number of services to home buyers including mortgages, valuations, insurance and loans.

It currently serves just over 2.5 million mortgages on UK properties. Lending awards for Halifax in 1997 included

National Lender of the Decade and Best Mortgage Loan Provider.

Halifax has an extensive network of branches. It is constantly looking at ways to improve

customers' surroundings and service and a number of branch design initiatives are taking place. The aim is to provide a relaxed, cheerful, inviting atmosphere where friendly, knowledgeable staff provide helpful, personal assistance.

Recent Developments

In 1995, Halifax merged with Leeds Permanent Building Society and announced plans to convert to plc status. It also built Halifax Direct, one of the most advanced computer integrated telephone environments in Europe which is able to handle up to 80,000 incoming telephone calls every hour. In 1997, Halifax Direct was named European Call Centre of the Year.

In 1996, Halifax took over the business of Clerical Medical, guaranteeing a significant presence in the independent financial adviser market. It also added to its estate agency network through acquisitions from Alliance and Leicester and Birmingham Midshires. Today, Halifax has 1,000 plc branches and more than 600 residential estate agency offices.

In February 1997, Halifax members voted overwhelmingly to convert the Society to plc status - a move made on June 2, 1997.

Promotion

The Halifax corporate 'X' logo was introduced in 1987 and was derived from the advertising strapline 'Get a little Xtra help'.

More recently, Halifax has a highly successful TV branding campaign developed by London advertising agency Bates Dorland. This features people joining together to form a variety of items such as the 'X' in the Halifax logo, a bridge and - perhaps most memorably - a house. Its advertising strapline remains consistent: "Get a little extra help" - a slogan that enjoys high brand recognition with 61% of consumers correctly associating it with Halifax, a BMRB International Omnibus survey showed in 1997.

When asked in qualitative interviews which advertising campaigns people can recall for banks and building societies, the Halifax 'House' commercial consistently enjoys high recall and positive responses. It has become a classic within the financial services advertising sector - well-executed, profile-raising and, as importantly, a succinct symbol for the organisation's activities which are personal finance and people-focused.

In 1997, a new TV campaign for Clerical Medical was launched. However, the first half of the year saw Halifax focusing the vast majority of its marketing and promotional activity on explaining and promoting the conversion to plc status to its members.

Sponsorship plays a part in Halifax's marketing and promotion. The company's first major deal was The Halifax Rugby League Centenary World Cup in 1995. The company looks to develop long term sponsorships to reinforce its corporate image in changing times. It fosters partnerships which can bring value for both sides.

In 1997, Halifax won the FinancialTimes/ Association of Business Sponsorship of the Arts award for strategic sponsorship, nominated by the Northern Ballet Theatre. It has so far won nine awards in the ABSA pairing scheme.

Halifax sees itself as part of its customers' daily lives. It therefore feels it has a responsibility to put back an investment into the community - a belief that also has a marketing and promotional benefit.

Brand Values

Halifax places a high value on equal opportunities and is a member of the Opportunity 2000 initiative. It understands that its staff are the living embodiment of the Halifax brand and for most consumers, the first point of contact with the organisation. It runs a number of schemes throughout the UK to improve employment opportunities for young people from ethnic communities.

Halifax set up its community affairs programme in 1989. To date, it has given nearly £8 million in direct grants to local charities and its average annual community budget is £1.6 million. Donations have helped the homeless,

the elderly, the disabled and supported debt counselling services. Its Visa Charity Card has raised almost £9 million for Mencap, the British Heart Foundation and the Imperial Cancer Research Fund.

Things you didn't know about
Halifax

One in five UK households has a relationship with Halifax.

The Halifax flotation in June 1997 was the biggest yet on the UK Stock Exchange.

The Transfer Document/Voting Pack for the flotation was the largest mailing Halifax had ever undertaken, involving 30 million items sorted into 8 million envelopes using 5,000 tons of paper. As part of its commitment to environmental protection, Halifax asked customers to recycle the transfer document and planted 30,000 trees.

Halifax has Europe's biggest business TV network for transmitting programmes to staff.

THE FINEST TOYSHOP IN THE WORLD

The Market

The retail toy sector has grown fiercely competitive in recent years. It has moved on from small independent toy shops to out-of-town superstores such as Toys-R-Us, department stores and even mail order but Hamleys, building on its worldwide reputation, has carved its own niche in this fragmented market.

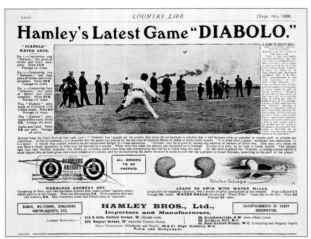

In the 1990s, consumers with disposable income are spending more than ever on their children, meanwhile children are increasingly sophisticated consumers and are no longer content with the simple dolls, games or toy soldiers that their parents may have enjoyed. Today's children want computer games, or the latest film spin-offs such as 'Buzz Lightyear' from the highly successful film 'Toy Story' or 'Teletubbies',

the big hit of 1997. And there is one place where parents know they will be able to buy them - Hamleys, the world's finest toy store.

Hamleys is renowned not just in Britain, but also around the world, for its range of toys and as a showcase for innovative new products. The company has been able to build on its international reputation and has now opened satellite stores in a number of countries and more are planned for the future.

Achievements

Hamleys is an established brand name which has successfully differentiated itself from other major toy retailers through its history, reputation and retail environment. In a recent review of the world's greatest brands by specialist consultancy Interbrand, Hamleys was classified as the ninth most powerful retail brand in the world.

The company's own-branded product range has grown to over 400 items which have generated over 20% in sales return at Hamleys' satellite stores. Utilising its worldwide reputation, part of Hamleys future strategy is to develop an exclusive retail offer based on a significantly increased own brand range and extensive ranges of major branded toy products - a number of which will be exclusive to Hamleys.

As well as the Regent Street and Covent Garden stores, the company now has an international presence having expanded into the European and Middle Eastern markets with shops at Schiphol Airport - Amsterdam, Changi

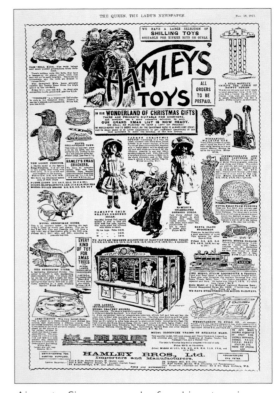

Airport - Singapore and a franchise store in Jeddah, Saudi Arabia. Hamleys sees the continuing expansion of its brand into major international cities and airports as a fundamental part of its future business strategy.

History

William Hamley first opened his toy shop in 1760 with the intention of becoming the finest toy shop in the world. The cramped Holborn shop was filled with rag dolls, tin soldiers, hoops and wooden horses and Hamley called it his 'Noah's Ark'. By the mid 1840s, Hamleys was a hugely successful 'joy emporium'.

William Hamley's grandsons opened a new branch of the shop in 1881 on Regent Street not far from Piccadilly Circus - Hamleys was there 11 years before Eros.

By 1921 the business was so successful that the Regent Street shop was redeveloped on six floors. Toy theatres, Punch and Judy puppets, pedal cars and miniature railways were among the most popular items on sale and helped to fill what had become the largest toy shop in the world. However, the depression forced the company into liquidation in 1931. It was saved by a man who had ridden on Hamleys delivery vans as a boy - Walter Lines, chairman of the Tri-Ang toy company, who bought it and rebuilt its reputation.

In 1938, Hamleys was awarded a Royal Warrant from Queen Mary - her granddaughters the Princesses Elizabeth and Margaret Rose both had Hamleys toys in their nursery. When Princess Elizabeth became Queen she too

awarded Hamleys a Royal Warrant.

Hamleys was bombed five times during the Second World War, but it didn't stop the business: staff wearing tin hats served at the front door rushing into the building to collect the toys that customers wanted.

After the war it was business as usual and Hamleys became as much a London attraction as Buckingham Palace or the British Museum. In 1981 it moved to its current premises 188 - 196 Regent Street and by May 1994 it had obtained a listing on the London Stock Exchange. It is still one of the largest toy shops in the world.

The Product

The Hamleys store in Regent Street offers up to 40,000 product lines - the widest toy range available in the world. It has created a unique retail experience through the stock density and range, active demonstrations and 'hands-on' experience of the product, friendly and knowledgeable staff and an atmosphere full of vitality and entertainment.

Toy demonstrations take place on all floors and at the peak pre-Christmas season there can be as many as 45 toy demonstrators in action. Hamleys also has a resident magician to entertain both children and adults. It is renowned for its in-store displays and award winning windows. The Christmas window displays generate significant media attention as well as attracting sizable crowds and potential customers.

Hamleys is one of the main tourist shopping destinations and attracts over five million customers every year - half of which are international tourists. On the lower ground floor of the Regent Street store there is the Hamleys Metropolis - a family entertainment centre with the latest and fastest electronic games.

Hamleys has developed close ties with all the major toy manufacturers and as a result has a worldwide reputation as a showcase for new product innovation and launches.

Recent Developments

Hamleys has taken the brand to international markets. Its most recent store opened in Jeddah, Saudi Arabia and the company says that it intends to open other stores in major international cities.

To take advantage of the opening of the Channel Tunnel, Hamleys has opened a tax free shop within the passenger terminal.

The fifth floor of the Regent Street store was recently redesigned and is now dedicated to sports, with everything from garden games and ball games to a huge selection of inflatables for water play. In-line skates, skateboards and clothing are well represented in what is a growth area for sports.

Another recent addition to Hamleys store development was the opening of the Manchester United shop where products range from shirts to hats, bags and mugs.

Hamleys has been developing an increasing Own-Brand offering. The product range includes everything from West End Barbie, a Hamleys exclusive, to a selection of classic games, collector soldiers and pocket money toys all bearing the distinctive Hamleys logo.

Promotion

Hamleys promotional strategy concentrates on PR activity, as it is perceived to be the media voice of toy retailing. The Hamleys press office is usually the first point of call for journalists wanting a comment on a toy related issue or a photographer looking for a great location. New product launches, in-store events and award winning windows all contribute to the marketing of Hamleys.

Brand Values

Hamleys is internationally recognised as the finest toy shop in the world. It is known for its extensive product range, its relationship with leading toy manufacturers which ensures that it is used as a showcase for new product innovation and launches, and for its activity, vitality and in-store entertainment which appeals to children of all ages.

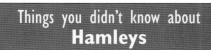

The Market

Heineken is one of the world's best-known beer brands thanks to a combination of widespread distribution and classic advertising. Its long-running 'Refreshes the parts...' advertising campaign has become an industry legend.

Heineken was founded in Holland by Gerard Heineken in 1863 and remains a family business today run by Gerard's grandson, Freddie. Heineken beer is distributed in the UK by the Whitbread Beer Company. It is available in two varieties in the UK: Heineken Cold Filtered and the stronger, premium brand Heineken Export - the original Heineken and the world's most widely distributed beer.

Heineken Cold Filtered is number three in the standard lager sector covering 'take home' and pubs and bar business, combined. Heineken Export is Whitbread's fastest growing premium lager with a 19% growth year on year.

Achievements

Heineken Cold Filtered is number two in the 'take home' sector with a 12% share and number four in pubs and clubs.

Heineken Export is now the third biggest premium lager brand in the take home sector with a 5.2% market share.

Heineken advertising has won numerous awards including a Royal Television Society Award for best use of special effects in 1994, a Eurobest Award, a silver and bronze at the

Cannes International Advertising Festival in 1993, highly commended IRL Awards, a Gold British Television Award, a bronze Creative Circle Award and the Press Jury's award at the Cannes International Advertising Festival in 1992.

History

The Heineken story began in 1863 when 22 year-old Gerard Adriaan Heineken bought a brewery, De Hooiberg, in Amsterdam. De Hooiberg was founded in 1572 and by 1863 was Amsterdam's largest. Heineken was an enterprising chap and from the beginning, he had a sharp eye for new developments in brewing and was responsible for introducing a number of innovations. He introduced 'bottom fermentation' of beer and travelled Europe in search of the finest ingredients. He established the company's own laboratory - a unique move at the time - to check the quality of basic ingredients and ensure quality control. He also performed pioneering work in the field of pure yeast cultures.

Heineken and Co enjoyed rapid growth and soon out-grew its central Amsterdam premises. In 1867, a new, larger brewery was built on the city's outskirts. Premium strength Heineken was first introduced to the UK in 1882 - it was a taste ahead of its time as British drinkers were used to weaker, standard strength ales and stouts.

Under Gerard's son, Dr Henry Pierre Heineken, the business continued to grow. With an emphasis on product quality, the company flourished into the twentieth century under Alfred H Heineken who oversaw the growth of the distribution overseas. Alfred was also responsible for establishing a dedicated advertising department modelled along American lines.

The Product

Beer is a product almost as old as humanity itself. Stone carvings dating back to 4000 years BC show beer already played an important role in the life of the Sumerians of Mesopotamia. Much has changed since then, but the brewing process today is - in essence - little different. Clean water, carefully selected barley, hops and yeast are the basic ingredients of Heineken beer.

Barley is first malted - allowed to germinate, then dried through a process known as 'kilning'. The grain is then crushed under large rollers although the husks - or 'chaff' - are left whole. Unfertilised flowers from the hop plant are dried to provide the third basic ingredient: hops. Water and ground malt are then mashed in a 'mash tun'. By heating this mixture to different temperatures using one of four brewing kettles - the main equipment used for brewing - starches are turned to sugars.

This sugary liquid is then filtered in the 'lautertun'. This has a sieve at its base which separates the husks from the liquid. The liquid seeps through this sieve and becomes clear, it is then boiled and hops are added. The hops give the beer its pleasant, bitter taste.

After boiling, the liquid is boiled again. Yeast is then added to turn the sugars to alcohol and carbon dioxide. Heineken's special A-yeast accounts for the beer's clarity, pleasant taste and aroma. It is then left to ferment for a week or so before the resulting 'green beer' is transferred to storage tanks where it matures over seven weeks at a temperature of zero degrees centigrade. The remaining yeast cells slowly continue to make alcohol and the alcohol content continues to rise - to 5%. Carbon dioxide produced which cannot escape gives form to the distinctive head on the beer. The final stage of the process is filtering under pressure to remove all elements making the beer cloudy without altering the taste.

Heineken Export is the original, full strength Heineken beer that is sold worldwide and has been brewed to the same recipe since 1873. It is a 5% ABV (alcohol by volume) beer with a smooth, easy to drink taste. Heineken Export is now sold in 177 countries - more countries than any other beer. Recent advertising campaigns have used the strapline: 'The World's Favourite Import'.

Heineken Cold Filtered was first brewed in the UK in 1956 and has been brewed by Whitbread since 1968. It is a line extension of the traditional Heineken - 3.4% alcohol by volume and brewed specifically for the UK to satisfy British drinkers' desire for an 'ale strength' lager. In blind taste tests, Heineken Cold Filtered is rated the best standard lager beating its nearest rivals including Carling Black Label, Fosters and Carlsberg.

Recent Developments

Both Heineken Export and Heineken Cold Filtered underwent extensive facelifts in 1998 with new packaging introduced in the UK during the summer.

Promotion

Heineken began its famous 'Refreshes the Parts...' campaign in the UK 30 years ago. Over this time, the campaign has run to 75 TV commercials and countless print ads. The idea

Heineken refreshes the parts other beers cannot reach.

Heineken refreshes the parts. So no money back.

Heineken refreshes the parts other beers cannot reach.

Heineken refreshes the parts other beers cannot reach.

for the creative strategy was presented to the then marketing director, Anthony Simmonds-Gooding, on board an Aeroflot plane by Frank Lowe. The first execution broke in 1974 - designed to entertain and claim the concept of 'refreshment' as Heineken's own.

Early ads broke conventional lager advertising rules. 'Piano Tuner' and 'Policemen', for example, took the action out of the traditional pub setting. Initial research suggested it was a risky strategy; the client, however, persevered. By 1976, perceptions of the brand were starting to change. By 1979, Heineken had become one of the most dominant brands in the UK lager market. The campaign really got into its stride in the 1980s when Heineken's confidence allowed bold creative executions such as 'Windermere' and 'Majorca'. During the Eighties, the brand braced itself for two new challenges: firstly, the rise of Australian lagers and secondly, the growth of premium beers.

Heineken's advertising responded with

the adjustment of the 'Refreshes the parts...' campaign to 'Only Heineken can do this' in the late 1980s. Punchy executions included 'Crimson Cow' and 'Telephone Box'. In the 1990s, a further shift took place with a new emphasis on the idea that when something isn't right, Heineken puts it right. Amongst the memorable ads from this time was 'Blues Singer'.

Meanwhile, Heineken Export's strategy was slightly different. With an emphasis on its premium positioning, advertising agency Lowe Howard Spink focused on the product's smoothness and premium positioning. The advertising played on the brand's strength and continental heritage with a series of ads featuring comedian Stephen Fry as a character known as the 'Smooth talking barsteward'. Heineken Export has most recently been advertised using the strapline: 'The World's Favourite Import'.

As a major international brand, Heineken has developed a number of major, international

sponsorships including the Round the World Yacht Race, Davis Cup Tennis, US Open (tennis) and the Rugby Union World Cup. In the UK, rugby sponsorship is a central part of promotion for the Heineken brand. Heineken currently sponsors the Heineken Cup, the northern hemisphere's premier club-based rugby competition, ITV's Five Nations coverage and all England internationals including games against Australia, New Zealand and South Africa.

In 1997, Heineken teamed up with Planet Hollywood to become the chain's preferred beer supplier in all restaurants outside the US - the first international, on-premises supply deal in the brand's 133 year history.

Brand Values

Heineken relies on the quality of its product - a promise central to its brand proposition which focuses on the beer's ability to refresh and its distinctive taste.

The Market

Heinz is truly a giant in the food sector. In 1979, the company's market capitalisation was $900 million; by 1997 it was $17 billion. Today, there are more than 300 Heinz-branded products available in the UK of which perhaps the best-known and best-loved is Heinz Baked Beans.

In the mid-Nineties, Heinz Baked Beans was involved in one of the most ferocious battles in marketing history. The UK food sector was characterised by the rapid rise of retailers' own branded goods. This put significant pressure on established brands, with fierce competition through price and positioning for limited shelf space in store. By the Eighties, the big five multiple retailers started to pull away from the pack. The huge baked beans market, a strategically important category, became a major battle ground as retailers began to re-appraise the role of own label. Already, Sainsbury's and Tesco were emerging as powerful brands in their own right. It was only a matter of time before the range and quality of their own label offerings would improve dramatically.

Heinz, however, stood its ground. It refused to enter the price war and continued to invest in marketing and promotion for the Heinz Baked Beans brand and introduced more sophisticated consumer targeting techniques. By taking positive action to protect its franchise, Heinz won the beans war.

Achievements

The Heinz umbrella brand spans hundreds of products and includes number one brands in ketchup, weight control foods (Heinz owns the

Weight Watchers brand), tuna, frozen potatoes, soups, beans, infant foods and pet food around the world. Today, the company has an enviable array of 25 'power brands' that enjoy at least $100 million in sales. Heinz Baked Beans is, for many Britons at least, the core product in the Heinz brand stable.

In the early Nineties, Heinz turned the baked beans business - which had effectively become a commodity sector - back into a brand-led business. Big retailers drew battle lines around the most essential products. Larger multiples offered own brand beans for 3p - less than the price of an empty can. Rather than become embroiled in the price war, the company launched a marketing and promotional counter attack underlining its heritage and product quality and to justify its value in the market. Heinz Baked Beans now enjoys a 51.1% share (value) of the baked beans market.

Today, Heinz is as well known for its product innovation as for the solid heritage of its core foods range. It has pioneered many technological developments in packaging and canning. It also regularly adds new products to refresh the product line.

History

Over its one hundred year history, Heinz Baked Beans has evolved from a luxury American curiosity available in Fortnum & Mason at a price few could afford, to become one of the most pervasive of all British grocery essentials.

In 1860, 16 year-old Henry J Heinz began bottling dried and grated horseradish from his family's garden in Pennsylvania. Unlike others, he packed his product in clear glass bottles so that his customers could see he was selling only horseradish without cheap fillers. By 1869, he had transformed the company and Heinz pickles and other bottled products appeared in many local shops. The product positioning was clear: no artificial preservatives, no impurities and no colouring. He also offered a money-back guarantee if his products failed to please.

Business prospered and in 1886, Heinz sailed to Britain. He brought with him five cases of products and called first at Fortnum's - who bought the lot. In 1905, British demand

was sufficient to merit the opening of Heinz' first UK factory, in Peckham. Twenty years later, Heinz' first custom-made factory opened in Harlesden, west London.

With the end of the Second World War it soon became clear additional manufacturing capacity was needed. A temporary factory was opened and remained in production for the next 30 years. In 1992, Heinz built a state of the art production plant in Dundalk, Ireland, for its Heinz pizza division.

Throughout the Sixties and Seventies, Heinz' percentage share of the bean market stabilised between 50% and 60%. The handful of branded competitors in the category seldom topped 5%, and own label knew its place - a slightly cheaper, but distinctly second rate alternative.

The baked beans sector once supported a range of smaller, independent brands such as Smedley's and Lockwoods. Soon these players found they could not compete. Heinz was in a

stronger position, but despite consistent advertising and a clear quality advantage, it too began to feel the squeeze. By the early 1990s, even Crosse & Blackwell, another powerful food brand, had conceded defeat in the beans sector. The only two branded beans remaining were HP and Heinz.

Heinz knew it could not rely only on its brand heritage. So it unveiled a strategy to develop its consumer equity and re-emphasise its role in the product category. The first step was a development of a new twist on the famous 'Beanz Meanz Heinz' campaign featuring Ian Botham, Cilla Black and Steve Davis. The campaign helped refresh the brand's image. The second step was to reduce the salt and sugar levels in the recipe without impacting on the unique 'Heinz taste'.

Another strand was major investment in the Heinz factory at Kitt Green, Wigan resulting in more efficient production and lower prices.

The Product

Heinz Baked Beans is the most famous of the company's 300 Heinz-branded products now available in the UK and most recently Heinz entered the frozen pizza market with Heinz Baked Beans Pizza.

The tomatoes for Heinz' distinctively flavoured tomato soups and sauces come from the Mediterranean where the soil and climate allows the tomato plants to grow unsupported in huge fields. This needs special varieties of plant and Heinz agronomists have worked closely with local growers to develop suitable strains. Endless testing and experiments in cross-fertilisation are undertaken to further enhance quality. Heinz is now one of the leading developers in hybrid tomato varieties.

As well as its established product range, Heinz is constantly looking to launch new products and invests heavily in its research and development centre where highly trained chefs recruited from Britain's top hotels and restaurants create new recipes designed not to lose their subtle flavours during large-scale, computer-controlled mass production.

In the early days, Heinz was a canny advertiser. It erected huge signs - all different - beside railway lines. Its pioneering press advertising made a strong argument for its beans' nutritional value. In 1927, Heinz' 'Joy of Living' campaign broke the mould with its message about the pleasures of eating. All advertising carried the 'no preservatives, no colouring' message. 'Picked and bottled in a day' was a slogan first used by the company in 1929.

With the growth of convenience foods in the Fifties, Heinz worked hard to ensure its advertising was closely in touch with social trends. So, one campaign in 1956 featured the line 'You and Heinz together' in response to evidence suggesting that housewives felt guilty if they let food manufacturers do all the work!

The first Heinz commercial was screened on September 24, 1955 - the first week of transmission by the new ITV. Sixty second black and white commercials for Heinz baked beans, tomato and vegetable soups, spaghetti and

shift-working mums and single parents rather than the typical saccharine images of food advertising. In one commercial, a single mum is seen balancing the demands of a young family and full-time job - and serving her kids Heinz Baked Beans for tea. The product is positioned as tasty, healthy, value for money and comforting.

The emotional richness of the ads was enhanced by a distinctive soundtrack using music by Zulu group Ladysmith Black Mambazo. Again, the umbrella branding was designed to re-enforce messages concerning different products in the range - notably, Heinz Baked Beans - communicated to consumers via direct marketing. In January 1998, a new improved 'At Home' was distributed to consumers.

Today, Heinz Baked Beans enjoys a 51.1% share of the UK baked beans market.

Brand Values

Undeniably, Heinz is a brand icon. It is a heritage brand familiar to generations of British consumers and widely appreciated for product quality and consistency. It is one of the most potent brands in the food sector, a trusted name for which consumers are prepared to pay a premium.

Recent Developments

Heinz unveiled its largest ever reorganisation plan in 1997. Known as 'Project Millennia', the strategy was designed to strengthen the company's six core businesses and improve Heinz profitability and global growth. Key elements include a commitment to increase media expenditure by 30% by the year 2000, overseas expansion, an 'Efficient Consumer Response' programme, value-added manufacturing, price-based costing and working capital savings.

Promotion

Heinz is responsible for some of the most famous and successful advertising campaigns of all time. 'Beanz Meanz Heinz' is one of the UK's most successful series of ads.

ketchup showed ingredients, depicting every day use and serving suggestions.

More recently in 1994, escalating media costs and enhanced database marketing technology prompted the company to increase investment.

Heinz built a consumer database. Around one million names were gathered via promotions run over the previous two years. Over the next two years, a further 3.5 million names were added via on-pack questionnaires, promotions and competitions. A quarterly full-colour customer magazine, 'At Home', was launched with news, views, competitions and offers.

Meanwhile, a new Heinz brand advertising campaign was developed to reinforce the parent brand's credentials. The 'United Nations' campaign broke in July 1995. It comprised a series of ten-second, slice of life vignettes depicting ordinary people enjoying Heinz products. The aim was to underline Heinz core brand values and remind consumers that Heinz and the home are inextricably linked.

By 1997, Heinz was consolidating its position with the 'Toast to Life' campaign. This focused on the emotional responses to the brand and its role in people's everyday lives. Five 60 second commercials portrayed latchkey kids,

Interflora™

The Market

Sending flowers is a traditional way of marking a special occasion. This simple act, however, is now backed by the latest advances in computer technology. Technology combined with the wider availability of an exotic range of flowers imported from all over the world and advances in design techniques means that floristry has become an increasingly sophisticated industry.

Although the British love flowers - each year they spend an average of £20 per head on cut flowers - economic uncertainty in the early 1990s signalled a very lean period for the floristry business. However, 1995 saw the beginning of an upturn in orders which has been maintained ever since as consumers recognise that one of the easiest ways to show you care is by sending flowers.

Achievements

Interflora is a unique organisation. It is not a franchise but a democratically-run network of 60,000 independent florists able to deliver flowers to 160 countries worldwide. A heartfelt message can be relayed from America to Russia, or from Dublin to Western Samoa. Interflora can deliver just about anywhere within 24 hours. This special service has even gone beyond this world - British astronaut Helen Sharman sent a message to Interflora from space, requesting a bouquet to be sent to her mother with the accompanying message: "Many thanks for supporting me in everything I've done, Love Helen".

Each member florist (there are 2,500 in the UK and Republic of Ireland) has an in-store terminal, linked to the main computer which processes orders from one place to another. Each year, over half a billion orders are sent through the Interflora network world-wide. Valentine's Day is traditionally the single busiest day of the year. In the UK, Interflora florists usually deal with around half a million deliveries on February 14th alone.

Interflora has played an important part in so many of the key occasions in consumers' lives from birth to funerals. For over 70 years it has handled sensitive situations with tact and sincerity. Interflora will also go to great lengths to meet the needs of its customers ensuring that deliveries are on time and that the flowers selected are appropriate. Interflora florists are renowned for their ingenuity and often have to sculpt very complicated designs in flowers, such as motorbikes, footballs, military coats of arms, pieces of furniture, 'Gates of Heaven', the poignant Mum and Dad and other floral tributes which help to convey messages of sympathy, love and respect.

History

Interflora's British operation celebrated its 75th anniversary in 1998. The business originally started in the US where two florists, frustrated that it took up to four days for their bouquets to journey by train across the country, agreed to telegraph requests to each other and settle up later. The idea soon spread and the Florists Telegraph Delivery Service was set up.

The idea reached the UK in 1920 when a florist in Glasgow and a nurseryman in Essex applied to become "foreign members" of the Telegraph Delivery Service. By 1923 there were 17 "foreign members" - enough for them to form a British unit.

In 1935, the British Unit ceased to be a part of the American operation and 11 years later, the British, Americans and the Europeans joined forces to become the International Florists Association. The name changed to Interflora in 1953 and the famous symbol featuring Mercury, the messenger of the gods, was adopted.

Since then, the Interflora network has grown enormously, allowing world wide deliveries.

The Product

The British Unit of Interflora is based in Sleaford in Lincolnshire and communicates with its members by a hi-tech computerised system which links every Interflora florist with the central database.

Interflora members have to meet strict criteria to join the organisation's network, as well as paying a membership fee. Interflora demands very high standards of professionalism so that customers know that they will receive quality service and products.

Interflora (British Unit) is a non-profit-making organisation. The £2.99 service and transmission charge is used to operate a rigorous quality control programme. When a florist applies for Interflora membership, he or she is required to conform to certain standards of floristry and service and also has to agree to participate in a 'mystery shopping' programme where members of the public order flowers which are then evaluated by a team of top florists.

Any complaints or queries about the service which can't be handled directly by the member-florist are addressed to the Customer Services department based in the Head Office, which acts as arbitrator. Interflora florists are always open to customer suggestions and are only too willing to please - however whimsical the request.

Certain deliveries are trickier than others - ships and hospitals are notorious! The 'disappearing hospital patient' syndrome can be a tough one, as increasingly, people are discharged from hospital at short notice.

Recent Developments

Interflora used new technology - the telegraph - when it was first formed and now takes full advantage of the Internet. The service is well suited for most Internet shopping mall developments including CompuServe, the international online service. Interflora has also developed its own Web site which was launched in March 1998. Many of those customers who order flowers via the internet are men who, Interflora believes are spared having to dictate a potentially embarrassing message to a telephone operator. www.interflora.co.uk is the website address.

Interflora also features on a major international airline's seatback monitors enabling travellers to send orders whilst in-flight, with the possibility of deliveries being made before the plane reaches its own destination!

Sainsbury's has developed Flowers Direct in association with Interflora to provide its customers with a freecall flower ordering service with the advantage of personal delivery from a skilled florist.

Promotion

Interflora supports its network of member-florists with national advertising campaigns. Perhaps the most memorable is that which carried the slogan: 'Say it with flowers' which was first used in 1938.

More recently, Interflora employed Ammirati Puris Lintas to produce advertising that would persuade people to change their buying habits from buying flowers in person for someone to sending flowers instead. The brief was also for advertising to change people's feelings about the quality of Interflora's work; and to create a contemporary identity for the brand. As a result of this work, APL won a Silver award in the 'New Print Campaign' category of marketing publication, Campaign in 1997.

The new advertising was developed to convince non-deliverers of flowers that from the recipient's point of view, flowers mean more when they are delivered by "the person from Interflora".

An Interflora delivery is exciting, frequently unexpected and implies special thought. The new campaign stimulates more Interflora deliveries by communicating the superiority and increased emotional impact of an Interflora delivery.

The style of photography focuses on the intrinsic beauty of the flowers, the envelope which accompanies them and the emotions they generate on receipt.

The campaign very much confirms the position of Interflora as pre-eminent florists.

Interflora has also run a successful campaign using 48 sheet posters across the UK and the Republic of Ireland featuring stylised flower images. The basis of Interflora's marketing policy is to ensure customers are aware of the range and flexibility of services available. This includes the 0500 434343 Freecall service linked to Interflora florists throughout the country, as well as the delivery of additional gifts such as chocolates, balloons and soft toys.

The organisation has also run a high-profile sponsorship programme with British Athletics over the last eight years. In 1996 it ran a tactical sponsorship programme which included the 1996 Interflora Valentine Classic in Glasgow featuring athletes such as Sally Gunnell and Linford Christie. It has also been involved with the Chelsea Flower Show, Crufts Dog Show, the World Ice Skating, the popular TV show, Gladiators and the World Canoeing Slalom Championships. Specially designed bouquets and attractive promotions also serve to link Interflora with other famous names such as the Nescafé 'Love Over Gold' promotion as well as BT, Cathay Pacific and Diners Club.

Brand Values

Interflora is not just about sending flowers it is also about the experience that the delivery represents. Interflora aims to ensure that this precious moment goes to plan, or in the case of a romance, has the desired effect!

The Interflora service signifies quality and professionalism, and a dedication to meeting the needs of its customers.

WHY, DURING the coldest Christmas on record, one person never felt so warm.

CHRISTMAS HAND-TIED BOUQUET, AROUND £25.

0500 43 43 43. Delivered straight to the heart.

Things you didn't know about Interflora

The international Interflora network operates in its own currency - the Fleurin. This has been used since 1948 and is loosely tied to the Swiss franc, a concept not dissimilar to the Euro but predating it by 50 years!

Interflora offers customers a twenty four hour seven days a week FreeCall Service. During shop hours, the number will connect a customer to their nearest Interflora florist. At any other time, the call is connected to a centralised Flowerline based at Interflora headquarters.

Interflora has relayed some interesting messages with flowers, such as: "Thanks for last night but can I please have the bath-taps back?" and from a soldier in the Gulf War: "I hope these flowers smell better than the camels round here!".

During the Second World War, Interflora set up an agency to provide military personnel with their own dedicated flower delivery ordering service. This extended to the Gulf War, when a special ordering facility was provided for military personnel living under canvas in the desert. When the tornado squadrons returned to base, Interflora provided the homecoming crews with flowers to give to their loved ones in celebration.

In 1996 a Gallup card survey confirmed that women value a delivery of flowers above a romantic meal or even a weekend away. What's more, the same survey also revealed that men enjoy receiving flowers, too. Contrary to the belief of almost 50% of the women surveyed, 70% of men said they would be flattered and pleased to be sent a bouquet of flowers.

Johnson's baby

The Market

Babies are big business. The total baby products market is estimated to be worth over £1 billion (in 1996/7). The babycare market, however, is a particularly fast-moving one. To be successful, manufacturers must constantly keep pace with an increasingly mobile population, shifting lifestyles and growing health awareness. They must accommodate advances in medical understanding and new technology which lead to steady product development. And, in recent years, they have had to combat growing competition from retailers' own brand rivals.

As the average age of mothers increases and more women return to work, two distinct types of mums have emerged - the traditional mum and the contemporary mum. The former is younger, of lower income and will sacrifice her personal spending to buy a complete range of products for her baby. The latter tends to be older, more affluent and increasingly demands multi-purpose goods which offer value for money. Contemporary mums also have a tendency to look for products which are hypo-allergenic, fragrance free and pH balanced, such as Johnson's Baby toiletries. And they are receptive to quality branding.

Achievements

Since the introduction of the brand more than 100 years ago, Johnson's Baby has prided itself on the quality, safety and trustworthiness of its products. Today, Johnson's Baby is top of mind for mothers and is considered the pre-eminent brand leader for baby toiletries. In June 1997, Johnson's Baby's brand share was 70.8% - up ten per cent year on year. Today, its products are the most used baby products in hospitals and more midwives use Johnson's Baby products than any other brand.

Products from the range have won numerous industry awards. A panel of five experts and 100 mums in the 1996 and 1997 Mother & Baby Awards voted Johnson's Baby Breatheasy Bath the Gold Award winner in the Best Skincare

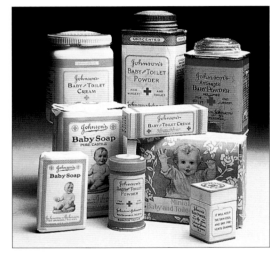

Product category. Johnson's Baby Skincare Cloth Wipes won the Gold Award in the Best Wipes category and the brand's Baby Nappy Rash Cream won the Silver Award in the Nappy Rash category in 1997.

History

The Johnson brothers - Robert Wood Johnson, James Wood Johnson and Edward Mead Johnson - set up business in 1885 producing surgical dressings from a factory in New Brunswick, New Jersey. The brothers' first products were improved medicinal plasters containing medical compounds mixed in adhesive. They soon diversified into a range of other medical products, including soft absorbent cotton and gauze dressing and 'kola' preparations for the relief of nausea.

Johnson & Johnson got into the baby business quite by accident, however. In 1890, following a complaint of skin irritation from using a medicated plaster, Johnson & Johnson started including a small can of talc with certain packs of plasters to soothe irritated skin. Soon, customers began asking for more of the powder - which lead to the birth of Johnson's Baby Powder in 1893 and the subsequent launch of the Johnson's Baby brand in the US. Thirty years later, Johnson's Baby Powder was launched in the UK. Today, the company's adult and baby talcs are brand leaders.

The Products

In the beginning there was Johnson's Baby Powder. The success of this, however, led to a wide range of other babycare products being launched. Today, Johnson's baby products span baby food and milk, wipes and toiletries. Johnson's Baby toiletries account for 5.8% of the total baby product market and are worth an estimated £58.3 million. Products include bath items, shampoo, lotion, powder, soap and oil.

Baby wipes is the fastest growing baby category, up 13.8% year on year by value. This category alone is currently valued at £81.4 million. Johnson's Baby Wipes are the number two brand in the wipes sector with 23.1% market share. However, the company is confident this is set to rise following recent innovations such as the launch of Johnson's Baby Skincare Wipes which use latest pop-up technology and the introduction of pop-up tubs for both Johnson's Baby Skincare Wipes and Top to Toe Wipes launched in 1998.

Other Johnson's Baby products include nappy rash and problem dry skin creams, oil baths, Breatheasy and Soothing Bath formulations, Mild Conditioning shampoos (including the brand leader: Johnson's Baby No More Tears shampoo) and nursing pads. Throughout its range, Johnson's answers mums' demands for value by developing dual functionality where it can. So, a number of the brand's products that clean, soothe or moisturise also relieve discomfort or irritation caused by nappy rash and sore skin.

Recent Developments

Johnson's Baby is committed to constant product development and innovation throughout its products' preparation, packaging and design. In April 1997, Johnson's launched the first Problem Dry Skin Range for babies designed to help relieve dry skin problems common amongst children aged up to two as baby skin is more sensitive and dehydrates quicker than older children's skin.

Johnson's also developed the first baby baths with decongestant and soothing benefits - Breatheasy Bath, the first decongestant formulation clinically proven to be mild enough for infants, and Soothing Bath formulated with camomile, a natural skin soothing ingredient designed to soothe sore, irritated or sensitive infant skin.

Promotion

Shortly after the First World War, Johnson's Baby Powder became popular with large numbers of US customers, meriting the largest advertising campaign in the company's history. Smiling babies featured in four-colour advertisements in most of the country's leading home magazine titles. The ads were so popular they were enlarged and displayed in shop windows.

By the mid-Sixties, Baby Powder advertising began to focus on the profound emotional bond between mother and new-born child - a theme which continues in today's advertising. A typical execution featured the image of a small child kissing his mother, accompanied by the words: "Your touch tells him everything. That's why we make our baby powder so pure and soft and soothing. It feels like love." More recent press ads have attempted to personalise the mother-baby relationship even further with the introduction of real people's babies referred to by name.

Today, the rise of retailers' own label products has had a significant effect on the market. As a result, marketing support for the Johnson's brand has been crucial for success. Johnson's Baby therefore invests heavily in quality TV and press advertising, point of sale material, educational literature and product sampling. In 1997, Johnson's Baby spent £5 million on marketing support for its Baby range. This included £700,000 spent on the national TV and press launch of Johnson's Baby Pop-up Skincare Cloth Wipes.

Johnson's recognises the importance of cultivating a close dialogue with mums and has set up two dedicated hotlines enabling consumers, retailers and health professionals to get additional information about its Baby products range. Education is also a core promotional activity for the brand with Johnson's producing numerous advice sheets and a Baby Skincare Guide.

Your touch tells him everything.
That's why we make our baby powder so pure and soft and soothing.
It feels like love.

Johnson & Johnson

Like all newborns, Emily Sweet can't instinctively close her eyes.

With thanks to Emily's parents and all at Queen Charlotte and Chelsea Hospital.

But with Johnson's No More Tears Shampoo, that's no problem.

Not only is Johnson's Baby Shampoo gentle enough to use on a newborn's delicate scalp and hair, it's gentle on the eyes, too.

That's because it's passed the rigorous Johnson's No More Tears testing. In fact, with this clinically proven formula, it's as mild as water itself. So if drips or splashes do get into a baby's eyes, they won't cause any discomfort.

And now we've added an extra protective ingredient to enhance the natural protection of hair and scalp to make clean hair healthy hair.

Yet our Baby Shampoo is still as gentle as it ever was.

Even for the newest of new babies.

Johnson's. From the day you were born

Brand Values

Johnson's is dedicated to making baby skin and haircare products of the highest quality. The core mild and gentle qualities of the brand have stayed constant over the decades. More recent product launches, product innovations and packaging redesigns reflect the demands of today's consumers.

For many years, the company's positioning in the marketplace has been: "Best for baby, best for you". This is still the case today as products continue to be developed for the youngest member of the household upwards, with many grown-ups valuing the hypo-allergenic and pH balanced properties of the mild and gentle range.

The core strapline on many of the brand's advertising campaigns is: "From the day you were born". Johnson's Baby's relationship with the consumer is based on a bond of trust, hence another of the brand's slogans: "The most trusted name in baby care".

No monitor could ever equal this.
But intouch comes closest.

baby reassurance monitor

Johnson & Johnson

The Market

Sales of sweets once again hit record levels in 1997, demonstrating that confectionery remains an integral part of people's everyday lives. The value of the UK confectionery market increased by 3% in 1997 to £5.2 billion. The average Briton spends £1.71 on confectionery and eats 277 grammes of it every week.

Today, the Kit Kat brand is estimated to be worth £225 million in consumer value - measured in total sales for 1997. The product is sold in more than 100 countries around the world, from Iceland to the Far East.

Achievements

Kit Kat is Britain's number one confectionery brand in value and volume (Source: Nielsen) with a staggering 44 bars eaten every second.

The brand has successfully introduced a number of variations to the traditional Kit Kat bar. In 1996, Nestlé introduced a limited edition Orange Kit Kat which caused a huge level of excitement across the country and generated an unprecedented 4,500 letters of appreciation from Kit Kat fans. In response to the overwhelmingly positive feedback from consumers, Nestlé reintroduced Orange Kit Kat two years later.

Kit Kat's success has been built on the brand's ability to flourish both as confectionery in the local corner-store and in the supermarket where it is sold as the No 1 biscuit.

Kit Kat has won numerous awards for advertising creativity and marketing effectiveness including Silver awards at the Cannes International Advertising Festival in 1991 and 1992; Gold in the 1993 Epica awards and Grand Prix in the 1990 Eurobest competition. In 1995, Kit Kat won Gold with its Burger King promotion in the ISP Promotional Awards.

History

Kit Kat was launched in 1935, although for the first two years it was known by a different name - Rowntree's Chocolate Crisp. No-one quite knows where the name 'Kit Kat' came from - it was first registered by the company in 1911. Many believe it was inspired by the famous Kit Kat Club - the Whig literary club which was

founded in the eighteenth century by Christopher Kat and reached the peak of its fame in the 1920s. Others have have cited the distinctive rectangular shaped paintings known as Kit Kats, hanging in the club, whose dimensions made them ideal for fitting in the confined wall space beneath the building's low ceilings.

The product was developed by Rowntrees' creative and productive marketing division headed by George Harris (1896-1958), the great grandson of Joseph Rowntree, and the company's chairman during the pre World War II period.

His strength lay in pinpointing new opportunities and pioneering new brands. Kit Kat was only one of a number of new products developed at this time: others included Black Magic, launched in 1933; Dairy Box (1936) and Smarties (1937).

Kit Kat was first launched in London and the south east although within a year its

success had fuelled distribution throughout the UK. By 1937, Kit Kat had become Rowntree's best-selling product - a position it has maintained ever since.

During the Second World War, Kit Kat was promoted to consumers as a valuable wartime food: brand advertising claimed it was "What active people need".

For most of its life, Kit Kat has been packaged in a distinctive red paper wrapper and silver foil. However, its colour did change to blue in 1945 when the product was produced with a plain chocolate covering due to shortages of milk after the Second World War. The blue livery was withdrawn in 1947 when standard milk chocolate Kit Kat was brought back onto the market.

Kit Kat advertising first appeared on TV in 1957 with the now famous slogan: 'Have a break - have a Kit Kat'. The campaign proved so popular it boosted sales by 22%.

During the 1960s, the first Kit Kat two finger multi pack was introduced - after just five years the six pack of two finger Kit Kats accounted for over 20% of the brand's total sales.

Sales also increased dramatically in the early 1970s following huge investment by Rowntree in new plant and equipment which significantly increased production capacity.

In 1973, Kit Kat's distinctive cream and red wrapper was updated with a new bright red and white wrapper. Since then, the design of the label has only changed twice - in 1993 and 1997. Subtle changes have been made to the oval shape in the centre of the wrapper, however. A new lighter, more lively typeface has also been introduced.

Kit Kat's success continued into the 1980s when in 1986 Kit Kat became the UK's leading confectionery brand. Today, Kit Kat continues to be manufactured at Nestlé Rowntree's factory in York - £6 million-worth of the product is manufactured each day. In 1994, Nestlé Rowntree invested a massive £28 million in its fifth Kit Kat factory on the site.

In 1993, Kit Kat was featured as the biggest confectionery brand in the world, with 11.3 billion Kit Kat fingers having been sold worldwide according to the 1995 Guinness Book of Records - 418 Kit Kat fingers every second.

Nestlé bought Rowntrees in 1989 following huge publicity - the high price paid for the company was primarily based on the strength of the Rowntree's brands - not least of all, Kit Kat.

Have a break. Peel a Kit Kat.

The Product

The basic Kit Kat formula has remained virtually unchanged since its launch over 60 years ago. However, there have been variations such as limited edition Orange (1996 and 1998) and Mint (1997) Kit Kats, both of which have proven enormously successful in generating consumer excitement and incremental sales.

Kit Kat is sold in different sized packs for different needs. The standard two finger bar offers an impulse purchase for children; the four finger bar is designed as an impulse purchase for all ages as a snack; the multi pack of two finger bars caters for teatime snacks, positioning the product as a biscuit.

Recent Developments

Kit Kat redesigned its logo in the autumn of 1997. The lettering was altered to give it a 3D appearance while retaining the famous red oval. The design of multi packs was also updated to maximise their impact on shop shelves, incorporating metalised film for extra freshness.

In early 1998, Kit Kat launched a joint promotion linked to animated TV sitcom The Simpsons to offer consumers £100,000-worth of cash prizes and Simpsons merchandise. The initiative was supported by a national poster campaign and contributed to Kit Kat's continued position as the UK's number one confectionery brand.

Soon afterwards, Nestlé re-introduced the Orange Kit Kat. This was followed by the introduction of special 'temperature change' packs and racks designed to encourage consumers to start eating straight from the fridge. The packs have been printed with inks that react to temperature change - when put in the fridge, ice crystals and a blue halo appear round the logo. Special branded chiller racks are being placed in all stores to encourage dual siting and ensure that Kit Kat is enjoyed during the summer at its very best - straight from the fridge. Summer is traditionally a slow time of year for chocolate sales.

In autumn 1998, Nestlé introduced for the first time a five fingered Kit Kat as a means of offering consumers a 'free fifth finger'. This was essentially a value promotion (25% extra free) but manages to incorporate a key brand property - ie a Kit Kat finger. This promotion has already caused an unprecedented level of excitement with the trade and it has generated enormous consumer appeal.

Promotion

Kit Kat's 'Have a break - have a Kit Kat' advertising slogan is one of the advertising industry's most famous and enduring copy lines. Research shows the line can be completed by 99% of the UK population (Nestlé Rowntree Research).

The brand's advertising strategy has long used a combination of different media which, in recent years, has been supplemented by product promotions.

In the early days, Kit Kat was advertised as "the biggest little meal" and "the best companion to a cup of tea".

The Biggest Little Meal in Britain!

FOUR big, crunchy, oven-crisp wafers. A lacing of finest butter. Creamy milk chocolate in between, and a thick layer of chocolate all round. That's Rowntree's Chocolate Crisp. The biggest little meal in Britain!

This particular type of chocolate block produces a slower rise of blood-sugar, which means that you don't get hungry again so soon. Result: longer endurance and staying power — and that's important these days.

2ᴰ

4210—R Rowntrees Nationals w.b. 2 Oct. 1939 5 x 4¼

Star of Kit Kat advertising throughout the 1950s was Kitty the Kat who emphasised the rich, full cream milk quality of the product. However, production improvements from the mid-Fifties improved product quality - particularly its crispness. So the kitten changed from reinforcing the brand's milk chocolate credentials to crispness - in ads, Kitty jumped to the snap of a Kit Kat being eaten. It was not until the end of the decade that 'Have a break - have a Kit Kat' became a regular advertising line.

More recent campaigns have included a range of 'slice of life' depictions of Kit Kat being consumed as a well-earned reward or pick-me-up during a break from work. In early 1998, Kit Kat ran a 'Football Manager' TV commercial in anticipation of that summer's football World Cup in France. The commercial shows a British football manager describing tactics through interpreters to his team made up of footballers of many nationalities.

Later in the year, 'Football Manager' was followed up with a commercial featuring the Russian-built Mir space station which has been dogged by problems during its life in space: Kit Kat goes into orbit and is delivered to beleaguered cosmonauts by ground control as a well-deserved break. Not only does Kit Kat

lift their mood but it also saves the day - or so they think. In the run up to Mir's decommissioning in 1999, it continues to be ever present in the news and media - ensuring that Kit Kat continues to be seen as topical and up to date.

Packaging has played an important role in the brand's promotion. Kit Kat's distinctive paper strap and silver foil is designed to add a sense of ritual to the consumption of the product - an aim underlined in the distinctive way in which the product is seen to be unwrapped and consumed in all its TV advertising. Consumers love to create their own personalised ritual in eating Kit Kat.

Brand Values

Kit Kat is a fine balance of milk chocolate and crisp wafer. It is carefully positioned as something special - a well-deserved reward to enjoy during a break from work, or play. Yet at the same time, it is part of everyday life - an ever present friend.

Lucozade

The Market

The UK soft drinks market is extremely competitive but only Coca-Cola and Pepsi have higher sales by value than Lucozade.

Lucozade is by far the most dominant brand in the energy and sports drinks market which is worth approximately £174 million. The market is extremely dynamic, experiencing an increase in volume sales of 64% since 1992. New brands are constantly being introduced. Product extensions and launches within the glucose energy sector, the largest segment of the market, have especially contributed to generating greater consumer interest and awareness.

per cent of the company's profit. During the 1950s, the brand went from strength to strength and became the biggest brand in Beecham's portfolio and in 1963 the 'Lucozade aids recovery' slogan was first used. In 1968, Lucozade was awarded a Royal Warrant.

By the 1980s, sales of Lucozade were flagging so it was repositioned as an every day energy replacement drink with the emphasis on the brand being a 'pick me up' rather than just for those who were ill. In 1980, the first new pack since 1927 was introduced - a new, conveniently-sized 250cl bottle. A new advertising campaign was developed starring decathlete Daley Thompson which used the line: 'Lucozade replaces lost energy'. In 1985, the product was launched in tablet form and the product range was then extended to include barley drinks in orange and lemon flavours.

Five years later, an isotonic sports drink was launched - Lucozade Sport - which is now firmly associated with the world of sport. Lucozade Sport was the official sports drink for the British Athletics Federation and sponsored the Premier League in 1992 and the English Rugby Football Union in 1995.

Lucozade provides approximately double the energy of other soft drinks due to its glucose content. It is particularly useful when energising nourishment is important such as during illness. It is also a valuable energy provider during sporting activities and boosts carbohydrate intake before and after exercise.

Lucozade Energy is a high energy drink specifically designed to get large amounts of carbohydrate into the body quickly. Lucozade Sport is an isotonic drink which is designed to replace fluids lost when exercising and give a boost of carbohydrate to working muscles by supplying carefully selected levels of sodium and carbohydrate. They are designed to be drunk before, during and after exercise supplying fluid to help fight dehydration and are available in orange, lemon and apple-citrus flavours. Low calorie Lucozade Sport is also available. Lucozade NRG is aimed at the teenage market as a trendy alternative to regular soft drinks whilst low calorie is predominantly for the female audience.

In 1985, Lucozade was introduced in cans and tablet form. Lucozade tablets were relaunched in 1989 with artificial colourings replaced by natural annatto and turmeric. New orange and lemon barley tablets were also added to the range. A year later, the tablets were renamed Lucozade Sport tablets and barley tablets reformulated to orange and lemon-lime.

Achievements

For over 50 years Lucozade was perceived and promoted as a drink for convalescents until it was repositioned in 1985 as an energy-providing soft drink to be used in sickness and in health. The range still contains all the essential qualities of the original Lucozade but the flavour bears no resemblance in taste to the original brand. In 1996, the brand was re-launched. The repositioning and re-launch of the brand boosted sales from £12 million in 1985 to £170 million in 1997.

History

Lucozade was first formulated by a Newcastle pharmacist in 1927 at the request of a consultant surgeon who wanted to give it to children recovering from 'flu. It was originally called Glucozade but by 1929 the name had changed to Lucozade. In 1938 it was bought by Beecham's. Beecham's was set up by Thomas Beecham, who started out in business in the 1840s selling herbal remedies from a market stall. Today, Beecham Group is a worldwide business with more than 200 products spanning prescription and proprietary medicines, toiletries, cosmetics, veterinary preparations and health and soft drinks.

Beecham began selling Lucozade in the classic yellow cellophane wrapped bottle as a drink for convalescents. Most of the product's early sales were through chemist shops. Within 15 years, Lucozade was generating around 50

The Product

Lucozade is a lightly sparkling soft drink that replaces lost energy and is available in a number of variants: Lucozade Energy available in original, orange crush, fresh lemon and tropical crush; Lucozade NRG Sparkling Fruit Explosion in orange and passion fruit crush and nectarine and lime flavours; Lucozade Sport isotonic drinks - orange, lemon and low calorie orange in both still and sparkling formats; and low calorie Lucozade with just five calories in each 300ml bottle.

Lucozade is a glucose syrup, a carbohydrate which provides a concentrated source of energy which is well-tolerated and readily absorbed. Glucose syrup is a starch which has already undergone some of the early stages of digestion which normally occur in the body. When it is ingested, the digestive breakdown of the carbohydrate is quickly and easily completed, providing an immediate source of energy. It also contains added Vitamin C.

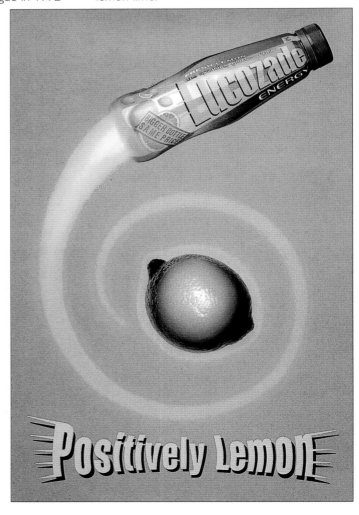

Positively Lemon

Recent Developments

Isotonic sports drink Lucozade Sport was launched in 1990. Lucozade NRG, a sparkling orange and passion fruit drink, launched in March 1995. Low Calorie Lucozade was launched in three flavours in 1997.

During 1998 all the four sub-brands of Lucozade (energy, sport, NRG and low calorie) have undergone a major packaging re-launch to keep them up-to-date with modern times:

Lucozade Energy launched a new 345ml bottle (300ml + 15% free) on all variants. These will be sold nationwide through all trade channels. Lucozade Energy is also now available in a 500ml PET bottle. These are available nationwide with a strong emphasis in forecourts.

Lucozade Energy and Low Calorie have both just launched exciting new advertising campaigns.

NRG has been carrying out successful sampling campaigns around various universities. This has gained product visibility focused within the target audience.

In 1996, Lucozade was relaunched with £14 million advertising and promotional support. The packaging was also dramatically redesigned with a new 300 ml curvy bottle. A year later, Lucozade NRG was relaunched. The relaunch saw a 100% increase in media spend on the product and an ad campaign starring footballer Alan Shearer was launched. The packaging was re-designed to highlight the 'energy' proposition and the entire range used brighter colours for greater impact. But perhaps most importantly the product was reformulated to deliver a new refreshing taste. The company introduced a widespread sampling campaign to get consumers to try the new product.

Lucozade has been an established drink for over 60 years. It is part of British heritage as well as our modern day lives. It is due to this enviable history that the energy advertising has taken a period of time from the past, in this case the 1960s, and adopted a Mods and Rockers theme based on the film Quadrophenia.

their boots, their hats... and a Lucozade Low Calorie bottle being held in front of their vital parts. They indignantly shout "What's that, Lucozade Low Calorie?". The advert follows, as the name suggests, from the film 'The Full Monty'.

Lucozade Sport was also backed by a TV ad campaign in 1997 which was aimed at making the product an essential part of training for all who play sport. It centred around Alan Shearer's training.

Lucozade is also an active sports sponsor. In 1992, Lucozade Sport sponsored the Premier League. In 1995, Lucozade Sport sponsored the English Rugby Football Union. Lucozade Sport has become a major high profile sponsor of many popular events today. In 1998, the brand backed Alan Shearer, the Football Premier League and nine first division football teams; the Lawn Tennis Association and Newcastle Sporting Club.

Brand Values

Lucozade is trusted as an effective way to quench thirst and replace lost energy and is

Promotion

Lucozade advertising has used leading sports figures including Daley Thompson, John Barnes and Linford Christie epitomising outstanding achievement and high energy. Latest advertising for Lucozade Sport features Alan Shearer. The brand has invested heavily in advertising since being bought by Beecham's in 1938. In 1954, the 'Replaces lost energy' claim was introduced. Three years later, 'Sustains energy' was added and in 1963 the 'Lucozade aids recovery' slogan was introduced.

The advertising firmly positions Lucozade Energy as an everyday drink, to allow you to do what you want to do.

The main character, Jimmy, is woken up by his friends. They're off to Brighton and Jimmy has forgotten. He is seen looking sleepy as he speaks to his friends and then shortly afterwards he is smartly dressed, drinking his Lucozade and bounding down the stairs to join his friends on their mopeds. You then see them riding off to Brighton. The advertising broke in June 1998.

Lucozade's low calorie variant was also backed by a new advertising campaign starring Sandra and Tracey - the 'Two Fat Slags' characters from the adult comic Viz. The Fat Slags are back and settling into their seats at the cinema, complete with big tubs of popcorn, to see 'The Full Mounties'. They are very excited. However this rapidly turns to horror when they see a line-up of gorgeous men spin round wearing

invaluable in sickness and in health. The core strategy for the brand is to concentrate on the energy and health proposition of the entire brand range while building bespoke identities for the four product categories: Sport for those who take fitness seriously; Energy - an everyday choice which consumers should be persuaded to drink more regularly; NRG which is aimed at youth; and low calorie. It is positioned as contemporary and youthful.

The Market

The toothpaste market is a mature business and as such, a highly competitive one. Two oral care companies dominate business in the UK and work hard to persuade consumers to switch from one brand to another. Habit, however, is a key feature of this sector and loyalty to brands is strong.

The UK oral care market was worth £470.5 million in 1997 (Nielsen). Sales were made up of toothpastes, which accounted for £291.2 million - a 7.4% year on year increase; toothbrushes (£118.8 million - up 6.6%) and mouthwashes (up 4.6% year on year to £60.5 million). SmithKline Beecham is the leading oral care manufacturer in Europe and number two in the UK market. The company enjoys a 21.7% share of the UK oral care market and a 15.6% share of toothbrush sales (Nielsen, Quarter 4, 1997).

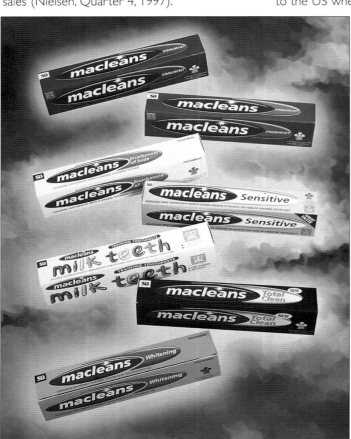

Achievements

SmithKline Beecham was the first to introduce an antibacterial agent into *Macleans* toothpaste in 1987. In 1995, the *Macleans* brand led the market with the introduction of *Macleans* Whitening toothpaste - the first mainstream toothpaste to whiten teeth on a daily basis. The brand was also the first to launch a variation harnessing the natural cleaning power of Bicarbonate of Soda.

Both *Macleans* Whitening and *Macleans* Sensitive were redesigned in 1996 to strengthen the impact of the *Macleans* umbrella brand. Since then, *Macleans* has reaped the benefits of umbrella branding to achieve its highest ever brand share.

History

Throughout civilisation man has always needed healthy teeth. Early tooth care methods were, admittedly, somewhat crude - a good abrasive was the key to cleaning but early solutions, such as crushed bone or oyster shells, damaged teeth. The earliest tailored solution was tooth powder which was applied to teeth with a simple stick. Added flavouring made the process a little more enjoyable. The first toothpastes, however, were not developed until the 1920s.

The *Macleans* story is a tale of two family businesses: *Macleans* Limited, set up in 1919 by Alex C Maclean and Beechams (now SmithKline Beecham) whose roots date back to the nineteenth century.

Alex Maclean was born in New Zealand, went to Australia for the gold rush then moved to the US where he eventually became a corset salesman. He subsequently brought his US business, Spirella, to the UK which proved successful until the managers quarrelled and split and Maclean set up business on his own manufacturing 'own brand' products for chemists.

The business was truly a family affair with Maclean's eldest son running the factory where he invented a tube printing process enabling different chemists' names to be printed on 'own name' toothpastes in small batches. In 1923, Maclean recruited top flight chemist Walter McGeorge who helped the company develop a range of new products and laid the foundations for *Macleans*' subsequent move into scientific medicines.

The pair's first major foray into toothpaste was with the launch of *Macleans*' pink formula Peroxide Tooth Paste in 1927 which was branded under different local chemists' names. The product proved extremely popular and a white variation was subsequently launched for sale under the *Macleans* name. The company scored a major coup when *Macleans* toothpaste was stocked by Woolworths which previously sold only Colgate tooth paste. The company continued to broaden its product base until in 1937 *Macleans* was bought by Beechams.

Beechams was founded by Thomas Beecham, the son of a farm labourer, who was born in 1820. The eldest of seven children, Beecham's formal education was brief and at the age of eight he started work - as a shepherd boy. By the time he was 20, however, Beecham had developed a number of herbal remedies for both human and animal use. He began selling them in country markets around Oxfordshire.

The turning point, however, came in 1847 when Beecham moved to Lancashire. The population in the country had grown rapidly with the Industrial Revolution. By the 1850s, Beecham was established in Wigan as a 'Chemist, Druggist and Tea Dealer'. He sold groceries and had a licence to sell medicines. Beecham had four products in his range - 'Female's Friend', 'Royal Toothpowder', 'Golden Tooth Tincture' and the celebrated 'Beecham's Pill'. At a time when people had an unshakeable belief in the value of purgatives, a laxative as effective as the Beecham's Pill quickly achieved widespread success.

Beecham's business expanded from a stall to a shop and then into mail order. His focus shifted - to manufacturing and national marketing. In 1859, Beecham's first newspaper ad appeared: for the Beecham's Pill. After Beecham's death in 1916, however, a long period of spectacular growth halted. It was only after Philip Hill, an entrepreneur, bought the Beecham estate in 1924 that the business' future was secured. Hill incorporated Beecham's Pills Limited as a public company in 1928. The company bought the estate's interests in Veno Drug Company, makers of Veno's cough medicine and Germolene antiseptic products.

Since 1937 Beecham's business and product range have grown dramatically. Today the company, now called SmithKline Beecham, owns brands including *Macleans*, Germolene, Aquafresh, Solpadeine, Oxy, Panadol, Lucozade, Ribena, and Horlicks.

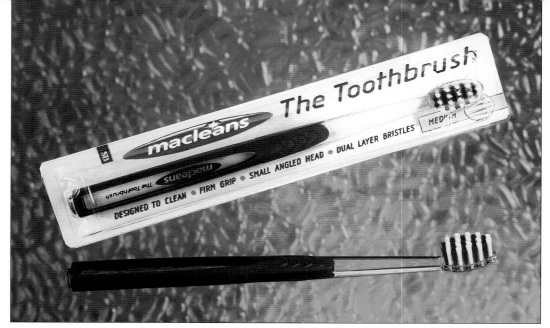

The Product

Macleans is one of two toothpaste brands owned by SmithKline Beecham - the other is Aquafresh which is the most purchased striped toothpaste in the UK.

Macleans has developed from its core Freshmint and Coolmint toothpastes into specialist pastes as these sectors have developed. *Macleans* Whitening is the brand leader in the mainstream whitening sector which now accounts for 4.5% of UK toothpaste sales. It offers all the benefits of an everyday fluoride toothpaste plus the additional benefit of whitening teeth. *Macleans* Sensitive is an effective everyday fluoride toothpaste which also contains Strontium Acetate - an active ingredient which relieves the pain of sensitive teeth. The latest product is *Macleans* Total Clean - its breakthrough formulation provides all round protection for healthy teeth and gums.

Macleans The Toothbrush was launched in September 1997 targeting confident, stylish adults. The 'designed to clean' positioning appeals to those seeking a simple yet effective toothbrush. It is available in medium and sensitive bristle variants, and features a small angled head and a firm grip as recommended by dentists.

Recent Developments

Macleans Sensitive was relaunched in July 1997 to capitalise on consumers' growing concern about the taste of their toothpaste. The launch was supported by a direct marketing campaign targeting consumers with sensitive teeth.

The launch of *Macleans* The Toothbrush in September 1997 was a logical extension of the brand. The toothbrush is distinctively designed to incorporate the *Macleans* logo's ellipse bubble shape. The launch was also intended to combat growing consumer confusion about the plethora of toothbrushes and confusing merchandise now available. The new brush's launch coincided with the arrival of the *Macleans* Total Clean 100ml pump dispenser.

The toothpaste, with special anti-microbial cleaning action, ensures teeth and gums are "totally" cleaned and protected.

Promotion

From 1994 the communications platform was: 'Tomorrow's oral health care products today'. Creative work was inspired by the Red Dwarf TV series.

SmithKline Beecham launched a new commercial for *Macleans* in March 1998 which broke new ground in oral care advertising by shifting the focus from product to lifestyle under the theme: '*Macleans* knows how to care for your smile' and the strapline: '*Macleans* Total Clean - Something to Smile About'. The ad traced a selection of characters at different stages in their lives - part of a £6 million spring campaign to boost the *Macleans* range.

The new 'Smile' campaign approach allows SmithKline Beecham to talk about the *Macleans* Oral health care brand in a way that is relevant and human, but also in an unconventional and engaging fashion. The consistent umbrella brand theme encompasses product specific communications such as Whitening, Sensitive and *Macleans* Total Clean.

Oral care for children has become increasingly important. With oral care education high on the government agenda, growing understanding of its importance has fuelled the development of a number of products specially designed for children. SmithKline Beecham sponsors a pre-school education programme called 'Healthy Teeth, Clean Teeth, Happy Teeth' to complement the government's initiative. The programme also supports the *Macleans* range of oral health care products for children.

In August 1996 *Macleans* Total Clean was launched - an advanced cleaning system for complete oral care.

Brand Values

Beecham's Pills Limited bought the *Macleans* brand for £2,300,000 in 1938. The deal brought *Macleans* toothpaste and Lucozade drinks into the Beechams' stable. The brand has a heritage spanning close to 100 years - yet has always maintained a contemporary feel. It has become synonymous with effective cleaning. The brand values are well encapsulated in the '*Macleans* knows how to care for your smile' theme.

Things you didn't know about
Macleans

The earliest tooth-cleaning materials included crushed bone, egg shell and crushed oyster shell.

There are 1800 bristles in a *Macleans* The Toothbrush head.

Prince Charles uses *Macleans* Fresh Mint toothpaste.

5,454,000 kilos of *Macleans* toothpaste are produced annually.

MANCHESTER UNITED®

The Market

UK football has come a long way in just twenty years. Today, it's not just a game - it's a sophisticated entertainment and leisure business.

The Nineties have seen a massive increase in the demand for football and anything associated with it. Eight out of ten people in the UK now have "some interest" in the game, according to a recent study by BMRB/Mintel (1996). And the increase in the popularity of football isn't just confined to the UK. An estimated 1.5 billion people watch the game regularly on TV around the globe - one quarter of the world's population!

Football has become increasingly commercialised. The larger clubs now reap the major benefits of sponsorship, merchandising and exploitation of stadia facilities for corporate hospitality, catering and non-match day activities such as conferences and banqueting.

Manchester United needs little introduction. It is arguably the most famous and financially successful football club in the world and is recognised in almost every country. In the UK alone it is estimated that 4 million support the club; 70% of these live outside the North West.

Around the world there are official supporters' clubs in Europe, the Americas and the Far East. Worldwide TV and media coverage has helped Manchester United become the most watched, best supported international football club.

As a business, too, Manchester United has grown at an impressive rate. The successful diversification of its business concerns has led to Manchester United now being considered as one of the most powerful brands in the world of football.

Achievements

Manchester United started 1998 holding the Premier League title. Eleven championships, nine FA Cups, one League Cup, one European Champion Clubs' Cup and one European Cup Winners' Cup confirm United's status as a dominant football force. And in 1996, Manchester United went down in history as the only club ever to achieve the 'double' of League and FA Cup, twice.

Success, however, is not just confined to the pitch. Since flotation in 1991, Manchester United's share price has increased nine-fold as financial results matched results on the field.

An increase in TV and sponsorship rights fees contributed to this, as TV rights increasingly reflect their true market value and sponsors better understand the power of football as a key route to the market.

The growth in official Manchester United branded merchandise has been via licences and through the growth of Manchester United's own merchandising operation. Official Manchester United merchandise is sold in high streets throughout the country. Retail sales now exceed £100 million a year.

Old Trafford, home to Manchester United, is growing in stature as an international venue in its own right. It is the UK's most visited club stadium and offers luxurious conference, hospitality and event staging facilities including a museum which is in the UK's top 100 most visited museums.

Manchester United is also breaking new ground in publishing and electronic media. The Manchester United Magazine is the UK's best-selling sports monthly now exported to over 25 countries and translated into Thai, Cantonese and Norwegian. And the Manchester United Web Site is a cutting edge site on the Internet.

History

Manchester United commands widespread respect worldwide - a reflection of its illustrious, generation-spanning history.

The Club began as Newton Heath LYR in 1878 and only became Manchester United Football Club in 1902. It was in the 1950s, however, that the Club became synonymous with success and its own unique style of football introduced by Matt Busby.

The Munich air disaster of February 1958 was a tragedy which both decimated the team and generated universal feelings of sympathy for the Club. Busby set about rebuilding the team and succeeded in assembling a successful side including the formidable trio of Best, Law and Charlton.

In 1968, Manchester United became the first English team to win the European Cup. Since then, the Club's popularity has been phenomenal. Even during the 26 year wait to win the Football League Championship once more, attendances outstripped those of any other UK football club.

However, despite a succession of very capable managers, none could measure up to Sir Matt Busby ... until the arrival of Alex Ferguson in 1987.

In 1990 the Club won the FA Cup then, in 1991 - the year Manchester United successfully floated - it won the European Cup Winners Cup. The run of silverware continued with the 1992 League Cup and in 1992/3, the Club became champion of the newly founded Premier League. The following season the team went one better winning the 'double' - the League and the FA Cup. In 1996 Manchester United went into the history books again as the only club ever to achieve the 'double' twice.

The Product

Manchester United's core product is and always will be football.

The development of the Manchester United brand, however, has enabled extensions into different market sectors. Merchandise now includes sportswear, clothing, videos, magazines, calendars, books, souvenirs and soft furnishings. On-site retail outlets now include three stores at Old Trafford, visited by up to 1 million people a year; off-site official merchandise can be found in several high street stores. Mail Order despatches merchandise around the world from its Old Trafford base which houses a state of the art call centre. The Manchester United Red Café at Old Trafford is the first of a planned international themed-video restaurant chain.

A Manchester United TV channel was launched in 1998. The 'lifestyle' channel was developed in partnership with BSkyB and Granada Media Group. It consists of Manchester United-themed programming ranging from archive footage to behind the scenes features,

exclusive interviews and quizzes.

The total offering may be viewed at Old Trafford itself with the intention this year to position itself more firmly as a leisure venue open 364 days a year, providing the ultimate Manchester United 'experience'.

Recent Developments

Ever-increasing demand for official 'association' with Manchester United has led to a recent review of development plans.

Traditionally, sponsorship opportunities at the Club have been limited: there's one Main Sponsor whose logo appears on team and replica shirts and there's a Technical Sponsor who designs and markets team strips. In 1998, however, Manchester United launched a 'Platinum Sponsorship' programme opening up additional sponsorship opportunities for eight non-competing companies with strong brand heritage who want to become 'Official Sponsors'. Demand for association with the Club extends beyond what happens on the football pitch. In an attempt to enable more people around the world to experience the "magic" of Manchester United, plans are underway for the launch of a £4 million Museum & Tour Centre catering for half a million visitors a year. This 'Manchester United Experience' will also be exported overseas with bespoke combined dining and retail outlets to launch in the Far East.

Manchester United TV, a lifestyle channel, was unveiled in 1998 to give the Club an even stronger media presence.

Promotion

Football is by far the most widely broadcast sport on TV in the UK, according to Sports Marketing Surveys research. In 1996, the top five sports based on TV coverage were football (3,500 hours); motor sport (1,800 hours); golf (1,700 hours); cricket (1,500 hours) and tennis (1,500 hours). In 1990 the World Cup was watched by 26 billion people worldwide. By 1998 this figure exceeded 40 billion (Source: FIFA).

Photo: Action Images

Manchester United has so far achieved its brand strength with relatively low-key marketing activities. Much of its success to date can be attributed to the change in footballing culture and shifting consumer perceptions of the product. Future marketing focus will be set firmly on non match day activities, particularly leisure-related activities designed to position Old Trafford as a key tourism venue. The Museum & Tour Centre will be at the heart of this strategy.

Brand Values

Manchester United is valued around the world for the quality, innovation and distinction of its performance on the football pitch.

In all other areas of its business too, brand strength comes from the delivery of strong product quality and brand values, particularly those tapping into the emotional selling proposition that football represents. It's an emotive sport which generates high passions.

Manchester United also has a reputation for extending the conventional boundaries of football and football-related activities. It is, at times, audacious and controversial. However, in everything it does it is professional and a perfectionist both on and off the field of play.

Manchester United's brand positioning is as a world class market leader - a unique positioning and one which the on-going business strategy is designed to sustain.

Things you didn't know about Manchester United

During the 1996/7 season, Manchester United commanded more than one billion TV viewing hours around the world - equivalent to one fifth of the world's entire population watching for at least one hour.

Approximately 2% of the UK population owns a Manchester United shirt - 20 times the 55,000 capacity of Old Trafford.

On a match day, approximately 20,000 people go through Manchester United's retail outlets before kick-off!

The Market

Eating out has always been a popular leisure activity. These days, it's a part of everyday life that many of us take for granted. However, it's easy to forget that a meal in a restaurant was once an occasional indulgence enjoyed by a privileged few. The popular catering revolution of the last fifty years changed all that. Today, dining out is a social activity enjoyed every day throughout the world by people of all ages and backgrounds. It is no exaggeration to say that virtually every taste is catered for - from exotic stir-fries and curries to hamburgers, pizza and good old-fashioned fish and chips.

The hamburger has become an icon of the late twentieth century. Its enduring popularity is rooted in a combination of value and convenience that makes it ideally suited to the increasingly frenetic pace of life in the nineties.

Achievements

McDonald's is the world's largest and fastest growing food service organisation, with more than 23,000 restaurants in 109 countries serving food and drink to 38 million customers daily. In the UK, McDonald's operates nearly 900 restaurants generating a combined annual turnover of more than £1 billion.

It is sometimes suggested that there are five stages in the life cycle of a brand: introduction, acceptance, growth, maturity and decline. McDonald's defies this principle. In the UK, the brand is nearly 25 years old and still being introduced into many towns, still being welcomed in new neighbourhoods and still growing in spite of increased competitive pressures. It is by no means mature and certainly not in decline.

Few other brands can match McDonald's for the power and ubiquity embodied in the company's familiar Golden Arches. In 1996, McDonald's was rated the world's greatest brand in a study published by leading international brand consultancy Interbrand. The study reviewed the performance of the world's leading brands and assessed each one for its strength and potential as a marketing and financial asset. Interbrand concluded: "Nothing compares with McDonald's for the power of a branding idea, the skill of its execution, and the longevity and width of its appeal. McDonald's is the quintessential American brand which has travelled the world on the strength of two quite distinct

phenomena - one cultural, the other commercial". Although McDonald's has its roots in the United States, it has become a citizen of the world.

History

The McDonald's story began 43 years ago in San Bernadino, California. Ray Kroc was a salesman supplying milkshake multi-mixers to a drive-in restaurant run by two brothers, Dick and Mac McDonald. Kroc, calculating from his own figures that the restaurant must be selling over 2,000 milkshakes a month, was intrigued to know more about the secret behind the success of the brothers' thriving business. He visited the restaurant which promised its customers "Speedee Service" and watched in awe as restaurant staff filled orders for fifteen cent hamburgers with fries and shakes every fifteen seconds. Kroc saw the massive potential and

decided to get involved. The McDonald brothers accepted Kroc's offer to become their first franchisee. On 15 April 1955, he opened his first McDonald's restaurant in Des Plaines, a suburb just north of Chicago.

Rapid growth followed. McDonald's served more than 100 million hamburgers within its first three years of trading and the 100th McDonald's restaurant opened in 1959. In 1961 Kroc paid $2.7 million to buy out the McDonald brothers' interest and in 1963 the billionth McDonald's hamburger was served live on prime-time TV.

The brand proved equally popular outside the United States. McDonald's had already established successful international markets in Canada, Japan, Australia and Germany by the time the British public welcomed the Golden Arches to Woolwich, south-east London in October 1974. By 1988, worldwide sales had topped $16 billion. Today, McDonald's is represented on all five continents, with a network of restaurants stretching from Beijing to the Arctic circle. What started as an American phenomenon has become a truly international brand.

The Product

From its early roots as a small, family-run hamburger restaurant, McDonald's has evolved into a multi-billion dollar quick service restaurant industry. While hamburgers and fries remain the mainstay of McDonald's business, the menu has been expanded to meet the

needs of changing consumer lifestyles and eating habits. An instinctive ability to anticipate and fulfil real consumer needs has been central to McDonald's success. A prime example of this approach was the development of the Filet-O-Fish sandwich. The product was conceived by Lou Groen, a Cincinnati-based franchisee whose restaurant operated in a predominantly Catholic area. Groen noticed that trade fell away badly on Fridays - a day of abstention from red meat for many Catholics. Having identified the reason, he set out to develop a fish-based product to meet the needs of the local community. The Filet-O-Fish sandwich was launched in 1963 and went on to become a popular menu item in many of McDonald's international markets.

Another franchisee - Jim Deligatti from Pittsburgh - was responsible in 1968 for the creation of McDonald's best known and most successful menu item ever, the Big Mac. Nine years later, the same franchisee was the driving force behind the development of McDonald's breakfast menu - a move that would change the breakfast habits of millions of Americans in the years that followed.

The spirit of innovation has played an important part in McDonald's growth. The company has invested heavily in new technology to find ways of continually improving the consumer perceived quality and convenience of the McDonald's experience. One of the biggest breakthroughs came in 1975 with the opening of the first drive-thru restaurant in Sierra Vista, Arizona. Once again, the idea sprang from the need to solve a local sales problem when servicemen from a nearby Army base were forbidden to get out of their cars in military fatigues. The drive-thru concept was an immediate success. Today, drive-thru accounts for more than half of McDonald's business in many of its international markets. While the basic drive-thru concept is still being introduced in McDonald's newer markets, the technology is already being refined in mature markets to find

ways of further enhancing levels of customer satisfaction. Canada is experimenting with the use of bar codes to automatically verify an order's content at the pick-up booth, while the US is testing a self-ordering kiosk for credit and bank card orders.

McDonald's is committed to providing its customers with food of the highest quality. This is achieved by using the best raw ingredients, sourced from approved suppliers and ensuring that food is prepared to a consistently high standard in the restaurant. As part of this commitment, McDonald's menu is continually reviewed and enhanced to ensure that it meets - and wherever possible exceeds - customer expectations. In the UK, McDonald's menu includes beef, chicken, fish and vegetarian products, as well as a full range of desserts, shakes and hot and cold drinks to cater for every taste. To help customers make informed decisions about their diet, McDonald's was the first quick service restaurant to make publicly available a complete ingredient listing and detailed nutritional analysis of all its products.

Recent Developments

Extra Value Meals and Happy Meals have proved two of McDonald's most successful product innovations of recent years. Extra Value Meals offer customers the chance to make savings when purchasing 'set meals' at a fixed price. Happy Meals offer young children the opportunity to have fun by enjoying their favourite McDonald's food along with a collectable toy presented in a special box.

Happy Meals and Extra Value Meals have been instrumental in building McDonald's family business and establishing the brand's ownership of value within the quick service restaurant sector.

Promotion

From the earliest days, McDonald's recognised the key role of marketing in the brand-building process. As Ray Kroc put it: "There's something just as basic to our success as the hamburger. That something is marketing, McDonald's style. It's bigger than any person or product bearing the McDonald's name." Advertising is certainly not the only cause of McDonald's success. It is, however, inseparable from it. To this day, a fixed proportion of restaurant sales is reinvested back into advertising and sales promotion in every market in which McDonald's operates.

McDonald's displays a rare ability to act like a retailer while thinking like a brand; delivering sales for the immediate present, while building and protecting its long-term brand reputation. In the UK, television advertising has been instrumental in transforming McDonald's brand image from that of a multi-national corporation to part of the fabric of British society. Through high profile brand advertising, McDonald's has developed a powerful emotional relationship with its customers based on trust and a fundamental warmth and humanity unmatched by its competitors.

In recent years, McDonald's has become increasingly involved in sports sponsorship. McDonald's uses its association with prestigious

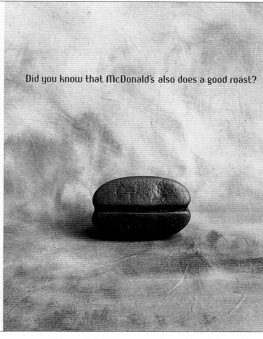

This is how we go about it. We choose 100% pure Colombian coffee beans.

The ones we use grow in only two small areas of Colombia. They are Arabica beans, which are the best quality.

They are also Excelso beans, which, we think, have the finest flavour.

In other words, before we filter the coffee, we filter the beans. Then we roast them to a rich, dark colour to bring out their full flavour.

Finally, we make sure that your cup of coffee is freshly brewed. Whether you drink it to wake you up first thing in the morning or to wake you up last thing at night.

When you've finished that cup, we'll be happy to pour you another one.

The service will always be polite and friendly. And, of course, it will be fast. But our coffee is never, ever instant.

Did you know that McDonald's also does a good roast?

global sporting events such as the World Cup and Olympic Games to reinforce its international brand stature, while tailor-made sponsorship programmes are used to address local market needs. This approach has been particularly effective in the UK where McDonald's involvement with 'grass roots' football right through to the Premier League has been leveraged to support the business at local restaurant level.

In addition to national advertising and promotional campaigns, McDonald's is strongly committed to local restaurant marketing. This commitment is an enduring testimony to founder Ray Kroc who held passionately to the belief that McDonald's should contribute to the

Two money saving tips from McDonald's

Avoid paying water rates

Extra Value Meals £2.88

communities which it serves. Local activity takes many different forms, ranging from free coffee mornings for senior citizens to fund-raising work with local schools, youth groups and hospitals.

Brand Values

Founder Ray Kroc developed his brand vision for McDonald's around a simple but effective consumer-driven premise of quality, service, cleanliness and value. Kroc's winning formula was quickly shortened to QSC&V - an acronym that would become and remain an enduring cornerstone of the brand.

If QSC&V is the cornerstone of the McDonald's brand, then trust is its bedrock. To its customers, McDonald's is a brand that can be trusted; placing the customer at the centre of its world; knowing the right thing to do or be even when the customer does not.

The key to McDonald's success has been its capacity to touch universal consumer needs with such consistency that the essence of the brand has somehow always been relevant to the local culture, no matter how different that culture might be from McDonald's origins. With one of the most powerful brands in the business, McDonald's looks set to enjoy healthy growth long into the future.

The Market

Biscuits are big business in the UK and are worth over £1.65 billion - twice the size of the wrapped bread market and four times the size of the tea market. The typical household spends

£4.67 per month on biscuits. That translates to around eight packets of biscuits being bought and enjoyed each month. Biscuits are bought for a variety of reasons: to snack, for a treat, to share with friends or as a gift on a special occasion.

The everyday biscuits sector is the largest in the market in volume terms, accounting for around 40% of all biscuits consumed. Biscuits in this sector are usually eaten straight from the packet or biscuit barrel. McVitie's Digestive, Rich Tea and Ginger Nuts are the top three best selling brands in the sector.

In the everyday treats sector, McVitie's Chocolate Homewheat Digestive is the number one brand, followed by McVitie's Jaffa Cakes. Products in this category tend to involve chocolate coatings and cream fillings.

But it is the chocolate biscuit bar sector that generates the largest sales revenue - more than 27% of the market. The sector is also one of the fastest growing, aided by the increasing popularity of packed lunches. McVitie's Penguin is one of the top brands in this sector. According to its familiar refrain, Penguin is 'The crunchy, chocolatey biscuit that's chocolate through and through'.

Achievements

McVitie's Homewheat Chocolate Digestive, Digestive and Penguin are all among the top ten biscuit brands in the UK. Other top selling brands include McVitie's Jaffa Cakes and Rich Tea. The combined value of the leading six brands amounts to £222 million.

McVitie's is category leader with a 23.2% share of the biscuit market, more than twice that of its nearest competitor. The heritage and longevity of McVitie's key brands are a testimony to the company's ongoing commitment to quality ingredients and high standards of baking.

An understanding of consumer lifestyles is essential. Recognising that fat is the nation's number one health concern, McVitie's introduced Go Ahead! in 1996, a range of biscuits, snacks, cakes and frozen foods that are up to 97% fat-free. One in two households purchase products from this sector making it the fastest growing

in the biscuit category. The Go Ahead! brand is already worth £50 million. It too is now one of the UK's top ten biscuit brands.

Independent consumer research by Millward Brown has shown that McVitie's is perceived well ahead of other brands on a variety of taste and quality considerations. Consumers recognise that McVitie's uses the best quality ingredients, has special expertise in baking, and introduces new and exciting biscuits to the range.

History

Digestive biscuits were first developed in 1839 by two Scottish doctors seeking to provide a remedy for flatulence. The original recipe contained a high level of baking soda, a well-known aid to digestion - hence the name.

McVitie's had been founded nine years earlier by Robert McVitie, a Scottish baker, who set up shop in Edinburgh in 1830. McVitie's bakery quickly became established as a quality outlet with branches across Edinburgh.

In 1888, company salesman Charles Price was made a partner in the firm. Now called McVitie & Price and specialising exclusively in the manufacture of biscuits, the business spread throughout Scotland and into England. The burgeoning reputation of McVitie & Price forced one fellow baker - Alexander Grant - to issue a challenge that he could bake better biscuits than those displayed by Robert McVitie. In good humour McVitie accepted the challenge. The end result of this contest was a new biscuit - the McVitie's Digestive.

The Product

Digestive and Homewheat Chocolate Digestive are probably the best-known McVitie's brands. Other core brands are Rich Tea, Hobnobs and

Ginger Nuts, which have all benefited from the launch of chocolate covered versions.

McVitie's first foray into the blending of biscuit and chocolate resulted in the Homewheat Chocolate Digestive brand. The name is derived from the biscuit's origins in the early 1900s, when wheat in the recipe was sourced from the home market while competitors imported ingredients.

The Hobnob brand, introduced in 1985, possesses a quirky character and more crumbly texture - a point of difference from other 'round brown' biscuits. Celebrity endorsement of Hobnobs has come from the likes of

presenter Shane Ritchie who has said, in celebration of National Dunking Day: "Whenever I feel like a good dunking, I always go for a Hobnob!" Actress Lorraine Chase prefers "A mug of Horlicks and a Hobnob". A chocolate Hobnob was subsequently launched and is now the biggest-selling variety.

The success of McVitie's Jaffa Cakes, with their 'smashing orangey bit in the middle' combined with sponge and dark chocolate, has given rise to Mini-Jaffa Cakes - a bite-sized version of the original.

Penguin is one of the most popular chocolate biscuit bars in the UK. It is estimated that over 470 million Penguin biscuits will be consumed in 1998. This classic brand, which celebrates its 65th year in 1998, has enjoyed a 23% increase in sales over the past two years, making it one of the fastest growing countline biscuit bars. The family has since been extended with the addition of Penguin Variety - a multipack of milk, plain, orange and mint chocolate biscuits - and Mini Penguin, popular amongst younger children.

Recent Developments

Core brands like Digestive are the foundation of the McVitie's business. But the recent success of Go Ahead! has shown that McVitie's responds well to new trends and the demand for different biscuits.

McVitie's aims to provide a biscuit for every occasion. In 1998, this was further exemplified with Penguin, when it entered the impulse confectionery market for the first time in a Pick-Up Pack format. This allows the £50 million brand to compete in a chocolate

confectionery market worth £1.8 billion. The portable pack contains three fingers of crunchy biscuit and chocolate cream, with 33% more chocolate than the standard variety.

The development of product packaging is part of a wider on-going commitment which aims to match products with contemporary consumer lifestyles. Packaging in different size formats offers the opportunity for purchase outside traditional retail stores such as airports, train stations and in office canteens.

McVitie's image was also enhanced in 1998 with the launch of a new corporate identity. The revitalised packaging on all 'core' brands features a much stronger sense of McVitie's identity and is designed to re-energise the biscuit shelves.

McVitie's continues to steer its brands into key positions within the biscuit market. The European market with a potential 326 million consumers, offers a huge outlet for future development and McVitie's has already joined forces with other prominent European manufacturers, securing a 12% share of the EC biscuit market.

Promotion

McVitie's supports its brands with a high level of marketing activity and invests heavily in television advertising.

A new TV advertising campaign launched in Spring 1998 supporting McVitie's Digestive and Homewheat Chocolate Digestive focuses on the special McVitie's 'moment' - a pause in the day. A dramatic slow-motion technique helps convey how pleasurable the McVitie's moment can be and that McVitie's biscuits make the moment truly special.

The reduced-fat Go Ahead! range has teamed up with fitness guru 'Mr Motivator' to feature in a nationwide television advertising campaign. The series of ads is designed to build awareness of the brand further and to promote the Go Ahead! range as a 'better for you' alternative to mainstream snacks. Each commercial is punctuated by the line: 'Go Ahead! make your day'. Other supporting activity for the brand includes Mr Motivator Roadshows, with the aim of encouraging the public to sample the range.

A band of mischievous orange characters, known collectively as 'Orangey Tangs', has taken centre stage with McVitie's Jaffa Cakes promotional activity. The five characters appear on various Jaffa Cake packs and McVitie's have constructed a dialogue with consumers where the 'smashing orangey bit in the middle' of Jaffa Cakes is under threat from the force of the

Orangey Tangs. Millions of Jaffa Cakes were 'saved' throughout the country by children collecting models of the Orangey-Tang characters.

Brand communication has become an important art at McVitie's. The company has created a consistently innovative approach to its packaging and promotions, ensuring that its products are made distinct and memorable in all their many markets. Marketing activity is continually researched to measure its effectiveness in a crowded multi-media environment.

Brand Values

McVitie's is a quintessentially British brand. It is an established part of our heritage which inspires trust and warmth. Consumers know they can rely on McVitie's to provide a wide

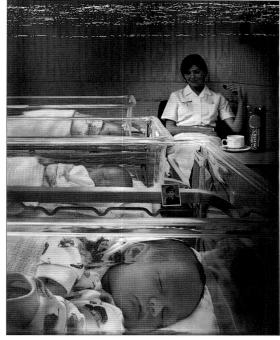

range of excellent quality, delicious biscuits which will appeal to all members of the family.

This is largely due to the longevity of the brand and the pleasure experienced by Digestive devotees and Homewheat Chocolate Digestive lovers over the years. In a highly competitive environment, McVitie's also manages to stay ahead, introducing new brands and line extensions that the British public love.

McVitie's successfully continues to marry its brand heritage with contemporary consumer trends to drive the biscuit market forward from strength to strength. It will continue to do so into the Millennium.

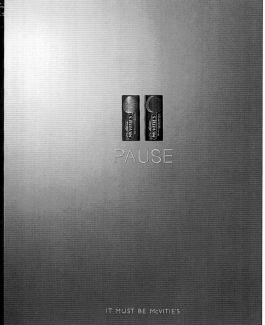

Things you didn't know about McVitie's

Over 6 million McVitie's Digestives are eaten each day and over 39 are eaten every second.

The first Digestive biscuit was baked by Alexander Grant at the McVitie and Price bakery in Edinburgh in 1892.

McVitie's Digestive sales are worth in excess of £40 million per year.

Homewheat is the original chocolate digestive - it was first baked in 1925.

Over 65 million packets of Homewheat are consumed each year; 70 Homewheat biscuits are consumed in the UK every second.

If you put all the Homewheat biscuits eaten in one year side-by-side they would stretch around the world more than twice.

In 1997, Britain p...p...pecked its way through 470 million McVitie's Penguin biscuits - more than eight Penguins per year for every man, woman and child.

McVitie's first introduced Penguins on television 32 years ago when Derek Nimmo said those magic words: 'P...P...pick up a Penguin'. Past Penguin advertising featured penguins playing football, visiting museums and playing bingo.

McVitie's Penguin is the UK's favourite chocolate biscuit bar with sales in excess of £50 million per year. The chocolate biscuit bar market is worth £480 million and is growing in value by 3% year-on-year.

1998
BIBENDUM

MICHELIN

The more we progress, the further you go.

The Market

During the twentieth century our lives have been changed beyond recognition by the advent of modern transport - cars, trucks, airplanes, trains and subway systems. Alongside this development has been the monumental growth of the world's tyre industry - now valued at $60 billion.

Despite some comparatively lean times in recent years, the industry has, in the Nineties,

showed signs of a renaissance as the price of raw materials - chiefly rubber - has stabilised and the leading tyre manufacturers improved their efficiency.

Today the market is dominated by Michelin (France), Bridgestone (Japan) and Goodyear (US). Other contenders include Continental, Sumitomo and Pirelli.

Achievements

The Michelin Group is the world's leading tyre manufacturer with almost a 20% share of the market and a consolidated turnover of FF 79.7 billion. Michelin is based at Clermont-Ferrand in France, but operates 74 manufacturing plants in 16 countries, five rubber plantations in Africa and South America, five testing facilities and five research and development centres in France, Japan and the USA. The company operates a comprehensive sales network throughout some 170 countries.

According to the Global Tyre Report 1996/97, Michelin topped the league of tyre manufacturers in both sales and brand value. Michelin has pursued an effective and consistent marketing strategy, capitalising on its corporate symbol - 'Bibendum' the Michelin Man - one of the world's greatest brand icons. The company has consolidated its status

through pioneering new tyre products which set standards for the entire industry.

History

Until 1889, the Michelin factory at Clermont-Ferrand, France, produced rubber products such as hoses and general farming implements. But a beleaguered cyclist with both tyres punctured changed all that when he arrived at the factory in an ox cart one day.

André and Edouard Michelin, the brothers who controlled Michelin, spent many hours repairing the tyres but they soon punctured again. This was because at that time, tyres were bandaged to wheels. Waiting for glue to harden while repairing a simple puncture was therefore laborious - it could take up to ten hours!

So, Edouard Michelin devised a solution - a detachable pneumatic tyre which could be removed and repaired in just fifteen minutes. His development was set to revolutionise the worldwide transport industry.

Having patented the detachable pneumatic tyre, the Michelin brothers sponsored a well known cyclist, Charles Terront, to enter a bicycle race from Paris to Brest. Using their tyres Terront went on to win the race by a full eight hours because he found it easier than his competitors to repair his punctures.

Michelin then organised a bicycle race from Paris to Clermont-Ferrand, secretly depositing nail booby-traps en route to cause punctures - giving them 240 opportunities to prove how easy it was to repair a puncture. A year later, over 10,000 cyclists were using Michelin tyres.

Michelin first used the Michelin Man as a marketing device in 1898. A series of posters was produced which showed the character drinking nails and broken bottles and claiming "Nunc est bibendum" - Latin for "Now is the time to drink" - to emphasise that Michelin tyres

ate up obstacles. At a Paris bicycle trade fair the following year, a man dressed as the Michelin Man attracted huge crowds to its stand and caused a sensation.

Michelin's great breakthrough, however, came with the car. The first cars used solid tyres but to demonstrate the efficacy of their pneumatic air-filled tyres, the Michelin brothers entered a motor race from Paris to Bordeaux. Driving an automobile nicknamed L'Eclair (Lightning) they finished ninth out of 210 competitors.

By 1905, a trading house had been set up in London and a manufacturing facility in Italy the following year. Building on the company's successes in car races around the world, the Michelin company bought a US rubber company and started manufacturing tyres in the USA in 1908.

When the First World War broke out, Michelin turned its hand to airplane manufacture and made 1,884 planes for the French war effort. After the war, Michelin developed tyres for passenger railways and began to expand the business internationally.

However, the Second World War brought tyre development to a halt until 1946, when Michelin registered the world's first radial tyre - known as the Michelin 'X' - the prototype of the broad-based pneumatic tyre we use today. This was a moment of enormous importance for the tyre industry and Michelin was soon kick-started into massive expansion to meet demand. It entailed a move into the US market in 1950 with the incorporation of the Michelin Tire Corporation, based in New York. In 1966, Michelin made its ultimate breakthrough in the US market when Ford decided to launch its new model, the 1968 Lincoln Continental III passenger car, complete with Michelin's radial tyres.

Throughout the 1960s, the radial concept had begun to dominate the tyre market. During the 1970s, Michelin underwent huge growth - 23 new plants to manufacture just radial tyres. In the US, still regarded as the prize market for car manufacturing Michelin became a leading supplier of tyre equipment. Michelin managed to stave off the worst effects of the ensuing worldwide recession with aggressive expansion plans, particularly in the Far East.

By the end of the 1980s, with the acquisition of the Uniroyal Goodrich Tire Company, Michelin was the world's leading tyre manufacturer.

The Product

Michelin produces over 3,500 types of tyre for virtually all types of vehicle including bicycles, motorcycles, cars, trucks, trains, airplanes and even the NASA space shuttle.

The company has been a pioneer of the tyre industry since 1889 when it developed the first detachable pneumatic

tyre. Other firsts have included: the tread pattern (1905); the twinned wheel used for buses and heavy goods vehicles (1908); rail-tyres "Michelines" (1929); the radial tyre, developed in secret during the Second World War and now the standard broad-based tyre design used for most motor-vehicles (1946); aircraft tyres including those for Boeing 777 (1980s); and tyres used for tube-trains, (first used in Montreal in 1951). Michelin has also developed tyres for rallying and racing cars and helped Ferrari win the Formula One World Championship in 1977.

A particularly successful brand extension is Michelin road maps and guides. André Michelin, an ex-official at the French Ministry of the Interior Map Department, supervised the publication of the first Michelin Guide in 1900. Up to this point, there had been minimal road-mapping, but Michelin ensured a constant stream of updated guides and now publishes 160 'Green Guides'.

Recent Developments
Michelin strives to ensure the safety as well as the durability of its tyres. In 1990, the company launched the 'Green Tyre' as a response to public environmental concerns. This tyre ensures rolling resistance with the road is reduced, to save fuel, and helps to reduce pollution. A range of 'Green X' energy-saving tyres, branded Energy, has been produced for cars, and in 1995, an Energy truck tyre range was developed, promising a 20% reduction in rolling resistance - the equivalent of a 6% saving in fuel.

In 1997, with its eye once more on the future, Michelin announced the development of the PAX system, a new tyre and wheel concept that allows a motorist complete mobility for 125 miles at speeds up to 50mph at zero pressure after a puncture.

The advance of silica technology in rubber

mixes has allowed Michelin to produce coloured tyres for motorists who wish to enhance the appearance of their cars.

In addition to developing new technologies, Michelin has undergone a complete corporate overhaul to ensure greater efficiency. Between 1960 and 1990, Michelin was on average

opening a new factory every nine months. In 1989 it acquired US-based Uniroyal Goodrich.

Michelin is now strengthening its presence in those areas of the world where the market for tyres is undergoing rapid expansion - the Pacific Rim, South America, Asia and Eastern and Central Europe. The company has taken a majority shareholding in a Polish tyre-making concern and has opened a factory in China.

Promotion
The Michelin Man, one of the most famous corporate logos in the world was 100 years old in 1998. This congenial figure built out of tyres, has been used in all Michelin's poster and TV advertising campaigns to date and features on all Michelin road-maps. His image has also appeared on key-rings, hot air balloons and toys.

The idea of the Michelin Man was conceived by Edouard Michelin at an exhibition in Lyon in 1898, when a stack of tyres struck him as almost lifelike. His brother André, with the artist O'Galop invented the Michelin Man and he was given the nickname Bibendum by Thery, a famous racing driver.

Early posters depicted Bibendum in various roles. An early O'Galop illustration showed him as a wrestler, flippantly kicking the dangers of the road into touch. Another artist, Grand Aigle, depicted Bibendum as a Tyrolean, while René Vincent portrayed Bibendum as the rescuer of a car with a puncture.

Bibendum has taken on many guises during his long life - a film star, a mime artist, a politician, a sailor - and he continues to evolve with changing times. He doesn't smoke anymore and since 1997 his body has become sleeker.

He is often seen in motorsport victory advertising as the Pilot, reflecting the name of Michelin's range of ultra high performance tyres and promoting the company's strong associations with rallying, touring car and motorcycle racing. Michelin's notable Formula One Grand Prix successes have been with Renault and Ferrari - particularly during the 1978 Grand Prix series. Michelin's involvement with motor-racing stems

from the company's earliest days when Michelin tyres showed their superiority over the competition in road-races.

To celebrate the centenary an exhibition entitled '1898-1998 - The Michelin Man,' showing the role played by Michelin in the development of the transport and tourist industries travelled the world.

Three books on the history of the Michelin Man were published in 1998. Michelin's Internet site provided information about Michelin celebratory events around the world and a competition was run to give net surfers a chance to win lots of prizes.

A range of products from babies play rugs to crystal miniatures featuring the Michelin Man's image are also available and Michelin was selected as "official tyre of the 1998 World Cup".

Brand Values
Michelin is a truly international brand with an impressive heritage. It is renowned for its ground-breaking achievements in the tyre industry which have been achieved through understanding and anticipating customers' needs. Consumers have come to expect consistently high quality and reliability from Michelin and it continually works to ensure ever greater travel safety. Michelin says it is always prepared to: "Take a great tread forward".

Things you didn't know about
Michelin

At the start of the century, the first electric car, known as 'La Jamais Contente' (Never Satisfied), was the first automobile to travel at over 60 miles per hour. It used Michelin tyres.

The Michelin Man - known as Bibendum - is so important to the company that only a very few select artists are permitted to draw him to ensure that he always looks the same all over the world.

During the 1930s, Michelin bought the beleaguered Citroën Car Company and restored it to the status of a great French car maker.

It takes seven years for a rubber tree to produce the raw ingredient for a Michelin tyre.

London's famously opulent Michelin Building, first opened in Fulham Road in 1911, was re-opened and refurbished in 1987 a by its new owners Sir Terence Conran and Paul Hamlyn.

Michelin is by far the biggest employer in the French town of Clermont-Ferrand, where its headquarters is based, employing 16,000 local people. There is a road, 'Boulevard Edouard Michelin' named after the company's co-founder and a bar, 'Les Bibs', after Bibendum, the famous Michelin Man.

One of Bibendum's recent feats was to run the London Marathon.

The Market

Business is buoyant in the UK small car market where sales grew from 450,000 to 566,000 between 1993 and 1997. Competition, however, continues to grow. Today, manufacturers must contend with high marketing and manufacturing costs and increasingly stringent legislation means that margins are under constant pressure.

This, however, has had a positive effect on the market as the struggle to gain competitive edge has lead to product innovations. A number of new small cars have recently been unveiled that will change the face of the car market as we know it. These include the Mercedes A Class, VW Beetle and the new Mini.

Achievements

Since its launch 38 years ago, the Mini has successfully carved its own niche in a highly competitive sector. Today, it has become one of the most widely known and popular car brands, a national icon and one of the few car brands to truly stand head and shoulders above its competitors.

The numbers speak for themselves. More than 5.3 million Minis have been produced so far. There are 500,000 Minis currently in everyday use in the UK alone. Elsewhere, the Mini is available in 20 countries. Production continues with more than three quarters of Minis made today now going to export markets.

History

The Mini was launched in 1959. It was conceived as a practical alternative to the motorcycle and side-car and as an answer to the raft of 'bubble cars' popular with the British public throughout the Fifties.

The car was the brainchild of Sir Alec Issigonis. He designed it from the inside out to provide drivers with an astonishing amount of interior and luggage space for a car just ten feet long. The transverse engine and front wheel drive layout were quite revolutionary at the time, and had a lasting influence on the rest of the car industry.

The Mini's minimal front and rear overhangs and diminutive size gave the car exceptional manoeuvrability and handling which led to it catching the eye of the motor

sports industry, including Formula 1 racing car manufacturer John Cooper. Its small size and compact shape meant it was ideal for taking corners at speed. The racing version, the Mini Cooper, quickly became a natural for racing and rallying. It won numerous races including the prestigious Monte Carlo rally which it won three times during the 1960s, securing the car's reputation as a motoring legend.

Even today, Issigonis' genius shines in the Mini. Nineties drivers find the car more appropriate for dealing with today's road congestion, pollution and impossible parking than many younger brands. "The Mini," motoring magazine Autocar recently claimed, "deals with today's motoring problems better than designs a quarter of its age ... economical,

reliable, desirable."

Small wonder, then, that the Mini is considered by many to be one of the greatest cars of all time thanks to its pioneering design, its powerful influence on the automotive industry and on society as a whole. In November 1995, Autocar magazine voted Mini Car of the Century.

Today, the future looks bright for the brand in the new Millennium, too. Some 38 years after the launch of the original, a new Mini was unveiled at the 1997 Frankfurt Motor Show. It is due to be launched in 2000.

The Product

Although the car has undergone a number of revisions the fundamental design of the Mini remains unchanged.

When the Mini was first introduced, Issigonis omitted space for a radio believing that music would interfere with the main business of driving. Today, however, Minis accommodate both car stereos and a heater - once an extra accessory - as standard as well as many more sophisticated features.

Thirty years since the first Mini Coopers were winning races, John Cooper again helped develop the current Mini Cooper 1.3i which uses the same engine as its forbears, but now includes fuel injection and a catalyst in its impressive design specs. John Cooper, meanwhile, still sells Minis from his dealership in Ferring, Worthing.

The current product line-up includes the Mini 1.3i and Mini Cooper 1.3i, both of which are powered by a 63PS fuel injected engine. All Minis use rubber-cone suspension, retaining the industry-leading handling characteristics which make it so enjoyable to drive.

Recent Developments

In October 1996, the Mini underwent the most extensive series of revisions in its history, gaining a driver's air bag, side-impact bars and seat belt pre-tensioners.

A new, sophisticated, multi-point fuel-injection system was added to the engine together with a wide range of additional improvements to make the car more refined and comfortable, while retaining all of the excitement of the original. Also added were a wide range of colours, trims, options and accessories so that customers can really make their Mini their very own.

Promotion

The Mini is a unique car and appeals to a particular segment of the market. Rover targets these customers very closely using direct mail, targeted black & white and colour press campaigns and event sponsorship, such as Mini Seven racing and the Italian Job charity run.

In the early days, the Mini enjoyed spontaneous advertising by Mini owners who liked sporting stickers in rear windows proclaiming: "You've just been Mini'd!' as it sped past larger, more cumbersome cars in traffic. Such inadvertent advertising enhanced the car's cult status in the Sixties which led to it winning a leading role in the popular 1968 film The Italian Job which starred Noel Coward and Michael Caine as the brains behind an audacious bank robbery in Rome.

Today, the Mini's advertising and promotion has kept pace with changing technology. The Mini has one of the most successful Internet sites in the UK, at www.mini.co.uk. This site receives an estimated 20,000 'hits' per day and has proved to be a highly effective direct marketing tool. It has won several prestigious awards including the Yell award for best commercial site on the Internet and a Gold Trophy at the Direct Marketing Association awards.

Mini Special Editions have always been popular and limited editions, like the Mini Cooper Monte Carlo, have become highly sought after collectors items.

The latest special edition is the highly desirable Paul Smith Mini, developed with the internationally renowned fashion designer for the UK and Japanese markets, was launched in 1998.

Brand Values

The Mini's core proposition is excitement - Rover likes to say it builds "the most exciting small car in the world". However, there are a number of other key brand values.

The car is entertaining - fun to buy, drive and own - which is why owning a Mini can become addictive. It's individual - unique within the car industry and able to reflect any personality its owner chooses, be it the sporty Mini Cooper or luxurious Mini Kensington. It's chic with an enduring style and sophisticated aura. It's classless - the Mini's cosmopolitan image cuts across traditional sectors and class groups, which is why the Mini appeals as much to the millionaire as to the man and woman in the street.

And, of course, it's quintessentially British.

MOËT & CHANDON

Fondé en 1743

The Market

"Burgundy makes you think of mischief,
Bordeaux makes you talk of mischief,
But champagne makes you get up to mischief."
Brillat Savarin

Of all drinks, champagne is surely king. It has been responsible for numerous bons mots and witty epithets. Noel Coward, for example, drank champagne at breakfast each morning - "Doesn't everyone?" he observed. Once a luxury for the elite, champagne has more recently moved into the mainstream as incomes have risen and attitudes changed. To some it remains a status symbol, to others a well-deserved luxury. It is always a pleasure.

This shift is reflected in the distribution of champagne which has expanded from exclusive outlets into high street off-licences, grocers and supermarket chains and by the number of brands now competing in the market. The traditional names - such as Moët & Chandon, Lanson, Piper Heidsieck, Champagne Mercier, Veuve Clicquot and Bollinger - are known as the Grandes Marques. They have been joined in recent years by cheaper, own label rivals competing for the mid-income customer.

The Eighties were a particular boom time for champagne brands. The bubble burst, however, with the Gulf War - champagne shipments plummeted by 34% in 1991 down from 21 million to 14 million in just one year. Grandes Marques, with their premium status, were hit particularly hard.

The rise of own label and the effects of recession therefore made the early Nineties a difficult time for champagne houses. Moët & Chandon, however, continued to achieve impressive sales growth and maintain its premium brand status.

Achievements

Sales of 75cl bottles of champagne through off-licences in Great Britain grew by 18% between 1996 and 1997. The champagne market growth was driven by Moët & Chandon which generated more than 20% of the total market growth and 55% of the Grandes Marques market (Source: Nielsen GB).

Moët & Chandon is clear brand leader with a share in total volume terms of the off-trade of 17.6% in 1997. According to shipment figures,

Moët & Chandon had a 15% share of total champagne shipments in 1996. Between 1985 and 1996, company turnover rose from £22 million to £50 million; sales rose from 3.18 million bottles to 3.3 million bottles over the same period. This is quite an achievement given that total UK champagne sales had crashed from 22 million to 14 million bottles between 1989 and 1991.

History

Moët & Chandon has been making champagne for over 250 years. With over 200 'crus', or vineyards, to choose from, Moët & Chandon's Brut Impérial is widely regarded as the ultimate expression of the art of champagne blending.

The House of Moët & Chandon was founded in 1743 by Claude Moët in Epernay, France, in an attempt to break the stronghold of the vineyards in nearby Reims. It worked. Today, Moët & Chandon is now the world's largest champagne house.

Claude Moët adopted the winemaking methods accredited to the Benedictine monk, Dom Pierre Pérignon. The Abbey of Hautvillers where Dom Pérignon resided was acquired by the Chandon family in 1825 and now houses a private museum. Before Dom Pérignon's experiments in winemaking, the Champagne area of France produced a still, rather murky-looking wine known as 'vin gris'. He achieved a major breakthrough by controlling the bubbles produced in the fermentation process, and used them as a marketing plus. He further transformed the wine by combining grapes from different vineyards to get a more balanced, blended result. His other innovations included gently but swiftly pressing the grapes and sealing the bottles with flexible Spanish cork rather than the traditional wooden plugs.

The region became known for its light, sparkling wines and Claude Moët was amongst the first to capitalise on this. Soon he was supplying some of the great names of French society, including Madame de Pompadour. International exports soon followed.

Claude Moët died in 1760 and was succeeded by his son, Claude-Louis Nicolas and, subsequently, his grandson, Jean-Rémy.

Business was difficult during the French Revolution with exports becoming virtually impossible. Production continued, however, and business flourished again in the early 1800s. When Jean-Rémy retired, the business was taken over by his son, Victor, and son-in-law Pierre Gabriel Chandon. From 1833, the company was known as Moët & Chandon and

by 1879 it was the largest vineyard owner in Champagne.

In 1936 Moët & Chandon introduced Dom Pérignon champagne - the first 'prestige' champagne to appear on the market. The company took control of Reims-based champagne house Ruinart Père & Fils in 1963 and in 1970 it acquired Champagne Mercier. A year later, the company bought Parfums Christian Dior and merged with the cognac house Jas Hennessy to form the holding company Moët-Hennessy.

In 1987, Moët-Hennessy merged with Louis Vuitton, creating LVMH Moët-Hennessy Louis Vuitton, a group with an unrivalled portfolio of luxury brands. Louis Vuitton brought with it three champagne houses - Veuve Clicquot, Canard Duchêne and Henriot (since sold), Champagne Pommery was acquired more recently.

Recent Developments

The Eighties boom followed by the Gulf War and recession hit all champagne producers hard. Inevitably, a number turned to discounting in the hope of retaining market share in the UK. Moët & Chandon worked to persuade distributors to keep their prices up, sticking to a value rather than a price proposition.

This, along with the company's decision to improve its relationship with the non-brewery-owned wholesale sector, eventually paid off. Between 1987 and 1991, the price of Brut Impérial jumped 50% from £11.99 to £17.99; between 1991 and 1998, the price rose further to £19.99 - a gentle and sustainable increase of 11%.

Since February 1997, Moët & Chandon has been the official champagne of London Fashion Week with the brand's involvement in the world of high fashion including features in many of the UK's colour glossy magazines.

In February 1998, Moët & Chandon launched Brut Rosé, its first new champagne product in more than 30 years. The champagne was positioned as a flagship for the Moët & Chandon range - an introduction to the full compliment of other Moët & Chandon products. In its distinctive copper and pink packaging, Brut Rosé is being marketed as an exclusive champagne.

Three sparkling wines and two spirits have now been added to the Moët & Chandon portfolio, although champagne remains 90% of the company's business.

— *Moët & Chandon. Turning nature into art* —

The Product

Champagne is one of the most versatile wines and can be enjoyed at any time of the day. Although certain styles of champagne lend themselves to different occasions, many people are mystified when it comes to matching champagne to food. As a result, many think only in terms of drinking champagne to toast a particular cause for celebration. There are, however, a number of different types of champagne.

Moët & Chandon's Brut Impérial Vintage has the weight to accompany a variety of different dishes, especially white meat and shellfish. An older vintage goes well with freshwater fish, game birds, foie gras and a number of cheeses. Moët & Chandon's Brut Impérial Vintage Rosé goes particularly well with meats and game, spring lamb and oriental foods. There are also dry demi-sec champagnes which make good accompaniments to desserts and blue cheeses.

Moët & Chandon wines are known for being soft and well-balanced - not dominated by one grape variety, whilst Moët & Chandon's approach to winemaking is careful to respect the fruit.

Moët & Chandon champagne is produced in the traditional way. Approximately 100 days after flowering, the grapes are ready to be picked by hand from the Moët & Chandon vineyards (in Epernay, Verzenay and Courtemont) which produce 25% of the company's requirements.

The grapes are then taken to the company's three pressing centres which still use traditional wooden presses. Grapes are pressed gently to ensure that no colour or harsh tannins from the skins taint the clear juice. 4,000kg of grapes first yields 2,050 litres of the finest juices from the first pressing. This is known as the "Cuvée" and is used to produce Moët & Chandon's champagnes. Grapes from different vineyards are then pressed and fermented separately.

The grapes then undergo a series of processes, starting from first fermentation which takes place at carefully controlled temperature levels. The still wines are systematically analysed and tested. The unassembled wines are stored separately for several months until they are further tested, tasted, compared and finally blended. This is a critical stage and a true art as the champagne maker's skill is based on creating a single blend which is far greater than the sum of its parts.

The blended wine is then bottled with the addition of sugar and yeast from a selected strain developed by Moët & Chandon's own laboratories which together induce the second fermentation.

It is this second fermentation, which takes place in the dark coolness of Moët & Chandon's 17.5 miles of underground chalk cellars, which creates the delicate sparkle of Moët & Chandon champagne. Legally, a champagne can be released for sale after 15 months but it is only after two years that the yeast imparts its full qualities. Moët & Chandon's non-vintage Brut Impérial is therefore aged for a minimum of two years whilst Moët & Chandon's vintage champagnes are aged for a minimum of four years.

Moët & Chandon produce their champagne in a different number of bottles including the Jeroboam (or double magnum - equivalent to four standard bottles); Methuselah (or quadruple magnum/eight standard bottles); Salmanazar (12 bottle equivalent); Balthazar (16 bottle equivalent) and Nebuchadnezzar (equivalent to 20 standard sized bottles).

Promotion

Moët & Chandon provides information for the consumer about different champagnes and how and when they should be drunk, whilst sustaining the magical mystique surrounding their products. They are eager to recruit new champagne drinkers to the brand.

Promotions, direct mail and merchandising play an important role in marketing Moët & Chandon products to the on-trade. Leaflets communicating both brand and wine values are a feature of off-trade promotions, along with offers involving trips to the House of Moët & Chandon in Epernay.

In 1994, Moet-London launched a first ever £1 million advertising campaign as a means of talking more directly to the consumer. The move reversed a long-standing strategy of not advertising in the UK.

Moët & Chandon allows visitors to its cellars and sees 100,000 people pass through its doors each year. Public Relations ensures the champagne is seen in the hands of the right people in the right places.

Moët & Chandon staff work with the catering industry to ensure the company's products are best served at all times.

Brand Values

Moët & Chandon is about heritage and quality. The company prides itself on the quality of its production technique and the mastery of its blenders and in addition, on a number of distinctive strengths - a genuine philosophy of winemaking, perfectly-defined styles, broad sources of grape supplies, proven expertise and a constant commitment to quality.

Things you didn't know about Moët & Chandon

Claude Moët founded the House at the age of 60 years old.

Napoleon Bonaparte once said of champagne: "In victory you deserve it, in defeat you need it". He honoured his old friend Jean-Rémy Moët with the Brut Impérial name in recognition of a long-standing friendship.

In this century alone, Moët & Chandon's sparkle has added to the lustre of coronations, including those of Edward VII and Queen Elizabeth II, and other major events: the 200th anniversary of American Independence, the Queen's Silver Jubilee and was even drunk on the first commercial flight of Concorde.

The late renowned artist Freddie Mercury started his most famous song "Killer Queen" with the words: "She keeps Moët & Chandon in her pretty cabinet..."

Madame de Pompadour once said: "Champagne is the only wine that leaves a woman beautiful after drinking".

The Market

Mothercare is the specialist retailer for the mother-to-be, new mothers, babies and children up to the age of ten. It positions itself as "The One Stop Baby Shop".

In Britain, the retail industry has undergone significant change over the past decade with the rise of edge-of-town superstores and the decline of a number of city centres. In the mother-to-be and mothers of young children sector the two markets have proven to be quite different and Mothercare has responded to this by retaining a strong presence in the high street whilst developing larger edge-of-town destination stores.

Mothercare's high street stores continue to be particularly suited to convenience shopping for items such as clothing, babycare and everyday household needs. Edge-of-town stores provide three of four times the space of the average high street store and convenient parking. This extra space gives the opportunity to display more comprehensive ranges, particularly of larger items like pushchairs and cots. Although customers may visit less, they are more likely to be pre-planned shopping trips, resulting in a higher spend.

Achievements

Mothercare was founded in 1961 as the UK's first specialist retailer for mothers-to-be and mothers with young children. It remains the only retailer focusing on this specific market segment.

In 1977 Mothercare received the Royal Society of Arts Presidential Award for Design Management. In 1979 Mothercare received the Queen's Award for Export Achievement and in 1996 Storehouse, Mothercare's parent company, received the award again in recognition of the rapidly growing international operation in both Mothercare and its sister company Bhs.

Mothercare prides itself on customer service and places great emphasis on making its stores parent and child-friendly shopping environments.

The chain won the Best Children's Clothes Shop category in the Tommy's Parent Friendly Awards in 1994, 1995, 1997 and 1998. In 1998 Mothercare also won a Parent Friendly Award for the Best Organisation for Dads.

Today, Mothercare also caters for children up to the age of eight (ten in Mothercare World and Childrens World). It operates a chain of 341 stores in the UK as well as an international franchise operation in 33 countries with over 160 franchise outlets.

Mothercare purchased the Childrens World chain of 57 stores from The Boots Company PLC in 1996. During 1997/8, all 15,000 square feet Childrens World stores were converted into Mothercare World. A new format for the remaining 30,000 square feet stores was unveiled in Romford in November 1997. This is the design blue print for the remaining 30,000 square foot edge-of-town stores.

History

The first Mothercare store focusing on mothers-to-be and mothers with young children opened in Kingston, Surrey in September 1961. In 1968, the age range catered for by Mothercare was increased to include children up to the age of five. In 1976 this was extended to ten year-olds. This was rationalised to eight year-olds in 1990.

Since Autumn 1962 Mothercare products have been available through mail order and as a result of the world-wide customer acceptance of the company's unique brand positioning and its authoritative product range the mail order business quickly moved into an international operation servicing over 130 countries. In 1968 Mothercare opened the first overseas store in St Gallen in Switzerland and this was followed in 1970 by the first store in Austria and in 1977 by the first store in Belgium. At this time all the overseas stores were owned and run by the UK operation however in 1984 Mothercare International began a franchise operation starting in the Middle East and this has expanded rapidly as appropriate partners have been

identified in relevant countries. The division will continue to expand in its targeted new markets.

Mothercare became a public company in 1972. Ten years later it merged with Terence Conran's Habitat chain to form Habitat Mothercare. In 1986, Habitat Mothercare merged with British Home Stores to form the holding company Storehouse plc. In 1992 Storehouse sold Habitat to the Stitching Ingka Foundation leaving Storehouse to focus on the core brands, Bhs and Mothercare.

Today, Mothercare has 284 Mothercare stores, 40 Mothercare World stores and 17 Childrens World stores. The company had a turnover of £481.3 million (including Childrens World) in 1997/8 and has more than 6,000 employees.

The Product

Mothercare sells products in a number of key areas: nursery equipment, maternitywear, babywear and childrenswear. Mothercare is renowned for selling a comprehensive range of nursery items including pushchairs, car seats, cots, co-ordinated bedding, feeding essentials and toys. All these items are tested and conform to relevant safety standards and where no standards are set they conform to Mothercare's own strict specifications. All clothing comes in durable, easycare fabrics which undergo rigorous quality control to ensure all fabrics and designs meet Mothercare's high specifications.

Mothercare is well known for its strength in product innovation. Currently, the company holds 24 patents for products it has developed and provides five main product groups, each aimed at the different unique stages of parenthood.

Maternity - Mothercare remains the dominant force in the maternity market providing a comprehensive range of clothing as well as specialist products and services.

Baby - the Mothercare baby range offers both function and fashion. Ranges are especially designed in consultation with midwives for early babies to reinforce the authority and expertise inherent in the brand. There are also exclusive in-house fashion brands such as Mini Club.

Young Children - clothing ranges for young children start at two years. Traditional areas of strength such as 'essentials' are now being developed with increased fashion and branded goods.

Nursery Equipment - Mothercare is the market leader in areas of the nursery equipment market, particularly in car safety, transport and bedding. Consistent growth has been achieved in these important markets through continued product development and by working closely both with manufacturers and suppliers.

Toys - following the acquisition of Childrens World, toys represent both a significant challenge and an opportunity. The management are tasked with defining the role of the Mothercare brand in the marketplace and establishing a clear strategy for the future.

As important as Mothercare's product range is its customer service. Mothercare aims to be the first choice for mothers-to-be and mothers of young children. It provides customer service desks in every store and, where space allows, a range of facilities including toilets, mothers' rooms and parents' rooms. The chain operates a Customer Care Line from Monday to Friday during office hours offering advice and customer support.

Additional services available in Mothercare include ordering products from other branches if they are unavailable in a particular store; home delivery; provision of spare parts for Mothercare own brand hardware; a bottle warming service and a maternity bra-fitting service. A new Personal Shopping Service was introduced in June 1998 which allows customers to make an appointment with an experienced sales adviser who can assist in their selection and offer them help and advice.

Mothercare also publishes a catalogue twice a year which is designed to offer advice and information on major purchases. All lines in the catalogue are available from Mothercare Home Shopping, the company's home shopping service.

Recent Developments

In 1992, a new look Mothercare store opened in the Harlequin Centre, Watford - the start of a refurbishment programme. By the start of Mothercare's 1995/6 financial year, 60% of the chain's trading space had been refurbished to follow the style of the Watford store. The programme has since slowed as the main stores have been completed and attention shifted to integrating the acquired Childrens World chain under the Mothercare banner.

In 1996, as a trial, four new Mothercare World stores successfully opened in Canterbury, Slough, Altrincham and Wakefield. These edge-of-town stores include successful elements from both Mothercare and Childrens World, such as fashion for children up to ten; an extensive toy range; a Clarks shoe concession and Mothercare's extensive range of baby fashion and equipment. Following the success of the first four Mothercare World stores, in March 1996, the first two conversions of Childrens World stores to Mothercare World were opened. All of the smaller Childrens World stores were converted to Mothercare World by 1997.

In November 1997, a striking new Mothercare World design concept was unveiled in the 30,000 square feet flagship store in Romford, Essex. The idea behind the new look is to develop a Mothercare World format able to cater for changing consumer tastes and needs well into the new millennium. The refurbishment of this store is the design blueprint for the remaining 30,000 square feet edge-of-town stores and offers an opportunity to increase Mothercare's prominence in its markets. Work has already begun on introducing elements of the new design into core High Street stores.

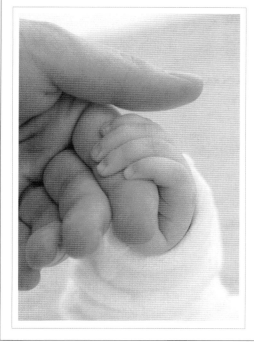

for a
helping
hand
in life's
greatest
adventure

Promotion

Mothercare has promoted the acquisition of Childrens World with an advertising campaign to support the stores which have re-opened as Mothercare World. During the refurbishment programme Mothercare World was promoted with the copyline: "You'll find a world of difference".

In 1998 Mothercare began developing their external communications strategy with a view to creating dominance in the 0 - 2 market and destination in the 2 - 5 market. This is seen as an evolutionary process with the initial campaign concentrating on reflecting Mothercare's core brand values.

To help the business achieve the aim of dominance and destination Mothercare has recently adopted six key strategic principles which guide all management actions:

'Winning people' encourages the right customer-focused attitude throughout the business as well as helping people to develop the right skills. The group's investment in information technology presents significant opportunities to re-skill and re-energise people at all levels.

'Great ideas' aims to make innovation part of the culture of the Mothercare brand and

management system. Everyone in the business is encouraged to contribute their own thoughts and ideas.

'Product obsessed' involves redefining the traditional design, buying and quality processes. The desire to create ranges and products that deliver outstanding performance and value is at the heart of the Mothercare brand proposition.

'Famous brand' status for Mothercare means being a brand that is close to its customers and understands their needs.

'Fabulous stores' will play an important role during the current year as Mothercare begins to update its core high street chain in addition to the further development of the large space, edge-of-town formats.

'Remarkable service' within Mothercare represents a significant point of competitive advantage with service and support knowledge being provided by in-store experts

Brand Values

Mothercare is the leading international name in products for mother-to-be and mothers of young children. The Mothercare brand name has become a symbol of safety, quality and value - strengths conveyed around the world by the distinctive Mothercare logos.

Mothercare is totally committed to safety, quality, integrity and excellence: it makes anticipating and meeting the needs of its customers around the world a priority.

Things you didn't know about Mothercare

Mothercare sells enough pushchairs each year to line the route of the London Marathon.

As the average parent pushes their pushchair for 30 minutes each day they walk almost 600 miles in a year.

If all Mothercare lorries left our warehouse at the same time there would be an instant 1 mile traffic jam.

Mothercare stores distribute over 400,000 Bounty Mother-to-be bags to pregnant women each year.

If all the sleepsuits we sold in one year were hung side by side on a washing line it would stretch from London to Inverness.

Mothercare has raised over £2 million for the Variety Club of Great Britain through the sale of gold hearts.

Nikon

The Market

The camera market is enjoying steady and consistent growth in the late Nineties: 1997 was the best year for camera sales since 1989 and the trend looks set to continue. Nikon currently has a 20% share of the total market - which includes both SLR cameras and compacts. The company has a 25% share of SLR camera sales and achieved its best ever market performance in 1997.

Achievements

Nikon's technological expertise has scored a number of worldwide firsts in photographic equipment. The company invented the autofocus SLR, the first camera with multi-pattern metering, the fish-eye lens and produced the world's first underwater AF SLR.

The F50 is Nikon's entry level SLR and was consistently in the top three best selling SLRs throughout 1997. The AF230, a starter level 35mm autofocus compact camera, has also consistently been a top three best seller. The A20, a starter level Advanced Photo System compact camera, is the sixth best selling APS compact and the second best seller of its class. Nikon has a large share of the professional market - its traditional base. The flagship F5 SLR consistently outsells its closest rival. The company is also a market leader in the 35mm film scanner market: in 1996, Nikon had a 43% share of the European market (Macarthur Stroud).

The F5, Nikon's flagship SLR, has won numerous awards since its launch in June 1996: Camera of the Year (People's Choice 1996); Camera of the Year (Amateur Photographer); Best Professional 35mm Camera (Photo Industry Awards 1997); European Camera of the Year (EISA); European Camera of the Year (TIPA); Camera Grand Prix (Japan); Grand Winner Popular Science (US); Camera of the Year (People's Choice 1997); Best Professional 35mm Camera (Photo Industry Awards 1998).

Nikon is one of five System Developing Companies for the Advanced Photo System - a photographic format which is now growing rapidly. Advanced Photo System now represents 30% of the camera market (value).

History

Nikon was founded as an optical company called Nippon Kogaku KK in 1917 by three of Japan's leading optical manufacturers. As a result, the company has incredible control over

the manufacture of its lenses and even makes its own glass. However, the company has only been producing high quality photographic equipment since the late Forties - photography is one dimension of a multi-faceted business whose existence was born out of two simple elements: light and glass.

Nippon Kogaku KK set up a glass research laboratory in the 1920s to evolve new methods and techniques for developing and producing high quality optical glass. By the Thirties, it was manufacturing camera lenses. During the second world war it produced optical equipment for government use. In 1946, production of non-military optical equipment resumed. The company's first 35mm SLR camera, launched in 1948, was the first product to feature the Nikon trademark.

The company fully entered the photographic market in the Fifties. Nikon's first SLR camera, the Nikon F, was launched in 1959. This true system camera, much loved by press photographers, was the first SLR to have the bayonet mount still in use on today's Nikons. By the end of the Fifties, the company had set up its first overseas subsidiary - in the US - and was increasingly known worldwide as Nikon.

Nikon's first camera with a built-in external CDS-cell exposure metre was the 1962 Nikon F Photomic. Nikon's FM2n fully mechanical SLR camera was introduced in 1983 and continues to be a popular and current model in the range - unchanged for 14 years.

The Product

More than 2,300 products carry the Nikon name, most of which owe their existence to the company's mastery of glass manufacture. Over 300 different types of glass are the essential components in products as diverse as camera lenses, scanners and sunglasses. The Nikon product range extends from microscopes and telescopes to binoculars, spectacles and sunglasses. In the field of healthcare, Nikon produces ophthalmic equipment, hearing aids and is also a leading light in the brand new field of telemedicine.

The Nikon lens mount has remained unchanged since 1959. This means the majority of Nikon lenses will fit all Nikon bodies - including the very latest models. The company is very proud of its policy of non-obsolescence. Nikon cameras range from autofocus SLRs such as the top of the range F5; the F90X; mid-range F70 and F50 entry level SLR through to manual SLRs such as the F3 and FM2; 35mm compacts and Nuvis Advanced Photo System Compacts.

The F5 was launched in 1996 and has since picked up numerous prestigious awards. Its innovative autofocus system features five separate detection sensors which cover five focus areas - centre, left, right, top and bottom. For greater accuracy and versatility, the F5 has a choice of autofocus modes. Dynamic AF mode allows you to select the priority focus area that best suits your composition. If a subject moves off the selected focus area, Dynamic AF instantly shifts to another one of the five areas to keep the subject in focus. There's also Single Area AF mode which is like having a choice between five carefully positioned AF spot sensors. Other features include fast and accurate Autofocus; a highly sophisticated metering system; exclusive 3D Colour Matrix Metering; spot metering and AF integration and five segment TTL flash control.

The Nuvis 160i, Nikon's new top of the range compact launched in November 1997, offers many impressive features. With its 4.2x zoom lens, the Nuvis 160i is the highest magnification zoom in Nikon's Advanced Photo System compact camera range.

Meanwhile the Zoom 800, launched in June 1998, is the latest stylish and lightweight addition to Nikon's 35mm format compact camera range.

Matching the refinement of the Nikon F5 is a range of flashguns. The most sophisticated of these has the capacity to fire a series of imperceptible pre-flashes of ever-increasing intensity just after the camera mirror goes up, but before the shutter moves. The reflections of these pre-flashes (up to 16 in total) are monitored and evaluated by the camera to automatically determine settings prior to the final flash, which can cover up to 42 metres.

Recent Developments

Nikon is now spearheading the digital revolution. Its Coolpix range of cameras is capable of storing images digitally and downloading them onto a computer. This highly developed business tool offers annotation and sound capabilities as well as image capture. Nikon's Coolscan range of compact film scanner can digitise and transmit images originally captured on film to anywhere in the world via a modem computer link and mobile phone.

Promotion

During 1998, Nikon focused on the importance of 'Nikon optics' throughout its marketing and publicity. 'Nikon optics' have been renowned since the company's formation in 1917.

Nikon publishes its own newsletter,' Nikon in Touch', three times a year. The publication is mailed to all Nikon SLR owners on the company's database.

Sponsorship plays a major part in Nikon's marketing strategy. The brand provides ongoing support for a range of major national and international sports and arts events including: the British Open Gold Championship; London Fashion Week; the London Symphony Orchestra and the Goodwood Festival of Speed.

The company also stages the annual Nikon Press Awards - the premier photographic awards event rewarding the best achievements

in professional photography each year.

Prior to 1998 the Nikon F5 provided the opportunity to communicate Nikon's leadership status. The "F5. Step Ahead" strap line underscored a series of press ads concentrating on product benefits. It helped reinforce the traditional Nikon image as the professional brand amongst its target audience. The campaign helped recapture the professional market as well as serious amateur photographers.

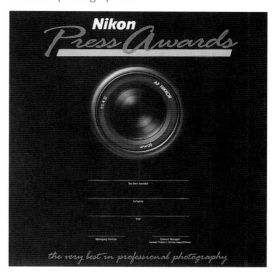

Brand Values

Mention the word 'Nikon' to just about anyone and the chances are they will immediately think of cameras. As a global brand it ranks among the most renowned and instantly recognised names. As a photographic brand, Nikon stands for high quality photographic equipment. Huge numbers of people around the world continue to use Nikon cameras first bought in the Sixties, Seventies and Eighties - an exceptional testimony to the enduring strength of these cameras and lenses and the quality of the products' design.

NIKON F5: 8 FRAMES PER SECOND WITH FOCUS TRACKING. WORLD RECORD.

3D COLOUR MATRIX METERING SYSTEM. • 1005-PIXEL EXPOSURE METERING SYSTEM.
5 AREA DYNAMIC AUTOFOCUS. • 1st SELF-DIAGNOSTIC SHUTTER CONTROL.

NIKON F5: 3D COLOUR MATRIX METERING SYSTEM. WORLD RECORD.

8 FRAMES PER SECOND WITH FOCUS TRACKING. • 1005-PIXEL EXPOSURE METERING SYSTEM.
5 AREA DYNAMIC AUTOFOCUS. • 1st SELF-DIAGNOSTIC SHUTTER CONTROL.

Things you didn't know about Nikon

Several of Nikon's cameras - including the F5 - have been styled by top Italian designer Giorgetto Giugiaro who, although involved in many different areas of design, has a background in automobile design and is best known for his Alfa Romeo, Fiat and Volkswagen models.

Thanks to its roots as an optical company, Nikon enjoys incredible control over its lenses and it makes its own glass.

Unlike other manufacturers, Nikon applies the same number of coatings to each lens element regardless of the type of lens. This multi-layered lens-coating process is an integral part of Nikon's lens design and varies for each one - bringing image contrast, light transmission and uniformity of colour balance across every single lens.

Nikon was the brand of choice during the highest ever civilian flight at an altitude of more than 30,500 metres. It has also been used in temperatures of below -50 degrees Centigrade during parachute jumps from over 8,000 metres, and by professional divers at depths of over 100 metres.

Astronauts on the 1988 Discovery space shuttle mission recorded their mission on modified versions of established camera models including the Nikon F3 35mm SLR.

In January 1993, a Nikon S3M fetched £28,000 at auction at Christies - many times its original price and a record for a camera at that time.

The Market

The UK market for bottled water is growing faster than any other sector of the soft drinks industry. In 1997, nearly 800 million litres of bottled water were consumed and it is estimated that by the year 2000 this figure will have grown to over one billion.

Apart from the weather, there are a number of other important factors influencing the growth of this market. One of these is a recent, radical change in the social and environmental climate. The benefits of a healthier lifestyle are now more widely recognised and the most natural drink for the health and fitness conscious is natural mineral water.

People prefer to drink a water that is wholesome and drinkable in its natural state rather than tap water and other waters that are treated with chemicals to make them safe to drink. Small wonder, then, that the UK bottled mineral water market is now valued at more £400 million and that growth is now driven by the growing number of brands competing for business. Bottled mineral waters are now sold in more retail outlets and take up more space on shop shelves than ever before.

Achievements

Perrier is the number one sparkling mineral water in the world (Canadean). The famous green bottle, instantly recognisable to consumers the world over, has changed little since it was first produced nearly 100 years ago.

Perrier is the mineral water most often asked for by name, according to independent research. It is brand leader in the UK (Volume: Value: Bottles: Source: Nielsen). And its brand presence is powerful - Perrier stands apart from its competition, separated by style, wit and quality. Its advertising strapline endorses this: "Perrier - Pour La Vie", which means: "Perrier - For Life".

Certain brands have an identity so long lasting that they have become 'classics'. Perrier is one of these. In one year, the brand organised the 'Perrier Pick of the Fringe', now known as the 'Oscars of alternative comedy', at the Edinburgh Festival. It was appointed official mineral water to London's International Fashion Week and it introduced the first-ever 'Perrier Young Jazz Awards' for young musicians. It has also made 'Sunday Lunch with Perrier' a national pastime and enables consumers to win a Sunday lunch at the most acclaimed restaurant in their area.

Despite fierce competition, Perrier remains a dominant force in the market. It sells twice as much sparkling mineral water (bottles) as any other brand in the UK through grocers and it enjoys the widest distribution of any bottled water brand in restaurants, pubs, clubs and hotels.

The UK natural mineral water market was built, almost single handedly, by Perrier. It has invested more in the market than any other brand and it is the best-known bottled water in the world. Perrier is currently exported to over 120 countries.

History

In 1994, Perrier celebrated its 90th birthday, although it has been around a lot longer.

As long ago as 218 BC, Hannibal discovered an effervescent spring in the Vistrenque Plain at Vergeze, France. The spring was conveniently situated just 200 yards from a road built by the Romans for travelling between Spain and Italy. The spring's reputation soon began to spread. Known as Les Bouillens - "the bubbling waters" - it also served Roman baths built nearby. The fall of the Roman Empire, however, led to a fall in the popularity of the bubbling waters. The spring soon faded into obscurity and only local villagers continued to visit - for the spring's health-giving properties.

However, the bubbling water was eventually bottled for sale. In 1863, Napoleon III ordered it should be bottled "for the good of France". The nearby town Vergeze was developed into a spa resort. Disaster struck in 1869 when the site was gutted by fire and it was only through the help of an Englishman, St John Harmsworth, that the Perrier brand came about at all.

Harmsworth went to Vergeze to recuperate after a motor car accident in 1903. Guided around the site by his doctor, Harmsworth was intrigued to see bubbling water gurgling from the ground. The villagers told him of its revitalising qualities. He drank the water and instantly recognised its commercial possibilities. So he bought the spring with the intention of bottling and selling the water. But it needed a name and striking packaging to succeed. So he decided to name the water in honour of the man who had introduced it to him in the first place - Dr Perrier. And the famous green bottle was based on the Indian clubs Harmsworth used for exercising.

St John Harmsworth was a visionary. He saw significant marketing potential amongst the expatriate community posted abroad, both in the military and civil service. During the reign of the British Empire, many ex-pats in far-flung lands believed the local water to be contaminated (and it often was). Quality water was therefore in short supply. Perrier provided an ideal alternative and - almost as important - it was a marvellous mixer with whisky.

The British loved it. Perrier was even favoured by royalty, receiving two Royal Warrants from Edward VII and George V respectively.

Harmsworth's marketing ploy proved successful. Perrier was advertised as the "champagne of table waters" and could be found in high-class establishments across the world but not in France - the country of origin. It was, in fact, easier to find Perrier in Singapore than in Paris. But this didn't harm sales. By 1922, six million bottles of Perrier were produced every year and by 1933, when Harmsworth died, this had risen to 18 million.

Perrier returned to French hands in the late 1940's when a French company, Societe Source Perrier, bought the brand. A new bottling plant was built, producing over 130 million bottles a year. The product became increasingly Franco-centric with only 20% exported abroad.

Until the 1970s, there was little marketing of Perrier in the UK and in 1972 only half a million bottles were sold. But it soon made a comeback when a subsidiary company Aqualac (Spring Waters) opened in London. The British rediscovered Perrier, spurred on by the brand's high profile advertising. By 1986, over 77 million bottles a year were being sold. In 1996, following its acquisition by Nestlé, the parent company was renamed Perrier Vittel Groupe Nestlé to reflect its expertise in both sparkling and still waters.

Today, the company markets Perrier in all five continents. It owns 56 bottled water brands but Perrier remains the flagship brand and the most international.

The Product

Perrier is one of the world's few naturally

bubbly waters. It springs from a source in the Vistrenque plain near Vergeze in Southern France, where a volcanic eruption beneath the spring thousands of years ago resulted in this unique water with natural bubbles. The water is of a very high quality. It is a refreshing, enjoyable drink and an excellent mixer. Particularly popular amongst today's clubbing, pub-ing youngsters is Perrier with a Twist, the first flavoured mineral water - a refreshing blend of Perrier with a dash of lemon.

Recent Developments

Perrier has always led the UK bottled water market setting standards and starting trends. It was the first brand to introduce sparkling mineral water in 330ml cans and the first to launch a flavoured water - Perrier with a Twist.

Perrier has adopted a powerful marketing strategy. It has a strong presence in all retail sectors and in hotels, restaurants, clubs and pubs and it is present at all the UK's famous annual social and sporting occasions. Perrier has long been established as an enjoyable drink in its own right.

Promotion

Perrier's advertising campaign launched in October 1997 was its biggest and wittiest campaign for years.

Like the hugely successful 'Eau' campaign,

star performer in the last two years. In 1998 its 'Win a Cruise to Tahiti' competition featured on the 75cl Tri-pack attracted new consumers to the brand and this was followed by the most exciting 'Win a Day at Wimbledon' competition which followed Perrier's appointment as the official mineral water for the Wimbledon Lawn Tennis Championships.

Brand Values

Perrier is invigorating, healthy, stylish and French. Skilful marketing has secured the brand star status in the soft drink sector. It has a name and packaging that are both instantly recognisable. It attracts enormous goodwill and commands universal respect. And it has become the natural choice for style setters and those who determine fashion in its widest sense.

which ran for over 15 years from the early Eighties, Perrier is again teasing the consumer with its subtle play on words. The ambiguous word in the campaign is 'pour'. Executions include 'Ready to Pour', 'Pour La Vie' and 'Pour Le Moment'. In English, the word expresses the enjoyment of pouring a glass of Perrier; in French, Perrier is 'For life', 'For the moment', or 'for' many other occasions. Each advertisement is a celebration of the exuberance and natural sparkle of the brand. Perrier is, after all, 'Pour La Vie'.

Perrier is youthful, fresh and sparkling. It is also innovative and active in the marketplace. The brand launched its first ever tennis bottle to celebrate the French Open in 1997 and as a lead up to Wimbledon the same year.

In the summer of 1997 Perrier invited consumers to take part in a 'Make us laugh' on-pack competition appearing on Perrier Tri-Packs. For Christmas 1997, Perrier produced a festive bottle highlighting its claim that 'No party is complete without Perrier'. This quickly became a collector's item. The bottle had a circus theme featuring clowns. Perrier's Tri-Pack has become a

Persil

The Market

The UK soap and detergents markets is one of the most competitive in Europe. It can be split into two main areas: low suds, for use in washing machines, and high suds products suitable for hand washing, twin tub and some top loading machines but not front loading washing machines.

It is the low suds market, however, that is continuously growing - in line with the profusion of new product launches and relaunches traditional to this sector. Growth has been spurred by competition - hence the need to take advantage of new technology in order to stimulate consumer interest.

The machine wash detergent market can be split into powders and liquids, with powders further split into concentrated and conventional. Powders account for 76% of the total market and liquids hold a 24% share value. According to industry predictions, in 1998 the detergent market in the UK will be worth £841 million. At present, Lever Brothers has a 27% share of this market with its Persil, Surf and Radion brands whilst Procter & Gamble has a 55% share with its Ariel, Bold, Daz and Fairy brands.

Achievements

Washing detergents are big business for Unilever, accounting for over £7 billion worth of worldwide sales. This represents a 22% share of the company's total sales. Persil is the flagship brand of Lever Brothers, a wholly owned subsidiary of Unilever plc. In the 88 years since Persil was first launched it has remained a staunch front-runner in the UK detergent market. Throughout its history, Persil has always been at the leading edge of new technology, and is consequently seen as both reliable - by virtue of its heritage and product performance - and innovative.

History

Persil was launched in 1909 as the 'Amazing Oxygen Washer'. The product was originally developed by two Stuttgart professors - Professor Hermann Giessler and Docteur Hermann Bauer. Persil was first owned by Crosfield until it was acquired by Lever Brothers in 1919.

At the time of its launch, bar soaps were used for washing clothes. The new Persil was a soap-based powder which was combined with an oxygen bleaching agent to remove staining in the wash. Persil functioned rather differently to the traditional bar soaps - it had to be stirred into a paste before being added to water. The conservative housewife was initially a little reluctant to desert her established cleaning methods but gradually responded - eventually convinced by the genuine 'whitening' power Persil offered and by its convenience.

The brand was advertised as soap powder that would do away with the dolly rub and washboard and the labour of rubbing clothes. Nothing could be easier. Clothes washed with Persil required only 'soaking, boiling and rinsing'. Up to the Second World War, when housewives started to spend their soap coupons on soap powder as well as soap, clothes washing methods had remained largely the same.

However, this all changed in the 1950s when the first reasonably-priced washing machine was introduced into Britain. As a result washing habits changed quite dramatically. By the late 1960s, as machines became more sophisticated there was a need for a low lather washing powder to prevent excess foam interfering with the spin drying and rinsing process, or causing overflowing. Mainly white fabrics were gradually replaced by coloureds, natural fibres by synthetic and before long, high temperature washing was superseded by the low temperature wash.

Responding to these changes, Persil established a continual programme of product innovation and improvement. In 1968, once the early twin tub machines had given way to the automatic front-loading drum machines which were more technically advanced than their predecessors, Persil launched Persil Automatic - a name that identified the newly-created detergent technology with the new machine technology.

The years since have seen enormous changes in the detergent industry. First, Persil made its detergents biodegradable, well ahead of legislation. Then, during the 1970s, Persil developed a new manufacturing process which enabled its soap powder to be reformulated and improved in both colour and solubility.

Throughout this period, Persil spearheaded a series of advances in stain removal. The 1980s saw the introduction of energy efficient ingredients such as enzymes as well as the launch of detergent liquids, which offered greater product convenience. A non-ionic polymeric soap-dispensing agent was launched in 1981 to improve solubility in 1981. New System Persil Automatic, with low temperature bleach (TAED) and proteolytic enzymes, was introduced in 1983.

Both innovations mirrored the technological development in machines, the changing washing load and increasing concerns about the environment. Similarly, environmental concerns fuelled the growth of concentrated detergents in the 1980s, but in recent years consumers have increasingly returned to using conventional powders.

The Product

The name Persil is derived from two ingredients - Perborate and silicate, both registered in 1906. Persil prides itself on being able to meet the consumer's washing needs whatever they may be. There is always a type of Persil to suit, be it

conventional or concentrated; powder or liquid; non-biological or biological action; specially formulated for coloured fabrics or for use with a twin-tub, top-loading or front-loading washing machine.

The main difference between biological and non-biological detergents is that biological varieties contain various enzymes which break down stains derived from protein, starch and grease at low temperatures - around 40 to 60 degrees centigrade. People concerned about their skin often prefer non-biological detergents. Persil produces both concentrated powder and liquid products. These products are dispensed using a 'dosing ball' and are therefore more economical as there is less product wastage than when using the detergent drawer of the machine.

In fact, the manufacturing process for the concentrated powders uses only 20% of the energy expended by conventional powder manufacturing methods and the process generates no emissions into the atmosphere. Persil's first liquid detergent was launched in 1988. Liquid detergents do not contain bleaching agents in their formulation and are therefore perceived as being gentle on fabrics. The other major advantage with liquids is that they dissolve easily and quickly, getting to work right away. This also makes them well-suited to hand washing.

was introduced in 1994.

New production processes have allowed Lever to include new ingredients. Every component of the powder has therefore been improved: a new active system; a new builder; a more effective enzyme system; a new perfume and a new bleaching system.

New Generation Persil and Persil Finesse were both launched in 1995. Persil Finesse was the first light duty detergent from a mainstream brand. It is non-biological, pH neutral and does not contain bleach or optical brighteners and was designed specifically to care for machine-washable delicate fabrics, like silk and wool.

Persil Power was the first powder based on a new production process, featuring a patented catalyst called the Accelerator (TM). However, negative publicity generated by rival claims resulted in this product being superseded by New Generation Persil.

Persil has since overcome this setback and, since 1996, has been simplifying the fragmented market. At the same time, it was worked to increase the efficiency of its detergents. The introduction of the polymer-based Stain Release System (TM), designed to aid stain removal, added to all Persil variants (except Finesse) has been accompanied by the convergence of the concentrated and conventional liquids into a single new one. Persil is now, once again, re-established as a strong force in the market.

emphasised the whitening benefit of Persil with the slogan 'Persil washes whiter'. Persil's whiteness was often compared with inferior brands in its advertising campaigns. This style of advertising was perpetuated into the TV age. And it worked. The consistency of message and familiar packaging built a huge brand loyalty that has been sustained over many decades.

Mums were the key washing figure in many households for many years. Persil's advertising reflected this through slogans such as 'Someone's Mum isn't using Persil' and the 'What matters to a mum' campaign which successfully balanced emotion with an informative and rational approach. Convenience became the key message towards the end of the 1960s as more and more women returned to work. Persil's main advertising theme centred around the theme 'A winning team - you, your automatic and Persil Automatic'.

In the 1990s, the main ingredients of Persil's advertising have been humour and information. Recent advertising has included the award-winning 'Artists Campaign' with posters in the style of famous artists, like Van Gogh and Degas, and has recognised that Mum is no longer the only user of the washing machine.

Persil's most recent campaign has helped consumers to understand the difference between all the Persil variants on offer and to reduce confusion about detergents in general.

Mrs Van Gogh's washing by **Persil**

Persil whites by Mrs Degas **Persil**

More recent additions to the Persil range have been Persil Colour in both powder and liquid formats and Persil Finesse. The colour products were introduced specifically to maintain the appearance of coloured fabrics for as long as possible through repeated washing. They do not contain bleach or optical brighteners which can, eventually, lead to a fading of dark colours or paling of pastel shades. Persil Finesse was specially developed for machine washing delicate fabrics such as silk and wool.

Recent Developments

The wide range of Persil products now available ensures that today's shopper can identify the ideal detergent for each specific wash.

The early 1990s saw the market becoming fragmented as manufacturers attempted to meet ever-more diverse consumer demands. The launch of Persil Micro Liquid in 1991 was a major step for the Persil brand as it was the first branded concentrated liquid detergent in the UK, meeting the demand for greater convenience and smaller packs. Liquid detergents have subsequently secured a reasonable share of the market, although sales of powder formats still outstrip liquids. Consumer awareness also led to the introduction of the Persil Eco-bag powder refill in 1993 and carton refills for liquids. Both proved particularly successful.

Another major innovation was the introduction of Persil Colour powder and liquid in 1992 and 1993 respectively, prompted by the changes in the make-up of the modern wash load which now includes more coloured items than ever. Concentrated Persil Colour powder

Promotion

All Persil packs carry the distinctive Persil logo and design. Persil aims to project itself as a heritage brand which has cared for the family's wash for almost 100 years.

The brand's cleaning and care credentials are communicated to consumers via advertising, direct mail and through a freephone Careline. The Careline was set up in 1993 to provide a facility for Persil consumers to seek expert advice and make comments or suggestions. The Persil Roadshow was launched in 1994. This set out to entertain, inform and involve consumers through demonstrations and sampling. In addition, Persil Funfit co-ordinates a reward scheme through schools for progress in physical education for children.

During the Second World War, Persil

Brand Values

Persil is a clean-cut family brand. It has always projected itself as caring and responsible, supported by its consistent and effective programme of research and new product development, which has produced detergents suited to each and every washing need.

Through the Persil Careline set up in 1993, consumers have direct access to Persil Advisors. As a result, Persil has been able to listen even more effectively to what consumers want from their detergent. It is therefore bright and innovative, uniting its dependable heritage with a modern, progressive approach. As a result, the Persil brand has inspired brand loyalty over many years.

Brooke Bond PG Tips

The Market

Tea is Britain's national drink. The British love it - so much so that they drink an estimated 180 million cups of tea every day. This equates to average daily consumption per person of 3.46 cups, 365 days a year. Or, to put it another way: tea accounts for four out of every ten cups of liquid drunk.

Its hardly surprising, then, that tea outstrips its nearest rival, coffee, in the UK hot beverages market. Annual tea sales amount to £65 billion - twice that of coffee. Tea has always been an important part of the UK grocery trade and remains so today. The UK tea market is currently valued at £550 million (Nielsen MAT, December 1997).

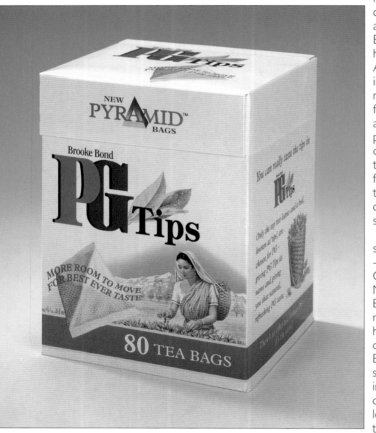

Achievements

Brooke Bond is the UK's number one tea company. Its flagship tea brand is Brooke Bond PG Tips. For more than 40 years, Brooke Bond PG Tips has been the UK's favourite tea brand and currently holds a volume market share of 20.2% (Nielsen MAT January 1998). And it is way ahead in one particular sector, packet tea, with a 26% volume share (Nielsen MAT, December 1997).

Founded over 125 years ago, Brooke Bond has had a long time to market its top tea brand. Awareness of Brooke Bond PG Tips amongst the British public is extremely high and has grown steadily since the TV campaign featuring the Brooke Bond PG Tips chimpanzees began in 1956. Today, these make up one of the longest running and most successful TV advertising campaigns of all time.

History

Although it is now a major UK company, Brooke Bond came from humble beginnings - a small high street shop in Manchester. It was founded by the son of a wholesale tea merchant, Arthur Brooke, who was born in 1845 above his father's shop in Ashton-under-Lyne, Lancashire.

At 19, young Arthur joined the Liverpool branch of a wholesale tea company. He then transferred to the company's head office in London but eventually left to join his father in business. The pair opened new branches throughout Lancashire, enabling Arthur to save around £400 - enough to set up in business on his own.

In 1869, Arthur Brooke opened his own shop in Manchester's Market Street, selling tea, coffee and sugar. It was a shrewd move as the location was opposite the Royal Exchange in a street always busy with housewives. In a break with convention, Arthur didn't accept credit, trading only in hard cash for his goods. An ambitious man, Arthur mixed his own teas, formulating specialised Quality blends and selling them in half pound and 1lb paper bags. His teas became an overnight sensation. Customers loved them so much that rival grocers were forced to sit up and take note. Within no time other retailers were asking if they could buy his tea at wholesale rates and sell it from their shops, too.

Arthur needed to brand his teas and settled on the name Brooke, Bond & Co - the name of his business. Oddly, there never was a Mr Bond, just a Mr Brooke. But the name had a certain ring to it - "it seemed to him to sound well", a contemporary observed. Brooke, Bond & Co was soon printed on every bag in its founder's distinctive copperplate script. Before long, customers associated the Brooke, Bond & Co logo with top quality teas they could rely upon.

Arthur Brooke was soon able to open more shops and started advertising the teas which had made his name. His tea, however, eventually earned itself a brand-name all of its own. At first it was known as Pre-Gestee, which means 'to aid digestion'. A change in the law, however, outlawed the description of tea as medicinal so the name was changed to PG Tips. This came from the top two leaves on the tea plant and a bud known as tips which provides the finest tea.

Arthur Brooke prospered and eventually opened shops throughout the UK. By the turn of the century, Brooke Bond and

Company Ltd had become primarily wholesale, built on three principles - intelligent buying of tea, sensible blending to satisfy the market and clever advertising. Inspired by a trip to the US, Arthur championed novelty and modern methods of salesmanship. Tin advertising plates were soon fixed to corner shops throughout the north of England promoting Brooke Bond teas.

In the 1930s, the Co-Operative Wholesale society was the giant of the tea trade in Britain. During the depression, the 'divi' (or dividend) was welcome. So the manager of Brooke Bond's Manchester shop set to work producing an economical tea blend to be marketed with special packaging and promotion involving a 'dividend card' comprising 60 perforated and gummed squares. Customers could save the stamps - each valued at an old penny - and hand in completed cards to grocers in exchange for five shillings. 'Dividend' tea was launched in November 1935 and became a bestseller.

Since then, Brooke Bond has continued to place high value on the qualities that helped Arthur Brooke's teas lead the market. Skilful marketing is behind the enduring strength of the Brooke Bond PG Tips brand. Considerable effort is taken to ensure that the quality of teas used and the blending process behind Brooke Bond PG Tips remain of a high standard.

The Product

Nowadays, all Brooke Bond's tea is blended and packed at the company's high-tech factory at Trafford Park, Manchester. The tea comes from plantations in South East Asia, India and Africa,

either direct from tea gardens or from auctions.

The Brooke Bond blending plant is computer-controlled, and was built as part of a £20 million investment programme. It is one of the most advanced of its kind in Europe. The plant was first built in 1921 to produce tea for Scotland and northern England. It now has the capacity to serve the whole of the UK as well as Brooke Bond's overseas market, and produces around seven billion tea bags a year.

Brooke Bond PG Tips is a blend of 28 teas. It is available in tea bags, the most popular form of tea accounting for 90% of all tea sold today, or loose. Originally, all tea was bought loose in packets or caddies. But in the 1950s, tea bags arrived in the UK. Although it took time for them to catch on, technical developments - such as a special paper bag which wouldn't break up in boiling water - made the tea bag ubiquitous.

Further innovations in the tea market included the launch in the 1980s of single-serve tea bags which enable a quick, easy brew made in the cup. Brooke Bond PG Tips One Cup was the first single serve tea bag to add a tag and string to the bag for easier handling, and a twin pouch for faster infusion.

Launched in 1990, Brooke Bond PG Tips Low Caffeine, with half the normal caffeine content of tea, appeals to the health-conscious Nineties tea-drinker.

Recent Developments

In 1996, PG Tips celebrated the 40th anniversary of its chimps advertising campaign. The celebrations were accompanied by a new TV advertisement featuring a compilation of key moments from the chimps' campaign, starting from the earliest black and white executions (when chimps drank packet tea).

The brand also ran an intensive programme of on-pack offers as a reward to consumers who had remained loyal to the brand and helped maintain its leading position since the 1950s. A record £25 million was invested in advertising and promotional activity during the anniversary year.

Brooke Bond PG Tips' new generation of Pyramid tea bags were also unveiled in 1996. The pyramid-shaped (or tetrahedral) tea bags took four years to develop and were a major advance in tea bag technology, promising a brew closer in flavour and quality to loose-leaf tea than any before.

The innovation has proven to be a tremendous success for PG Tips - it has helped grow the brand's volume share by an estimated 20%. Much of this has not only been due to improved taste and the new, robust caddy pack packaging but also the innovative way in which the bag was launched. A totally integrated approach has been taken from traditional media including TV, press and posters as well as bus ticket advertising, strategically placed post-it notes, bus-sides and much regionally focused sampling using door to door involving characters from the adverts and PG's own "rocket men".

Promotion

The hot beverages market is a highly competitive business. To keep ahead of its competitors, Brooke Bond PG Tips relies on a top quality product and memorable advertising. The idea for a family of chimps to endorse the taste of Brooke Bond PG Tips tea was conceived in 1956 shortly after the launch of commercial television. The campaign was inspired by news at the time of chimps' tea parties at London's Regents Park Zoo.

The first advert showed the chimps enjoying a party in an elegant country mansion, drinking tea from silver tea-pots and bone china tea-cups. The commercial was a huge success. It led to a further 100 TV commercials which were to prove enduringly popular. Subsequent executions covered a range of chimps in unusual situations, such as as workmen digging the Channel Tunnel; cyclists in the Tour de France race; as racing car drivers and mechanics.

The Tipps family, was introduced in 1992. These ads featured parents Geoff and Shirley Tipps with their children Samantha and Kevin. The common thread running throughout was that of a cuppa as the ultimate reward (or consolation) after a busy day.

The chimps campaign also coined a number of memorable catchphrases, such as: "Avez vous un cuppa?" and "It's the taste". Celebrity voices used to support the cast of chimps have included Cilla Black, Bruce Forsyth, Peter Sellers, Stanley Baxter, Kenneth Connor, Pat Coombs, Arthur Lowe, Irene Handl, Bob Monkhouse, and Kenneth Williams. In 1998 the chimps were rested to allow the popular comedienne Caroline Aherne (alias Mrs Merton) to promote the brand for a time.

Running alongside the TV commercials has been a picture card campaign. Since 1954, Brooke Bond PG Tips has inserted picture cards into its packs, inspiring generations of collectors.

Brooke Bond PG Tips has also contributed to high profile charity campaigns, including Comic Relief where almost £1 million was raised. Another popular charity with which the brand has long been associated is the World Wide Fund for Nature (WWF UK). Brooke Bond PG Tips has featured WWF in on-pack promotions and has contributed significant funding towards WWF conservation projects.

Strong packaging design has also played an important role in Brooke Bond PG Tips' marketing strategy, contributing to its distinctive brand identity. Brooke Bond PG Tips packs are well-known for their familiar red, green and white livery and the tea-picker logo. Brooke Bond PG Tips tea bags also bear a watermark motif, depicting a tea leaf overlain by the PG logo. This has been further strengthened by the introduction of the robust and innovative caddy pack.

Brand Values

Brooke Bond PG Tips enjoys a strong brand heritage and reputation for top quality tea. Research has shown that the British public associate Brooke Bond PG Tips with a sense of security, comfort and continuity - everything we long for in a cuppa. Some of the brand advertising's most recognisable punchlines say it all: "Britain's best-loved tea"; "The unbeatable taste of PG"; "Everything we love in a cup of tea" and: "It's the taste".

Things you didn't know about
PG Tips

Brooke Bond started to blend tea in tea in 1869.

Currently, around 35 million cups of PG Tips are drunk every day.

Each tea brand consists of a number of original teas blended to produce a familiar taste. PG Tips, for instance, the UK's favourite tea, is a blend of as many as 28 original teas.

Relative to average weekly earnings, tea is cheaper today than it was in 1700 and 1850 - around 2p a cup.

Tea is also believed to be an aphrodisiac and is recommended in ancient medical books as a way of improving your sex life.

Tea was discovered when leaves from the tea plant accidentally fell into the boiling water of a Chinese Prince and he liked the taste.

Philishave®

The Market

The market for men's electric shavers in the UK is worth over £57 million a year. This figure accounts for sales of nearly 1.4 million models - battery, mains and rechargeables. Although the annual number of shavers sold has not changed significantly in the past few years, the type of model sold has changed and the value of the market has increased quite substantially.

As in other electrical personal care product markets, users like to 'trade up' to new and better models as they are introduced. In the case of shavers, this means highly sophisticated rechargeable models with many additional features. While sales of battery and mains models fell in 1997, sales of mains/rechargeable models were up by over 9%.

Almost one in two of all men's electric shavers sold in the UK is a Philishave.

Achievements

For nearly 60 years, Philishave has been the world's number one name in men's electric shavers. Throughout that time Philips has invested continually in the brand to maintain its performance as a world-beater. From the moment that the first Philishave was unveiled to the public in 1939 at the spring exhibition in Utrecht, the brand has regularly attracted attention. In 1998, the introduction of the new Philishave Cool Skin marked another milestone in the history of the brand.

History

The introduction of the first single head rotary Philishave on the eve of the Second World War could have seen the end of the brand before it even began. In fact it was an instant success and even the German occupation of Holland didn't prove too great an obstacle to sales. Philips, the company behind the product, persuaded the Germans that manufacturing dry shavers was essential as soap for wet shaving was in short supply.

Immediately after the war, a 'shaver product development programme' was started. Two years later one of the world's most famous designers, Raymond Loewy, created the 'egg' look on which all subsequent designs have been based.

In 1951, new designs incorporated two rotary shaving heads and a few years later, the triple-head rotary shaving models so well-known today were introduced. Each year, over 12 million Philishave models are manufactured at Philips' factory in Drachten, Holland. They are marketed in over 145 countries throughout the world with over 3/4 million being sold in the UK.

The Product

Philishave is undoubtedly one of the most important products in the Philips Electronics portfolio. Its name is a combination of the manufacturer's name - Philips - and 'shave'. Watersheds in the product's evolution have included the 1980 introduction of the 'lift and cut' shaving system and the 1996 introduction of the Reflex Action series. However, none has been more important than the launch of Philishave Cool Skin in 1998.

Recent Developments

Philishave Cool Skin introduced a third shaving system on to the market - a system which gives the user a true wet-shave experience without the risk of nicks and cuts and skin irritation. This revolutionary new shaver dispenses a special moisturising emulsion which helps to give the user an unexpectedly close, comfortable shave, leaving the skin feeling fresh, smooth and invigorated.

The launch was the culmination of a three year research and development programme by the Philips Personal Care Institute and Beiersdorf, the company responsible for the successful Nivea for Men range and the company which has produced the special Philishave Cool Skin emulsion.

The moisturising emulsion is dispensed at the press of a button and the three Philishave Reflex Action 'lift and cut' rotary shaving heads, specially manufactured from corrosion-free stainless steels, combine with the emulsion to give a superbly close and comfortable shave. Because the emulsion is made by Nivea, it is perfectly suitable for use on the most sensitive skin.

It is estimated that the new Philishave Cool Skin System gives an important four hours of 'extra life' to a clean-shaven face. The Nivea for Men moisturising emulsion sachets click easily into the back of the shaver and each sachet contains enough emulsion for up to ten shaves. The shaving heads are easy to clean under running hot water as the shaver is completely waterproof and the emulsion water soluble.

Philishave Cool Skin is attractively styled in midnight blue with canary yellow buttons and can be recharged in eight hours

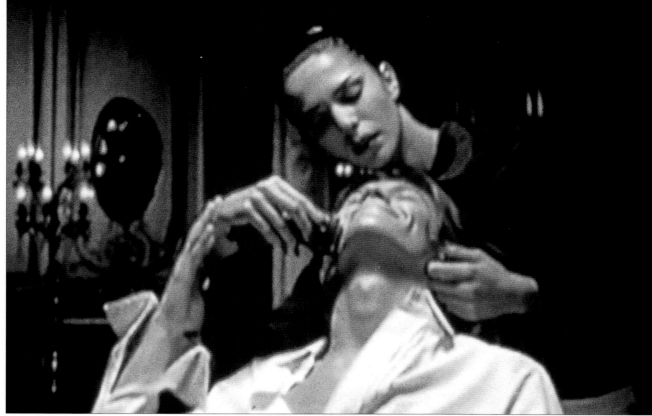

Both Philishave and Philishave Cool Skin got year-long advertising and promotional support in 1998. PR activities included sponsorship of the high profile Philishave Parachute Team which 'dropped in' to sporting events around the country.

Brand Values

The success of Philishave is based on its precision engineering, strong marketing and awareness of the need for continuous innovation. The launch of Philishave Cool Skin neatly illustrates this. The company is confident the combination of a break-through in shaving performance, innovative design and advertising is ensuring the new product's future success.

to give up to 55 minutes (approximately 18 days) of cordless shaving.

There are estimated to be 150 million men throughout Europe who shave, 60% of whom do so with a blade while 40% use an electric shaver. For nearly 60 years Philishave has dominated the dry shaver sector, gaining brand leader position in all its markets through a continuous programme of innovation and promotion.

When it was decided to look into the requirements of blade users to see if there was any way to move them back into the dry shave method, Philips found that there are several types of wet shavers. There are those who are unquestionably happy with their blades, who are too conservative to change and who like the ritual of wet shaving. But there is another group of men - around one in four of wet shavers - who are open to change because their present method can cause nicks and cuts and skin irritation. This group is younger than the 'happy sector', aged from 15 to mid-thirties. Philishave Cool Skin has been designed for this young group and in the UK alone it is estimated that this could account for up to two million young men.

Significant research among blade users throughout Europe resulted in very positive results. In test panels, Philishave Cool Skin was preferred to wet shaving because it left the skin feeling smooth and gave a comfortable 'gliding' feel to shaving. It was felt it nourished and cared for the skin, leaving a feeling of freshness. And, most importantly, there was no skin irritation. It was also felt to be easy to use, hygienic and pleasant.

57% of blade users questioned said they would consider exchanging their razor for a Philishave Cool Skin.

Philishave Cool Skin
PHILIPS

Promotion

Two major factors have contributed to the long term success of Philishave. First, it's a top quality product which has been consistently supported by massive investment to ensure that the brand stays ahead of its competitors and Philishave Cool Skin is a prime example of this. Secondly, the company's long-term commitment to support the brand has involved high profile advertising and promotional campaigns.

In 1997, Philishave was supported year-round in the UK. The brand was promoted on TV, in the press, at point-of-sale and with an active PR programme. In 1998, stunning cinema and press ads devised by the world famous photographer Helmut Newton launched Philishave Cool Skin to young and about-to-be shavers. The campaign adopted a 'tongue-in-cheek' approach to underline the revolutionary nature of the new shaver - both emotionally and physically.

PIRELLI

The Market

The deep-rooted and far-reaching economic recession of the early 1990s badly affected the world-wide tyre industry. A decreasing demand for the product led to increased competition and a downward pressure on price. The majority of tyre companies were forced to make difficult strategic decisions, with redundancy programmes and plant closures becoming all too common.

In order to achieve success in a highly competitive global market, Pirelli realised it would have to become world-class. This was achieved by rationalisation of production, the introduction of the Japanese philosophy 'Total Productive Maintenance' and a dedicated workforce. As a consequence, Pirelli is now considered to be a world leader in the tyre industry.

Achievements

Pirelli has been at the forefront of tyre technology with innovations in design, market segmentation and service standards. With a record like this it's easy to understand why, in total market share, Pirelli is among the leading players in the UK (out of 107 brands currently available) and is the sixth major player world-wide. It is the clear leader in terms of ultra high performance tyres fitted to the world's most prestigious vehicles.

Pirelli is the only company in the UK to receive Jaguar's coveted award, 'In Pursuit of Excellence' for five consecutive years.

Success in motorsport signifies that a company is at the leading edge of technology and innovation and much research has shown that companies which are involved in motorsport are also successful in the market place. Pirelli therefore benefits from its success in rallying in both marketing and technical areas, with many of its latest road tyres being derived from rally technology.

The pressure to reduce costs led to the concentration of production in fewer factories and specialisation, allowing benefits from economies of scale. This drive to improve efficiency and flexibility culminated in the Pirelli organisation adopting a Japanese initiative called 'Total Productive Maintenance' (TPM). Its Turkish factory was the first to implement the TPM philosophy and very quickly the improvements in factory output, efficiency, cleanliness and the reduction of machine breakdowns were visible to all. TPM is now implemented in all Pirelli tyre factories and in 1995 Pirelli Carlisle became the first UK tyre factory to gain the Japanese Institute of Plant Maintenance Award, and is now regarded as one of the leaders in this activity.

History

In 1872 Giovanni Battista Pirelli, a twenty-four year old engineer, established Pirelli & Co. in Milan where, a year later, he set up the first general rubber goods factory.

By the end of the century, with the manufacture of insulated telegraph wires in 1879, submarine telegraph cables in 1886 and the birth of the first bicycle tyre in 1890, the diversification process had begun. The first passenger car tyre dates back to 1901. In the wake of product diversification, encouraged by the company's fast growth, geographical diversification occurred: cable factories were opened in Spain in 1902, Great Britain in 1914 and Argentina in 1917.

In 1927, the first oil-filled cable was constructed, a fundamental technological breakthrough. The tyre front saw the launch of Superflex Stella Bianca. International expansion continued: in 1929 cables started to be manufactured in Brazil and tyres in the United Kingdom. Production of general rubber goods was begun in Spain in 1917, Argentina in 1919 and Belgium in 1938. From the 1920s onwards, racing drivers such as Nuvolari, Ascari and later Fangio, began to score a lengthy series of victories with Pirelli tyres; to date the company boasts over 80 successes in as many international Grand Prixs and six World Driver championships, not to mention 18 victories with Alfa Romeo and Ferrari in the legendary Mille Miglia race.

After the Second World War, in 1948, the Cinturato radial tyre was born; it was to leave its mark on tyre history. Geographical expansion

continued: factories for the manufacture of cables were set up in 1953 in Canada and in 1956 in Mexico, and for general rubber goods factories were set up in France in 1957 and for tyres in Greece and Turkey it was 1960.

The Sixties and Seventies saw further expansion. The Veith tyre company was acquired in Germany. Cable manufacturing activities were set up in Peru in 1968 and Australia in 1975. The power cable activities of General Cable (US) were purchased in 1978 and those of Trefimetaux in France and the Ivory coast in 1980. These were also the years of the union with Dunlop in 1971: a venture which had the merit of being a forerunner of the concentration trend in the rubber industry which was to manifest itself later but which was strongly conditioned by the external environment during its existence. The union was severed in 1980. In those years Pirelli invented the low profile tyre which remains the most significant technological innovation since the radial tyre. During the same period a real revolution occurred in cables: fibre optic cables appeared on the scene. It was Pirelli in 1982 who first started producing the fibre in Italy, at Battipaglia. Manufacture was immediately extended to other affiliates abroad.

As for the majority of companies in the west, the Eighties were years of growth for Pirelli. Many acquisitions were made: Metzeler and Armstrong for tyres; for cables, Filerige and, at he beginning of the 1990s Standard Telephone Cable's land telecommunication activity. The Tyre Sector was grouped under Pirelli tyre Holding NV, listed on the Amsterdam Stock Exchange, and the Cable Sector under Pirelli Cavi SpA.

In 1992, within the previously mentioned restructuring of the group, the non-strategic businesses of the diversified products sector were sold, while cables and tyres moved firmly on to their international relaunching phase.

The Product

The most significant breakthrough in tyre construction - one that would revolutionise the industry - was the introduction by Pirelli of the first fabric belted radial tyre, the Cinturato CF67, in 1951. This was continuously developed and by 1975 a new series of radials for cars emerged, starting with the P3 and followed in subsequent years by the P4, P5, P8 and the now legendary P6 and P7.

The introduction of low profile tyres for cars, truck and agricultural vehicles, developed since the mid 1970s, has been of major importance. In the early 1980s came the development and introduction of tyres with low rolling resistance, which reduces power

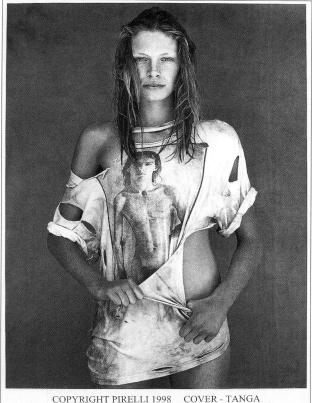

COPYRIGHT PIRELLI 1998   COVER - TANGA

absorption and therefore saves fuel. Pirelli's history is one of continual development and setting new standards of tyre technology.

Recent Developments

In the UK, the product development group moved to Carlisle in 1995 from its previous base at Burton on Trent. Shortly afterwards, Carlisle was designated a Pirelli Technical Competence Centre alongside other centres in Italy, Brazil, Germany and the US. The objective was to develop new or substantially modified product lines in line with market requirements.

The tyre development process commences at the early stages of new vehicle chassis design and all such requirements are benchmarked against previously supplied Pirelli products or more commonly competitors' tyres. An indoor test facility houses a wide variety of tyre testing equipment and machinery and because of the importance of safety, high speed and durability, performance testing features highly.

Complementing the indoor testing of tyres is

additional testing, conducted on an outdoor test track. Tyres are evaluated on cars supplied by the manufacturers. Low speed evaluation takes place on local roads under normal operating conditions. However, to test the tyre to its full capabilities the facilities at Leyland and MIRA in the UK are used in addition to the Pirelli Vizzola test facility in Italy.

The mould profile and pattern designs are created in Italy utilising the latest techniques of finite element analyses (FEA) and computer modelling. The initial specification is followed by development loops interspersed with joint test evaluations with the customer. This process continues until a satisfactory specification is agreed.

Recently, Pirelli introduced its new P3000 Energy tyre which reduces fuel consumption. P3000 is a green tyre with low rolling resistance, made possible by 'New Age technology' where the tyre compound, structure and pattern combine to provide an innovative new formula. With P3000, users can have a product designed to safeguard the environment without sacrificing cost efficiency, performance or safety.

Promotion

Pirelli has secured a strong marketing presence with its calendar and advertising campaigns. The Pirelli Calendar was first launched in 1964 and has since then gone from strength to strength and is one of Pirelli's most powerful

communication tools. Pirelli's advertising campaigns have always been innovative and memorable using strong images, linked with celebrities in the film and sporting world who have included Sharon Stone, Carl Lewis, Marie Jose Perec and more recently the Pirelli-sponsored Inter Milan Footballer, Ronaldo - enforcing the Pirelli strap-line "Power is Nothing Without Control".

Brand Values

In all parts of the world, tyres and cables are essential to national economies in the areas of transportation of people and goods, and transmission of energy and information. Pirelli's business is centred on these key markets in which it is among the world leaders and innovators.

For more than a century the company has grown as a truly multinational corporation, deeply rooted in local markets throughout the world and building upon our two core product sectors - cables and tyres.

Pirelli's technological and research capacity in terms of professional skills and resources continues to be a great source of strength. This, coupled with close involvement with customer requirements, enables the company to operate successfully from bases around the world. A high priority is extended to continuous improvement in the environmental impact of processes and products.

THE PIRELLI CALENDAR. 1984.

JANUARY

M	T	W	T	F	S	S	M	T	W	T	F	S	S	M	T	W	T	F	S	S
					1	2	3	4	5	6	7	8	9	10	11	12	13	14	15	
16	17	18	19	20	21	22	23	24	25	26	27	28	29	30	31					

The Market

The sugar confectionery market is extremely competitive and much more fragmented than the chocolate market. This is a market where many brands and brand extensions fail and it is largely driven by impulse purchases.

Relatively low start up costs for sugar production mean that there are a large number of brands and manufacturers. In 1993 there were over 1,000 different confectionery brands on the market. About half the market is accounted for by companies with less than a 5% share.

The UK mint sector is valued at £220 million. Nestlé Rowntree, the maker of Polo has a 28% share, while its rival, Trebor Basset, with four mint brands in its portfolio - Trebor Extra Strong Mints, Trebor Softmint, Trebor Imperials and Trebor Mild Mints - has a 46% share.

With sales of £46 million, Polo is the UK's top selling mint brand. Polo has 20.5% value share of the mint market, while its nearest competitor, Trebor Extra Strong Mints has 17% value share. Polos are eaten by equal numbers of men and women. The highest proportion of Polo eaters (20.8%) are aged between 16 and 24 years old.

Achievements

Polo recorded its best ever sales year in 1973 and from then until the early 1990's the volume never fluctuated by more than a few per cent. However, by 1993 Polo sales were beginning to decline.

The company's response was to relaunch Polo in 1994, backed by an extensive advertising campaign focusing on the personality of the Polo brand and to launch three variants in addition: Polo Spearmint, Polo Strong and Polo Sugar Free.

In 1993, before the launch of the Polo variants, Polo had a 15.6% value share of the market. This grew by 1995 to 20.4% following the successful launch of the variants and the effects of their individual TV advertisements. The variants revitalised the Polo brand and also stimulated market growth by attracting new consumers.

Polo is now a family of individual but related products, each with its own position in the market. It was the fastest growing confectionery brand in 1995. In that year it once again enjoyed volume sales in line with those in the 1970s and the 1980s - in fact by 1995, volume level was only 2% below Polo's record sales year of 1973.

History

Confectionery company Rowntree developed a mint with a hole in 1939. George Harris, the company's chairman - who was responsible for the introduction of Kit Kat, Smarties and Black Magic - was convinced that there was a place in the market for a small peppermint, provided that it was advertised extensively. War time restrictions, however, meant that the product was not actually launched until nine years later. Polo was initially launched in London and the South East in 1948 and was priced at 2d to appeal as much to adults as to children. The brand was rolled out nationally in 1952.

By the beginning of the 1950s, supply difficulties which had been caused by the aftermath of the Second World War were almost entirely resolved and Rowntree started to develop the Polo range. Polo Fruits were launched in 1954 and in 1961 three mint variants were launched - Spearmint Polo, Polo Crystal Mints and Polo Candy Mints. Unfortunately these three products cannibalised the original, more profitable peppermint line. As a result they were withdrawn in March 1963.

Polo continued to grow as a single product throughout the Sixties, Seventies and Eighties, maintaining market leadership.

The brand was relaunched in 1994 when Polo was renamed Polo Original and three new variants were introduced - Polo Spearmint, Polo Strong and Polo Sugar Free - to stave off increasing competition in the sugar confectionery market.

A range of limited edition Polos were introduced in 1996, Polo Fizz Fruits, Polo Tangy Fruits, Polo Gummies, as well as Polo Holes - shaped pieces which exactly match the hole in the centre of an original Polo. These were only available for a four week period. People became so caught up with the Polo brand that sales of tubes increased while Polo Holes were on sale. People were buying the Holes to actually fit in the holes of the Polo sweets. Polo Holes created enormous positive PR for Polo and was a sales success story.

Following this, Spearmint Holes were launched for a limited period in 1997 and achieved similar success.

The Product

Polo mints are highly compressed rings of sugar and glucose. They are flavoured with high quality peppermint oil specially selected to give a smooth, clean, fresh flavour.

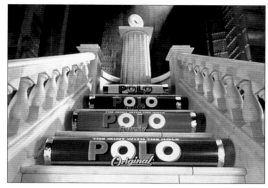

Polo Fruits are an assortment of fruit flavoured boiled sweets available in five flavours: strawberry, blackcurrant, lime, orange and lemon.

Recent Developments

The relaunch of the Polo brand resulted in Polo regaining its position as the UK's No.1 selling mint.

In 1996, Polo Strong was relaunched with new packaging and increased mint strength. An image of bus wheels was used as part of the relaunch to convey the idea that the mints are so strong that they could carry a double decker bus.

After extensive consumer research, the company launched Polo Supermint in June 1998 backed by a £1.5 million TV ad campaign. The product is wickedly powerful and comes in miniature form. The mint delivers instant refreshment in a discreet and convenient way and is packed in a plastic dispenser with a unique 'pop locking' opening device.

Promotion

Polo is the only mint brand to have been consistently advertised on television. Following the 'Mint with the hole' ad, the company ran a campaign for many years called 'People like Polo' which focused on the wide range of people who enjoyed the brand.

In 1994 Nestlé Rowntree spent £4.6 million relaunching the Polo brand and introducing its new variants in a bid to bring consumers back to the brand. Each variant was supported by a specific ad to communicate its launch.

In addition, Nestlé Rowntree also ran tube card advertising and a campaign on tube trains with its own version of 'Poems on the Tube', extolling the virtues of Polo in verse. Its press advertising and the tube card ads won a

number of creative awards including Campaign Press & Poster Awards and a D&AD nomination.

Polo Sugar Free has a tightly defined target audience - people concerned with calorie and sugar intake. This group is mainly made up of young women who seek out products which offer weight control benefit. When launched in 1994, Polo Sugar Free had its own launch ad - the message focused on 'the low calorie mint'.

The ad campaigns were highly effective. By the end of 1996, the Polo Spearmint variant had captured 29% of the mild mint market and the Sugar Free variant had gained 45% value share of the Sugar Free market despite being launched in the last quarter of the year.

Fruits and to the brand's limited edition confectionery.

The product is also associated with smoothness and refreshment. New variants have the inherent values of the original Polo but also have their own 'personalities'. Nestlé Rowntree describes Polo Spearmint as fun, cool, hip and unconventional; Polo Sugar Free is light-hearted, fresh and healthy, bursting with personality; Polo Strong is smooth, confident, calm and collected.

Brand Values

It is the hole in Polo which differentiates it from other mint brands in the market, giving it a 'play factor' in the mouth. This unique quality has been extended to Polo

Centre half.

Polo. The mint with the hole.

Second half.

Polo. The mint with the hole.

The Market

During the 1990s, the UK sportswear market has become increasingly competitive as brands have sought to capitalise on its significant growth (both value and volume). The market, which includes 'apparel' and 'footwear', is now worth £2.2 billion.

The major brands are sold through dedicated sports retailers such as Sports Division, JJB Sports, JD Sports and Intersport as well as through department stores such as John Lewis.

Although sports participation remains a key driver, much of the recent market growth has been stimulated by non-sports usage. The endorsement of sports brands by stars of music and entertainment has cemented these brands' evolution from the sports arena and gym to now include the high street and night club. This has also had the 'knock-on' effect of making the market's profile slightly younger.

Reebok's targeting has acknowledged these shifts, concentrating on 12-24 year olds with 15-19 as the core and separating 'Fashion led' and 'Performance led' consumers. These two groups are markedly different. The 'Fashion led' consumer includes both males and females who are highly brand and image conscious. They shop frequently and are well informed about new technologies and launches. In contrast to the 'Performance led' consumers, they are unlikely to use their sportswear for sport.

'Performance led' consumers' active participation makes them less concerned with image and more concerned with genuine performance.

Achievements

As a brand, Reebok is traditionally associated with fitness and running. This perception has firm foundations as Reebok's emergence as a 'superbrand' coincided with and capitalised upon the fitness boom and the rise of aerobics especially.

Over time, this heritage has posed increasingly testing questions for Reebok. In particular, how could a brand associated with non-contact unisex activities like fitness and running gain credibility and valuable market share in contact sports dominated by men. In recent years, perhaps Reebok's greatest achievement has been its ability to retain its dominance in its heartland (fitness) whilst successfully entering a new market (football).

Having pin-pointed football as a focus for brand attention, Reebok quickly understood the importance of 'credibility' in that market. It also realised this was something the brand lacked. To address this, Reebok not only began to develop better product but recognised how marketing, and in particular sponsorship, could help in the task. Ryan Giggs, who plays for Manchester United, was chosen to endorse Reebok boots. Since then, Giggs has been the focus of much of Reebok's football related marketing.

Giggs selection was not just dependent on his footballing skills but also on his wider appeal to non-footballers and women. It was clear that Reebok's endorsement of Ryan Giggs could not just sell more boots but could benefit the brand image more broadly.

Since Reebok began concentrating on football, its place in the market has risen from 8th to 3rd, increasing its market volume share from 4% to 11%. Crucially, while this has been going on, Reebok have retained their place as the largest fitness brand, now commanding 36% of market volume.

History

Reebok began life in 1895 although it didn't come to be known as Reebok until 1958. Originally known as Fosters, the company was founded by Joseph William Foster who was a keen runner and a member of Bolton Primrose Harriers, in Lancashire. Initially he was forced to make his own running shoes because he could not afford to buy a pair, but by 1900 he had refined his skills to such an extent that he set up his own business making handmade shoes for local athletes.

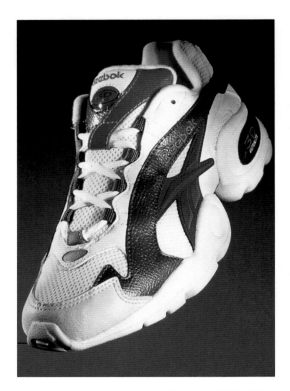

In 1904, the Foster's Spike helped athlete Alf Shrub set three world records at a single meeting in Glasgow. Word quickly spread about Foster's spiked running shoes and by 1908 they were worn by many Olympic and professional athletes. Foster also developed a self-measurement chart for feet to give runners a custom fit. The Fosters Deluxe Spike remained a top running spike for nearly 50 years.

Foster died in 1933 and was succeeded by his sons, James and John. Five years later CB Holmes competed in the Empire Games in Australia wearing Foster spikes and won both the 100 and 220 yards in record time.

Over time the company expanded and moved into other sports. In 1958, Joe Foster, Joseph's grandson, joined the company and continued to create custom footwear for top athletes. But after completing his national service, he decided to start a companion company. First named Mercury Sports it was then changed to Reebok, the name of an African gazelle.

The company continued to expand and in 1979, Paul Fireman, an American marketer of outdoor equipment, spotted Reebok shoes at an exhibition and gained the license to sell Reebok in North America.

In 1982, Reebok introduced Freestyle - one of the first women's performance shoes specifically designed for aerobics. Crafted from leather in a range of colours, it became the best selling shoe of all time. Under Paul Fireman's stewardship this heralded the beginning of the fitness boom and led to the development of an entire line of Aerobic/Fitness shoes. Three years later, with Reebok established as a household name, it became a public company and in 1987 became the largest athletic footwear company in the world.

Today Reebok has a global turnover in excess of $3.5 billion.

The Product

Reebok produces a wide range of sportswear including clothing and footwear as well as other sport related items such as caps, bags, footballs, eyewear, watches and fitness equipment.

Given the importance of technology in the marketplace, the majority of Reebok's running, fitness and basketball shoes incorporate one of its proprietary sole technologies - Hexalite, DMX and 3DUltralite; this is the performance platform of the brand. Another key area of Reebok's footwear business is 'Classics' - essentially a sub-brand which has become a sports fashion icon. The shoes themselves have simple white leather uppers and do not feature any specific sole technologies.

In apparel, Reebok have a number of named ranges aimed at differing segments of the consumer market. 'Essentials' is the collection of simple training wear which is available for men, women and children and forms the core of the range. 'Freestyle' is a range of women's apparel which is more overtly branded, appealing to the younger end of the market, whilst for men, 'Athletic Department' apparel offers a strong performance range in classic sporting colours.

Recent Developments

In footwear, Reebok has developed a market leading set of footwear technologies -

Hexalite, DMX and 3DUltralite - each of which have marked significant breakthroughs in their field.

Hexalite is a unique sole material made up of small hexagonal cells which offers unique cushioning. Beyond other cushioning systems, Hexalite understands that runners move in three dimensions and consequently that cushioning technologies need to be able to perform under both sheer and compression forces.

DMX (DynaMic eXchange) is a sole technology which features a number of linked air-filled pods which fill and empty with the movement of the wearer. Because the shoe responds to the individual wearer it can provide the exact cushioning that particular person requires - in essence, the ultimate cushioning system.

3DUltralite is a material made of speciality blown rubber compound which allows a shoe's mid-sole and out-sole to be combined in one unit. As a consequence it makes shoe's made with 3DUltralite amazingly light. Abel Anton won the 1998 London Marathon wearing a pair of Marathon Racer 3D Ultralite - Reebok's lightest ever running shoe. As competition has increased in the sportswear market, Reebok has been looking at new and innovative ways of reaching its consumers, a good example of this being the naming of The Reebok Stadium in Bolton, Lancashire.

Reebok's commitment to Bolton Wanderers has gone way beyond just kit or club sponsorship but has extended to actually assisting in the construction of a new all seater stadium. The 25,000 capacity ground replaced Burnden Park, Bolton's home for the past 102 years.

In addition to this marketing activity, Reebok have recently become increasingly involved in charity, in particular helping the British Red Cross. With the help of stars like Ryan Giggs, Reebok has launched a shoe amnesty which seeks to collect 12,000 pairs of trainers for recycling and distributing to the Third World.

Promotion

One of the key distinguishing factors of promotion in the sportswear market is the immense importance of sponsorship. In the main, consumers believe the brands used by top performers are intrinsically high quality. Consequently, from a marketing point of view, ensuring endorsement from top performers is a short cut to high quality perceptions. Needless to say it can also be a very good means of gaining PR as well.

In the UK, Reebok has concentrated much of its marketing budget on securing full value from sponsorship deals. With football being of such great importance of late, Ryan Giggs has been the sole focus of three major

advertisements - Field of Dreams, Theatre of Dreams and Doppelganger.

More recently Reebok have built awareness of their relationships with Peter Schmeichel and Dennis Bergkamp (as well as Ryan Giggs) in the 'Other Careers' campaign.

Beyond individual sponsorship arrangements Reebok also sponsors Liverpool FC, Aston Villa FC and, of course, Bolton Wanderers.

Outside football, Reebok has key sponsorships with the British Athletics Federation and the Welsh Rugby Union and on a global basis it sponsors leading names in athletics and tennis.

Brand Values

Reebok is the sports and fitness resource that creates possibilities for personal achievement. The very strong performance tradition of the brand, especially in the fitness and running categories, mean that it is perceived as authentic and innovative. This authenticity and constant innovation provides the Reebok consumer with products that create possibilities for self-expression at all levels of sports participation.

Things you didn't know about
Reebok

Reebok is the oldest sports shoe company in the UK.

First named Mercury Sports Footwear, it was then changed to Reebok after the African gazelle.

Abel Anton won the 1998 London Marathon wearing a pair of Marathon Racer 3D Ultralite - Reebok's lightest ever running shoe.

Reebok has been strongly involved in human rights since 1988 when it first joined forces with Amnesty International and sponsored Human Rights Now, an international concert tour.

In November 1996 Reebok announced a programme to label its soccer balls with a guarantee that the balls were not produced using child labour. This is believed to be the first time a guarantee of this kind was placed on such a widely distributed consumer sports product.

Samsonite®

The Market

The world of international business is growing fast. New technology has fuelled significant developments in global communications. Meanwhile, improvements in transport links around the world have led to more people than ever travelling abroad for business and for pleasure.

For those supplying goods and services to the international traveller, the challenge is to keep up with technological developments in other fields - ensuring that travel goods meet consumers' growing expectations of value, quality and dependability.

This is certainly the case for the makers of luggage and particularly for Samsonite, the market leader in travel bags, suitcases and accessories.

The UK is Samsonite's fifth largest market in Europe.

Achievements

Samsonite is the world's market leader in durable and stylish luggage, regularly setting new trends with unique, patented designs. The company achieved turnover in Europe of 10.140 billion BEF in 1997. As well as pioneering new luggage technology and rigorous quality testing procedures, Samsonite has also developed a range of travel-related accessories. The company's aim now is to be perceived not only as the world's leading luggage manufacturer, but as the world's leading travel products brand.

History

Samsonite was founded in 1910 in the US. Its founder, Jesse Shwayder, wanted to produce the best and strongest luggage available anywhere. His first redesigned suitcase used the best materials available and was, he claimed, as strong as the legendary Samson. The suitcase was an immediate success and the company adopted the Samson-ite name.

Samsonite first came to Europe in 1965 with luggage imported from the US. The new concept of hard side luggage and attaché cases was an immediate hit and it was soon decided to start producing luggage in Europe. Production of hard suitcases began in 1966 from its European headquarters in Belgium. By 1974, production had outgrown capacity and the European business moved to a larger base.

During the 1980s, four Samsonite production sites were added in France, Spain, Italy and Hungary. Local manufacturers also produce for Samsonite under co-operative agreements in Bulgaria, the Czech Republic, Slovenia and Russia. Since 1991, all the European subsidiaries have come under the control of the holding company, Samsonite Europe NV, based in Oudenaarde, Belgium.

The Samsonite brand is built on its reputation for quality and reliability - a solid foundation thanks to constant investment in state of the art technology. The company prides itself on constantly redefining standards for durability, versatility, ergonomic design and security.

The company's European headquarters and main production facilities are in Belgium. Samsonite Europe currently distributes more than 25,000 suitcases and travel bags every day.

The Product

Every piece of Samsonite luggage has been designed to take the worry out of travelling - to withstand the rigours of airport baggage handling, to be extra light, extra manoeuvrable and extra protective and to take on with style and grace whatever the world of travel has in store.

Samsonite products can be divided into two main categories - 'hard' and 'soft' luggage.

'Hard luggage' involves moulding and assembly of plastics. It is produced according to one of two basic manufacturing processes: injection moulding - requiring polypropylene, and vacuum forming - requiring ABS grains. Injection moulding forces molten plastic pellets into a cooled mould under high pressure. Vacuum forming is achieved by heating ABS grains into flat sheets which are then re-heated and pulled under vacuum across the cooled mould.

'Soft luggage' production requires synthetic materials, such as polyamide, polyester, vinyl or polyurethane. Although computers and other technology have become a key part of the production process, high quality craftsmanship remains indispensable.

The Samsonite product range is extensive, spanning suitcases and attaché cases to beauty and garment bags, in both hard and soft cases.

At the top end of the range is the 950 Series/Deluxe range, for example. This selection of chic and sophisticated cases are ABS shells trimmed with full grain cowhide leather and matt nickel fittings. A revolutionary product in this range is the 'Ultra Transporter' - a case with six wheels and innovative interior hanger pack divider to keep suits wrinkle-free.

At the other end of the scale is the recently-launched Trunk & Co range of backpacks, casual bags and accessories aimed at younger consumers. One selection in the range, Bungees, comes in bright colours with handy functions. Samsonite positions these through strong branding at affordable prices.

Rigorous testing is done on all Samsonite products. The company prides itself on assuming the worst will happen to its products and ensuring they'll cope. So, for example, fully loaded cases are subjected to free fall at room temperature and at minus 12 degrees Centigrade in the 'drop test'.

In the 'tumble test', a fully loaded suitcase is placed in a rotating drum with a number of obstacles. After 25 spins, the suitcase survives intact, fully functional and with only a few scratches. To test Samsonite luggage's wheels, cases are placed on a conveyor belt and dragged for several kilometres.

Such diligence has paid off. A number of Samsonite products have been awarded ISO 9002 and GS quality certificates for achieving the highest level of quality in process control at certain stages of production.

All Samsonite products come with a three year guarantee against possible defects in material and workmanship on rigid suitcases, beauty cases and attachés, all handy cases, soft suitcases and garment bags. All other soft products are guaranteed for one year against defective workmanship and zippers.

Recent Developments

There are many different destinations and ways of travelling today - from a luxury cruiser to a 'red eye' flight to New York, from a Caribbean holiday to a long-distance Saharan trek. Samsonite works to offer the right piece of luggage for every occasion.

The company is dedicated to ensuring its luggage is fully equipped to satisfy the Nineties' business professionals' work travel requirements. In 1996, Samsonite brought out the first side-loading 'mobile office on wheels'. A year later, Samsonite launched the first 'upright' on wheels which can be pushed and pulled, and which has an organised interior - the 'Ultra Transporter'.

To ensure its brand image keeps pace with the technological developments pioneered for its products, Samsonite introduced a new brand image in 1997. The new 'Worldproof' strategy is built on the brand's traditional strengths - quality, reliability and innovation. It has now been integrated into all communications.

The company has also developed a range of travel accessories ranging from neck rests and eye shades to luggage straps and adapter plug kits.

Promotion

Samsonite's 'Worldproof' theme is about providing the traveller with comfort and confidence. It underlines Samsonite's claim that its products are designed and manufactured to cope with all eventualities. It also underlines Samsonite's positioning as a provider of solutions - meeting travellers' demands for versatility, durability, flexibility and security.

The new strategy was introduced in an international advertising campaign launched in June 1997. The first ads featured Samsonite's 'Ultra Transporter'.

A series of press ads in striking colours featured pictures of places around the world juxtaposed with an image of a Samsonite product. One, featuring an African woman with clothes piled high on her head, was accompanied by the strapline: 'Zanzibarproof'. Ads ran in newspapers and magazines. A second wave comprised ads on taxis and roadside poster sites at airports, as well as a TV campaign in Germany during the year-end period.

'Worldproof' has now been integrated across all Samsonite's communications including leaflets, labelling and point of sale displays.

Another recent promotion involved a tie up with the James Bond movie 'Tomorrow Never Dies' for promotion of the Epsilon hard side range. A 'Tomorrow Never Dies' competition was launched in-store offering prizes including a trip to Thailand, mobile phones and CDs.

Endorsement and recommendation are central pillars in Samsonite's marketing and promotions strategy.

Rigorous testing of products ensures they meet independently measured standards of durability and reliability. Samsonite products are therefore regularly recommended by the international press, independent consumer groups and word of mouth. The company's commitment to quality is underlined by the fact that every item is guaranteed.

Samsonite also works hard on its relationships with retailers. It recently launched a retail service called 'SONNET' via the Internet. This allows electronic ordering and selling, providing retailers with up to the minute price information and product availability.

Another recent investment was Samsonite's new, fully automated warehouse and distribution centre which opened in February 1998.

Brand Values

Samsonite stands for top quality engineering, dependability and styling. Reliability is an essential part of the Samsonite brand. The company depends on consumers' confidence that its products will outperform the rival brands and provide unparalleled durability, portability and style. The positioning is summed up in Samsonite's recently introduced brand proposition: 'Worldproof'.

The company has also worked hard in recent years to communicate its brand values to a new generation of younger consumers. It has developed selected items targeted at the younger, non-business professional - such as the Trunk & Co and Sammies ranges. The aim is to combine Samsonite quality with a trendy, young and dynamic image.

Things you didn't know about Samsonite

In 1916 a photo was taken of Jesse Shwayder, his father and three of his brothers, standing on top of a suitcase. This image served as the company trademark for many years.

The first magnesium suitcase was made by Samsonite in 1956.

Samsonite Europe currently produces more than 25,000 suitcases and travel bags every day.

Samsonite unveiled the first handy case - a new concept in luggage for women.

To test the handles of its cases, Samsonite suspends a fully loaded case by its handle then raises and lowers the case thousands of times.

Samsonite Europe manufacturers over 5 million suitcases and bags a year.

Save the Children Y

The Market

Children deserve the best start in life but sadly, many children around the world are deprived of hope and opportunity through no fault of their own. Poverty, conflict and natural disasters

continue to throw millions of people's lives into turmoil and sadly it is often children who are the first to suffer and who are least able to defend themselves. Of course, charities continue to respond to major emergencies around the world - but what is less well known is the enormous amount of work which goes on to try and prevent disasters, and to find long-term solutions to the many problems faced by the world's most impoverished communities.

Achievements

One of Britain's favourite charities is Save the Children. Its determination since 1919 to improve the quality of life (or even save the lives) of children everywhere has won it many supporters, elevating it to the ranks of one of Britain's best-loved and well-known charities.

It is difficult to sum up the achievements of an organisation like Save the Children. A headcount of those who have benefited from the dedication and hard work of the charity would be impossible. Save the Children is perhaps best known for its high profile emergency work, particularly in Africa. And indeed this forms a major part of its work. But as important, is its long-term work, both in Africa and in over 50 countries around the world, including Asia, the Middle East, Latin America and the Caribbean.

In addition, Save the Children works in Central and Eastern Europe, particularly in former Yugoslavia, to tackle the problems faced by disadvantaged children. In the UK, issues such as homelessness, health, early years services and young people leaving care are tackled. Wherever possible, young people are involved in order to encourage them to become active citizens, and the focus of Save the Children's UK work has shifted from direct service provision to innovative ways of working that can be applied more widely.

Save the Children aims to be a child-focused organisation, seeing the world through children's eyes wherever possible and not making adult assumptions about their lives, yet remaining staunchly practical.

Save the Children aims to make the most

of its expertise by influencing decision makers on issues affecting children and their families. With almost 80 years of practical involvement and expertise, when Save the Children draws attention to a particular issue, local, national and international organisations often sit up and listen. In this way, Save the Children is able to extend the benefit of its work to thousands more children.

History

One of the unsung heroes of the twentieth century must be Eglantyne Jebb, the founder of Save the Children. She launched the charity in 1919 on the following precept: "Save the Children must work for its own extinction. It must not be contented to save children from the hardships - it must abolish these hardships". Eglantyne firmly believed - and it cannot be disputed - that the children of the world are our future.

Save the Children has proved a persistent and effective force in trying to eradicate the problems that beset so many of the world's children. It has upheld Eglantyne's philosophy that children's needs have to be met not only in times of crisis, but at all times.

Eglantyne was moved to pioneer Save the Children's first campaign by the appalling plight of starving Austrian children after the First World War.

Since then, Save the Children has worked hard to secure assistance for those affected by persecution and discrimination and develop long-term programmes across the world.

The Product

The majority of Save the Children schemes focus on building links within communities in a drive towards self-sufficiency. Overseas, long-term projects include the provision of clean water, mother and child health schemes, immunisation, agricultural self-sufficiency schemes, and work with disabled children, helping to integrate them into their communities.

Save the Children champions the rights of all children to a happy, healthy and secure childhood. This means speaking out if it thinks children are being badly treated. For example, working with child soldiers in Liberia, children whose childhoods have been stolen - victims of violence who have in turn become violent. Here, Save the Children tries to restore some normality in their lives by bringing them back into the community.

Save the Children puts the reality of children's lives at the heart of everything it does. This means understanding the culture and context of children's lives. For example, Save the Children is rightly shocked by child labour but believes that it is important to look beyond the emotional response to what working children think and say. Not all work done by children is harmful to them and many children simply have to work to boost the family income - ban one type of work and they may be forced into worse alternatives. Far better to protect children from exploitation and to provide opportunities for schooling that can fit around non-harmful work. This pragmatic response has come out of Save the Children's efforts to listen to working children and their families and understand their situation.

Save the Children often works closely with the United Nations and other leading organisations. It does this in partnership with the International Save the Children Alliance, a body of independent sister organisations from across the world which aims to be a truly international movement for children.

Obviously, the main product of a charity is its core values. Save the Children's work is firmly based on the Rights of the Child, first drafted by its founder Eglantyne Jebb in 1923, and outlined here in its original form:

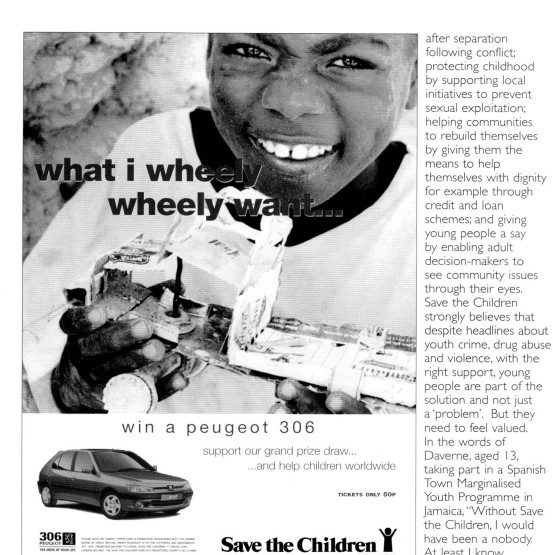

what i wheely wheely want...

win a peugeot 306

support our grand prize draw...

...and help children worldwide

TICKETS ONLY 50P

Save the Children

after separation following conflict; protecting childhood by supporting local initiatives to prevent sexual exploitation; helping communities to rebuild themselves by giving them the means to help themselves with dignity for example through credit and loan schemes; and giving young people a say by enabling adult decision-makers to see community issues through their eyes. Save the Children strongly believes that despite headlines about youth crime, drug abuse and violence, with the right support, young people are part of the solution and not just a 'problem'. But they need to feel valued. In the words of Daverne, aged 13, taking part in a Spanish Town Marginalised Youth Programme in Jamaica, "Without Save the Children, I would have been a nobody. At least I know somebody cares."

and corporate fundraising. It also receives national and international government support and funding. In recent years, Save the Children has raised over £70 million annually to help improve children's lives. To maintain this level of income requires an experienced and creative team of fundraisers in what is an increasingly competitive environment.

One of the most successful elements of Save the Children's fundraising has been the partnership it has built up with leading industries through its corporate development department. A leader in its field, it raises around £4-£5 million from the corporate sector each year.

The emphasis of Save the Children's relationships with companies is on partnerships for mutual benefit - delivering commercial advantage whilst generating substantial funds for its projects with children.

Save the Children has a professional fundraising team made up of staff who come largely from the corporate sector, who work closely with companies to help understand and meet their business objectives. There are a wide range of ways in which a company can work with the charity - staff fundraising, payroll giving, promotions, sponsored events - many of which result in public interest and media coverage. In addition, Save the Children works closely with trade unions, other NGOs (non-governmental organisations) and leading companies, to give advice and help influence opinion on ethical working practices, such as child labour.

Brand Values

It is hard to define the brand values of an organisation as wide-ranging as Save the Children which works to improve children's lives around the world. Save the Children's core values, however, are to be child-focused, seeing the world through children's eyes; ambitious but practical - setting its sights high but accepting that its main responsibility is a practical one; independent - Save the Children is not beholden to anyone, never compromises its integrity and is prepared to be radical and outspoken if necessary; open - communicating its work clearly and honestly; collaborative - seeking to work with others whenever it can; accountable - to those it serves and by whom it is supported. Professionally and financially, it is sound, scrupulous, efficient and effective.

Registered charity number 213890

1. The Child must be protected beyond and above all consideration of race, nationality or creed.

2. The Child must be cared for with due respect for the family as an entity.

3. The Child must be given the means requisite for its normal development, materially, morally and spiritually.

4. The Child that is hungry must be fed, the child that is sick must be nursed, the child that is mentally or physically handicapped must be helped, the maladjusted child must be re-educated, the orphan and the waif must be sheltered and succoured.

5. The Child must be the first to receive relief in time of distress.

6. The Child must enjoy the full benefits provided by social welfare and social security schemes, must receive a training which will enable it, at the right time, to earn a livelihood, and must be protected against every form of exploitation.

7. The Child must be brought up in the consciousness that its talents must be devoted to the service of its fellow men.

Save the Children is still governed by these principles. It has developed a reputation as an effective, highly professional organisation which never reneges on the core values on which it was founded. Eglantyne Jebb stated: "We all of us deplore child suffering, but few of us realise just how much of this suffering is really unnecessary". Save the Children serves to remind us of this at all times.

Recent Developments

In 1991 the UK government ratified the UN Convention of 1989 which adopted the Rights of the Child manifesto espoused originally by Eglantyne Jebb and which forms the backbone of all Save the Children policy.

Areas of particular success include the charity's expertise in the field of family tracing, helping thousands of children find their families

Promotion

Save the Children enjoys a high profile amongst the British public with an impressive 96% prompted awareness.

The active involvement of its president, HRH The Princess Royal, in addition to its professional fundraising and publicity team and volunteers around the country ensures Save the Children maintains a high profile and maximum exposure. The active support of a range of celebrities and some of the UK's top companies enhances this profile.

Save the Children maintains its independence and security of income by attracting and receiving funding from a variety of sources: volunteer fundraisers in branches around the country, shops and trading, legacies, donations

spice up your life

make the most of it

lift your spirits learn new skills   get involved

make a difference

volunteer with us

Save the Children

The Market

Most of us associate adhesive tapes with the home and office where products such as Sellotape Original are commonplace. However, over the last 50 years, the adhesive tapes market has diversified - it now encompasses applications especially developed for the DIY market. Due to technical developments, adhesive tapes now compete with conventional fixing methods such as screws and nails. The European consumer sticky tape market is currently valued at over $335 million per annum.

Achievements

Sellotape was first launched into the stationery trade in the 1930s. Since then it has become synonymous with clear adhesive tape - the word Sellotape even has its own entry in the Oxford English Dictionary. Consumer awareness of the brand is very strong - around 98% of UK consumers recognise the Sellotape brand name and in unprompted research it was placed in the top ten of well-known brands. (Source: The Stationery Market in the UK, Volume iii, 1993-1998 MPA International).

The Sellotape brand is Europe's favourite cellulose tape. It is the number one office tape in the UK, Ireland and Holland and enjoys the number two position in Norway. Elephant Tape is the star Sellotape DIY tape and is the fastest growing tape in the DIY market. Outside Europe, Sellotape is the clear brand leader in New Zealand and number two in South Africa.

History

The first known use of adhesive sticky tape was around 1600, when it was used to repair lutes. Over 200 years later sticky bandages were first used during the American Civil War. However, the industrial use of adhesive sticky tape was pioneered by Henry Ford, the American manufacturer of the Ford motor-car. Masking tapes were used in Ford's spray-painting process where different coloured cars were assembled.

The Sellotape brand dates back to 1937 when Colin Kininmonth and George Gray coated cellophane film with a natural rubber resin, creating a sticky tape product which had been based on a French patent. They registered

their product under the name Sellotape. Manufacturing soon commenced in Acton, West London.

Today, Sellotape consumer products are popular in the commercial stationery market as well as being widely stocked in the retail sector where the product is available from stationers, high street shops, supermarkets, confectioners, tobacconists and newsagents and DIY stores.

Sellotape is a truly international brand. It is now sold in 119 countries and operates manufacturing sites in Dunstable in the UK and Auckland in New Zealand.

France, the source of the original Sellotape patent sixty years ago, is now the focus for future growth of the brand. In 1997 the Sellotape Company acquired the consumer interests of Barnier SA, a respected player in the French DIY market. The Sellotape brand has now been launched in France with a range of energy saving products - Calfeutrage. A wide range of other tapes, including masking and electrical tape, will be introduced in the future. Presented in modern and distinctive packaging, backed by the latest merchandising techniques, Sellotape will set new standards for DIY tapes in France.

The Product

Sellotape Original is Europe's biggest selling clear cellulose tape. The only environmentally friendly, biodegradable tape on the market, Sellotape Original is manufactured from cellulose, a natural wood pulp product. Its natural origins provide a number of intrinsic benefits over rival products. It is naturally static-free for no-tangle handling, easy to tear and biodegradable. And it is stickier than most other clear tapes.

Constant innovation has resulted in extensive development of the consumer product range.

The company has carried out extensive consumer research to design a complete range of over 70 products to suit every 'sticky' need around the home, office, garage and garden, with applications as diverse as binding books to repairing a broken hose - there is more to Sellotape than wrapping parcels.

Elephant Tape, the tough all purpose DIY tape is Sellotape's most successful innovation for the DIY market. Likewise Rug Gripper, Sellotape's latest new product which stops rugs, mats and carpets from slipping, has further grown the DIY tape market.

Recent Developments

Despite very wide awareness of the Sellotape brand, the company has never rested on its laurels. The brand was relaunched in 1995 in order to penetrate new markets and demonstrate the company's creativity and innovation with new products. The introduction of its new corporate identity - The Sellotape Company - allowed the company to grow in different directions and extend its product portfolio to new market sectors. The new identity has freed the brand from its old generic image.

Brands are now targeted at different market sectors in a way which distinguishes Sellotape from its competitors.

The Sellotape Office brand name contrasts with traditional retail products and provides a range which targets the needs of the office market including the 'Small Office, Home Office' sector with new products packaged with upbeat graphics. Other products especially designed for office use include Velcro fasteners for display purposes and a whole range of packaging tapes and dispensers for the mailroom.

In the retail market too, new packaging has been introduced with Sellotape Original using the familiar blue and yellow corporate colours and other products receiving different colour schemes and graphics, enabling shoppers to differentiate between products at a glance.

This product differentiation is now being extended to Sellotape products in the DIY market with tapes for painting, fixing, repairing and packaging, designed for impact on the shelf and for easy identification by customers in-store.

The company has also introduced a range of adhesive products for children under the brand name Stick It!. The range was launched with collectable tape dispensers moulded into the form of snail characters and is to be developed with innovative new licensed characters, such as the 'Barbie' registered doll, supported by a promotional programme to build the market among children and their parents.

The continuing new product development and drive into new markets has been fuelled by the opening of a new state of the art manufacturing plant at Dunstable in 1998 and the launch of Sellotape into the French DIY market.

Promotion

Innovative and creative promotional concepts are an innovative part of Sellotape's marketing strategy to add value to the Sellotape brand and generate customer demand.

In the commercial stationery market, the company runs ads in the trade press and also promotional campaigns to support its trade customers, encouraging office staff to specify Sellotape as their preferred office tape. In 1998 a promotion for Sellotape Original and larger boxes of Velcro offered office purchasers film processing for the cost of a stamp and 50p postage.

This kind of support activity enables Sellotape to sell at premium prices and generate strong sales for its trade customers. Electronic point of sale data shows that Sellotape promotional packs achieve the highest stock turns of any stationery products in the supermarket.

In 1998 Sellotape targeted the home interest press with a series of ads promoting its DIY range of products including Elephant Tape and Rug Gripper. 'Back to school' products were supported by consumer competitions and editorial in children's comics and women's titles aimed at mothers.

Brand Values

Sellotape offers simplicity and convenience, where other adhesives, liquid glue for example, can prove messy and difficult to handle.

Sellotape has a distinct proposition and has built a highly valuable brand name which enjoys strong customer loyalty.

The new strategy, based on market segmentation, puts great emphasis on innovation and reinforces the reputation for quality that Sellotape has built up over the last 50 years.

Quality is synonymous with the Sellotape brand name, together with reliability and innovation. The same rigorous standards are applied at each production location and the sharing of best practice ensures continuous improvement in customer service.

Sellotape's biodegradable qualities resulted in environmental awards in 1996 and 1997 from the British Office Systems and Stationery Federation.

Stick It! is a trademark.
Super Snails is a registered trademark.
Elephant Tape is a registered trademark.
Barbie & Associated Trade Marks are owned by and used under licence from Mattel Inc. © 1998 Mattel Inc all rights reserved.
'Dennis the Menace' and 'Nasher' are trade marks of DC Thompson and Col Ltd © DC Thompson and Co Ltd 1997.
Sellotape is a trade mark of Sellotape GB Ltd.
Velcro is a registered trademark of Selectus Ltd in the UK and Republic of Ireland.

Things you didn't know about
Sellotape

On average, we each buy one roll of Sellotape per year.

A passenger's life was dramatically saved on a flight from Hong Kong to London in May 1995 when a coat hanger, Sellotape and a bottle of brandy were used in an emergency mid-air operation.

If all the rolls of Sellotape Original sold in one year were joined together they would reach the moon and back.

The Market

The value of the UK confectionery market in 1997 increased by 3% to £5.2 billion. More money is now being spent on confectionery than on tea, newspapers and magazines - combined! The children's sector of the confectionery market is extremely competitive and was estimated to be worth £477 million in 1997. It has experienced 14% growth in volume since 1995, from a combination of internal brand growth, brand extensions and new product launches. Recent new product launches include Giant Smarties, Milky Way Stars, Milky Way Crispy Rolls, Fruitang, Polo Gummies and Cadbury's Astros. Smarties continues to lead the field.

The same children's brands have remained popular for generations because of the influence of parental endorsement - brands bought by parents are usually the ones that they enjoyed years ago. The challenge for manufacturers is to maintain the traditional appeal of these brands but also to keep them contemporary for today's consumers. Limited editions are becoming increasingly popular in this market. The Blue Smarties promotion launched by Nestlé Rowntree in 1988 was so successful it led to the permanent inclusion of blue Smarties in 1989. Smarties have experienced further success in the limited edition arena, launching a completely orange tube of Smarties in 1995. This promotion was such a hit with consumers many still remember it today.

Achievements

Smarties is the UK's number one children's confectionery brand by value and was worth £49 million in 1997. Seasonal Smarties products, such as giant tubes and Easter Eggs, are worth £21 million a year.

The brand has become so popular that it has been able to successfully enter new markets capitalising upon its powerful values. The Smarties name has now been licensed to cover stationery and footwear.

History

Smarties were first introduced in 1937 by sweet maker Joseph Rowntree following successful test marketing in Scotland. They were simply called 'Chocolate Beans' and were initially priced at 2d. Chocolate Beans were renamed 'Smarties' and packed in the famous tube a year later.

In 1938, Britain had more than 300,000 sweet shops and the average consumption was seven ounces per week per person - double the average American intake. More than 350 confectionery companies competed for this enormous market but Smarties soon established a strong following.

In 1969, Rowntree merged with Mackintosh and in 1988 both were taken over by Nestlé to form one of Britain's biggest confectionery companies.

Since the brand's launch in 1937 Smarties has always consisted of eight fun colours. The only

permanent change ever made to the coloured shells happened in 1989 when light brown Smarties were replaced by the bright blue Smarties we see today. The other seven Smarties colours are red, orange, yellow, green, violet, pink, and dark brown. The centres of Smarties have experienced more change with the original light brown Smarties having coffee-flavoured centres, and the original dark brown Smarties made of plain chocolate. Today all Smarties have a milk chocolate centre, and the Orange Smarties are the only Smarties with a permanent flavoured, orange, centre.

The Product

Smarties are produced by pouring molten chocolate between two extremely cold metal rollers. These rollers have a dimpled surface so that when the two rotate they form Smarties' distinctive shape. A process known as 'panning' is used to apply the crisp sugar shell to the chocolate.

Smarties are available in four standard pack formats - tubes cartons, three and four tube multipacks and mini carton packs. As every child knows, Smarties tubes include coloured caps featuring letters of the alphabet. The tubes and their tops are used for spelling and school lessons as well as for model building. Although all 26 letters of the alphabet are embossed on the caps, there are more vowels than consonants to reflect the frequency of letters written in English.

Recent Developments

Launched in June 1997 Giant Smarties are the 'Big Brothers' of Smarties - they have everything that is great about Smarties, but just more of it. The target market of ten year olds love Giant Smarties because they deliver the taste and colour of Smarties, with added street credibility for older kids.

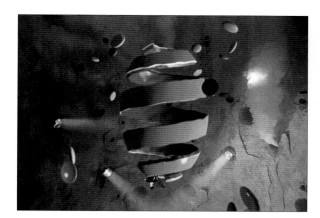

Since launch Giant Smarties have received consistent advertising support and have so far proved a resounding success, a major force behind the outstanding 27% volume brand growth Smarties experienced in 1997.

Smarties Mini Eggs are colourful, mischievous little chocolates with spirit and imagination. Positioned as a special Easter treat for eight to twelve year olds, they offer permission to indulge for anyone who is a child at heart. Since their launch in Easter 1997 Smarties Mini Eggs have established themselves as a strong competitor in the Mini eggs sector. Available in both bag and tube formats Smarties Mini Eggs helped grow the Mini egg market in 1997.

Nestlé Rowntree has recently introduced a Smarties licensing programme. A key objective of this programme is to increase brand visibility for Smarties amongst the target market of children aged between three and nine. A further aim is to reinforce Smarties brand appeal by adding excitement and innovation to the overall Smarties proposition.

The Smarties name was first licensed in the footwear category in the Autumn of 1997. The footwear range mirrors the colour, fun and quality aspects of the Smarties brand and has proven incredibly successful with children and mothers alike. Distribution continues to expand, with the Smarties footwear range now available in mail order catalogues, and leading high street retailers including Clarks, Russell & Bromley, Olivers and Barratts.

The licensing programme continues to grow, with the recent launch of colourful and exciting Smarties stationery products. The range includes a fun pack of Smarties colouring pens and a chunky nib Smarties writing pen from top quality manufacturer Berol.

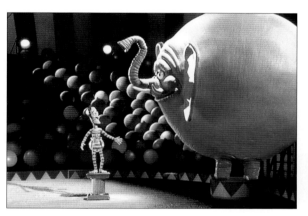

Promotion

The brand is aimed at children aged between three and nine. It is with this in mind that the following brand positioning was developed: "Smarties is my chocolate coloured with fun which really excites my imagination."

Communication has been built around a distinctive personality. Smarties has the bright and boisterous personality of an inquiring, mischievous eight year old. Everything is an adventure, everything is open to question, nothing is taken for granted (or accepted because adults say so). Lively, sociable, keeps up with playground fashions without being obsessed by them. Always on the look out for a bit of fun and adventure, always surprising so you never know what's coming next. But still, endearingly, a child.

Smarties have been consistently supported since their launch and Nestlé Rowntree will have spent approximately £4 million in advertising and promotional support for the brand in 1998. The slogan 'Only Smarties have the Answer' has been synonymous with the brand since the mid-1980s. Smarties ran three campaigns in 1998, encompassing TV, Satellite and Comic media. The 'Innatube' advertisement supporting the core brand is an enduring and engaging execution which appeals to all ages, inviting the viewers into a vibrant Smarties world.

Brand Values

Smarties' core brand values are as salient today as they have ever been. Children delight in the colour and vibrancy of the Smarties, together with the play value inherent in both the product and the tube. The chocolate in Smarties and the fact that there are 'lots' are also key brand values. For mums it is the pleasure in seeing their children enjoying their Smarties, which taps a rich nostalgic vein reminiscent of their own childhood.

We challenge you!

start eating Smarties —then try to stop!

TASTED these gay little chocolate beans? Then we're quite sure that you haven't been able to stop!

Everybody's eating Smarties! Four favourite "chocolate" flavours — milk, plain, coffee, orange — in a variety of bright attractive colours. Buy a tube of Smarties today. Made by Rowntrees.

PRICE PER TUBE or loose at 4d. a ¼-lb. **2ᴰ·**

For parties, or to give as presents, you'll like the attractive gaily coloured cartons of Smarties. Price 6d. and 1/-.

SONY

The Market

Television, video and sophisticated audio equipment have over the last decade become an integral part of our lives rather than a luxury. However, the world is braced for a revolution which will blur the divisions between electronics, telecommunications, computers and the entertainment industry. New media will offer consumers the benefits of interactivity, multimedia and online services.

As Nobuyuki Idei, the president of Sony Corporation, told Fortune Magazine in June 1995: "The digital revolution will shake out the total business platform so that brand image and production power and even the best technology won't be enough. We have to recognise that in the future, most of our products will become part of a larger digital network. From now on, Sony's work is to build bridges between electronics and communications and entertainment, not mere boxes."

Achievements

1996 marked Sony's 50th anniversary and the Japanese consumer electronics giant had plenty to celebrate. And, 1998 marked the 30th anniversary of Sony's presence in the UK. The company has been at the cutting edge of technology since it was founded by Akio Morita and Masaru Ibuka in 1946 and has had a major impact on the way in which we live our lives. Few companies are better-placed to drive the digital age into homes and businesses around the world over the next 50 years and beyond.

Sony has developed a wide range of products which have now become part of the mainstream. It invented the first magnetic tape and tape recorder in 1950; the transistor radio in 1955; the world's first all-transistor television set in 1960; the world's first colour video-cassette recorder in 1971; the Walkman® in 1979, which has now sold almost 150 million units and has become a way of life for a generation; the compact disc; the first 8mm Camcorder; the MiniDisc in 1992; and the launch of the DVD in 1998. Sony is entering one of the most exciting eras in multimedia technology.

Sony is not just a market leader in consumer electronics - through research and development, it has made considerable inroads into the world of professional broadcasting, telecommunications, PC technology and now, the Internet. Its increasingly high profile as an entertainment company through its divisions, Sony Music Entertainment Group and Sony Pictures Entertainment Group, is set to consolidate the international recognition it enjoys.

Sony is also one of the most respected companies worldwide. Its ability to innovate and its constant drive for self-improvement earned Sony worldwide sales of $45 billion in 1995. The company now employs nearly 163,000 staff.

The key to the success of the brand is how it meets the challenges of change. For fifty years Sony has led the market in terms of innovation and this is the challenge for the next fifty years. Products will no longer be developed with just hardware in mind. The convergence of technologies - PC, telecommunications, consumer electronics, entertainment and PC software is now a reality.

History

Sony was born out of the chaos in Japan at the end of the Second World War. Fired with a vision for a new future and with an abundance of talent and marketing skill - but with a market capitalisation of the equivalent of £850, 20 employees and no machinery - Akio Morita and Masaru Ibuka founded Tokyo Tsushin Kogyo (Tokyo Telecommunications Engineering Corporation), in 1946.

Their declared aim was to: "Avoid the problems which befall large corporations while we create and introduce technologies which large corporations cannot match." They believed the reconstruction of Japan depended on the development of dynamic technologies. By developing innovative high-tech electronics products, Sony was able to expand its operations outside Japan into the United States, Europe, Asia and other regions. In 1998 it celebrated its 30th anniversary in the UK.

Sony's most famous product - and one which created a whole sector was the Walkman personal stereo. The prototype Sony Walkman was produced in 1978. At that time, engineers at Sony had been developing a stereo cassette recorder based on the compact Pressman (TCM-10) cassette recorder but it had proved difficult to install recording and play-back mechanisms in such a small unit.

Undeterred, Sony set about finding a solution and produced a system equipped with a play-back only mechanism, and such high quality sound reproduction that the product was simply

begging to be marketed. Its chief attraction was its size - used with set of lightweight headphones it could be used anywhere. The name Walkman was chosen because it reflected the product's debt to the Pressman technology, and because Walkman summed up the sense of mobility which characterised the product.

At first, the Walkman was poorly received by retailers. Eight out of ten Sony dealers were convinced that a cassette player without a recording mechanism had no real future. However, its compact size and excellent sound quality attracted consumers. During 1980, the Walkman was hailed as one of the most popular new fashion products and young consumers adopted it as an essential part of their lifestyles. In its first two years on the market, Sony sold 1.5 million Walkman units.

Fierce competition from rival products, spurred Sony to research and develop improved products to ensure that it continued to lead the market. The WM-20 model, often called the 'Super Walkman', was engineered to the same size as a cassette-tape case. Walkman sales have topped 150 million units worldwide and it has become the single best selling consumer electronics product ever produced.

The Product

Sony operates in the electronics and entertainment markets. It manufactures video equipment including digital video and still cameras; televisions, announcing in 1997 the first ever completely flat television screen, and looks towards digital television in 1998; audio equipment, specifically supporting MiniDisc as a replacement for the cassette tape; CD-Rom drives and computer monitors and much, much more. Sony has always been involved in the development and production of recording media.

This precipitated Sony's acquisition of CBS Records in 1988, and Columbia Pictures Entertainment in 1989, which today form Sony Music Entertainment and Sony Pictures Entertainment. Sony Music Entertainment has produced a string of best-selling albums from artists such as Michael Jackson, Mariah Carey, Sade, Pink Floyd, Pearl Jam and Oasis.

The Picture Group has achieved almost a 19% market share in the US box office, propelled by a number of hit films which have included Sleepless in Seattle, Philadelphia, Jumanji, Men In Black and the highly acclaimed Sense and Sensibility.

Sony Pictures Entertainment also holds a stake in STAR TV's music service, Channel V, and is a partner in the German music channel Viva and the Latin American pay-TV channel HBO Olé and satellite service HBO Asia. The company also operates satellite channels in India and Latin America under the name Sony Entertainment Television.

The fruits of Sony research are not only limited to the enjoyment of the average consumer. Sony's professional product range is used for a variety of applications by broadcast stations, production houses, educational organisations, research facilities, and medical institutions.

be perceived increasingly as an IT brand as well as a consumer electronics brand.

Sony is also a leading player in the developing DVD industry. DVD has been launched across Europe, US and Japan and this format is the next major milestone in the consumer electronics and multimedia industry. DVD is a single layer disc holding more than seven times as much information as today's CD and comparable to a full-length feature film. This new format for carrying audio and visual information gives home cinema experience true substance.

1998 has been one of the most exciting years in the world of technology and that the digital age means that products in the home will, for the first time, be able to be networked together. Sony is moving towards fulfilling its president Nobuyuki Idei's strategy of building new products for "digital dream kids", the next generation of consumers in a digital future.

media attention and curious glances from the general public. By the time the Walkman was officially rolled-out, Japan was in a state of high excitement. Within three months, the entire stock of 30,000 units had been sold. Production couldn't match demand. The Walkman had arrived. This PR continues, and in the UK Sony launched a film makers strategy to support amateur film-making. This has taken shape in supporting the Edinburgh Film Festival and workshops.

Around the world, this marketing ploy exacted similar results. Additionally, in the UK, Sony uses large-scale home entertainment and consumer electronics events to give the public a chance to sample Sony products and experience the exciting range of software titles available. In 1997-1998 Sony exhibited at The Big Bash Motor Show, Ideal Home Exhibition, ER Show, Hi-Fi Show and Live '98.

...the ref wants them back ten yards...

WEGA
Widescreen
Be there.

Recent Developments

Sony continues to be at the forefront of new product development.

The Sony MiniDisc, launched in 1992, is pegged to be the replacement for the compact cassette. With a diameter of just 6.4cm, MiniDiscs are available in two formats - pre-recorded and recordable blanks.

Sony has also become a major player in the games industry. Its games software publishing division Sony Interactive Entertainment develops games titles for all games platforms, including the PC.

Sony has also developed its own games console, the Sony PlayStation, with 32-bit processing power, which was first launched in Japan in 1994 before a worldwide roll-out during 1995. The PlayStation offers real-time 3D graphics to ensure an arcade games-playing experience in the home. To date, an estimated 3 million units have been sold.

Sony has also taken advantage of the PC boom, manufacturing electronic components such as chips and pick-ups, and began to market its own Sony-branded PC in 1998. The company says that its long term strategy is to bring its expertise in the home entertainment market to the less innovative PC market. Sony will then

Promotion

When it comes to marketing, unlike its main rivals in the consumer electronics market, Sony has not proved to be the biggest spender. The phenomenal strength of the Sony brand worldwide is surely a testament to the company's reputation for producing innovative products of exceptional quality and value. As Idei said in 1995: "Marketing is not just a function within Sony - it is a cornerstone of our business philosophy. We are dedicated to a process of constant technological innovation, and marketing plays a vital role in this process".

Sony's advertising uses a combination of TV advertising, national press, consumer, trade and specialist magazines. For example, with the launch of the MiniDisc, editorial features, plus single and double-page spreads appeared in newspapers, youth and lifestyle magazines, as well as the music press. This promotional activity worked in conjunction with an upbeat, youthful TV commercial, shot in New York. Specific youth and music-loving markets were targeted through a Pan-European campaign rolled-out on MTV. The TV advertisement for Sony's Wide screen televisions featured a man skydiving in his armchair. The stuntman in the starring role later said that this was the most difficult stunt he'd ever done.

However, Sony doesn't just rely on brilliantly executed advertising campaigns to secure public attention.

Back in the 1980s, slick PR strategy ensured the Walkman was launched in a blaze of publicity. Sony was canny in its pre-launch marketing, encouraging famous Japanese singers and young Sony employees to sport Walkmans while out and about, exciting both

In a world where technology is moving forward quickly, Sony puts its full marketing muscle behind explaining the benefits and range of products available to the public today. And continues to search for ways of doing things others don't.

Brand Values

Sony signifies innovation, state of the art technology, superior quality and durability. It pursues a policy of continuous improvement - known in Japanese as 'kaizen' - reflected in its considerable investment in research and development. Sony continues to strengthen its leading position in the markets in which it operates through strengthening its product range and developing for the future.

'Sony', 'Walkman', 'MiniDisc' are trademarks of the Sony Corporation, Japan. 'PlayStation' is a registered trademark of Sony Computer Entertainment Inc.

St Michael
FROM
MARKS & SPENCER

The Market

A number of key influences have shaped Europe's huge retail sector in recent years. Companies eager to increase their share in an already competitive market have plunged into a spate of mergers and acquisitions in an attempt to secure greater buying power. At the same time, added pressure has come from the emergence of discount retail operations. As a result, retailers have sought to extend their networks abroad and have undergone major restructuring programmes to increase efficiency.

Marks & Spencer has expanded into new markets overseas but has continued to focus on the core of its business - high quality products at value for money prices.

It has a 15.5% share of the total clothing and accessories market and 5.8% of the total footwear market. Today, Marks & Spencer has the highest pre-tax profit of any retailer in Europe (Times 1,000, 1996).

Achievements

In the UK, Marks & Spencer is a well-loved institution affectionately dubbed 'M&S' or 'Marks & Sparks'. The St Michael brand, is the only brand sold at Marks & Spencer and just under 80% of all St Michael merchandise is made in the UK.

The St Michael brand is quintessentially British with a reputation for high quality and service. It is this which has enabled Marks & Spencer to open stores not only across the UK but throughout the world.

Marks & Spencer currently operates a total 711 stores world-wide, from Birmingham to the Bahamas, with a total sales area of 13.8m square feet. It is a highly lucrative business. In 1996, group turnover amounted to £7.8 billion, with

pre-tax profits of £1.1 billion. It was the first retailer in the world to be awarded a prestigious AAA credit rating which indicates the stability and strength of the group.

The company is one of Britain's largest exporters of clothing. It has been awarded the Queen's Award for Export Achievement on four occasions, most recently in 1995. In 1996 Marks & Spencer won a Queen's Award for Technological Achievement for the second time.

Marks & Spencer was voted 'Europe's most respected company' by the Financial Times in 1994.

History

Marks & Spencer was founded by a young Russian refugee, Michael Marks, who arrived in the north east of England in the early 1880s. He started out selling haberdashery from a tray in the villages close to the industrial centre of Leeds. However, he had ambitious plans and borrowed £5 from a local wholesaler Isaac Dewhirst to enable him to buy fresh stock and set up a stall in Leeds market. His first advertising slogan was straight-to-the-point. It stated: "Don't ask the price - it's a penny." This helped Marks get around the problem of his poor English.

Less than ten years on, Marks was operating a chain of stalls across the north east. He formed a partnership with Tom Spencer, a cashier at the IJ Dewhirst wholesale company, which accelerated the growth of the business.

The family's involvement in the company continued when Michael's son, Simon Marks was named as a director in 1911 and became chairman during the First World War. During this period the Marks & Spencer penny price point disappeared. In 1917 Simon Marks was

joined on the board by his friend and brother-in-law Israel Sieff. Together they were to chart the next stage in Marks & Spencer's history. Both became chairman of the company at different stages, and were later granted peerages.

During the 1920s, the company introduced the revolutionary practice of buying stock direct from manufacturers, thereby forming long-lasting, close relationships with suppliers, many of which have continued into the present day. Many of the ground-rules which have been key to the company's success were initiated at this time by Marks and Sieff.

The company registered the St Michael trademark, which distinguished all Marks & Spencer goods, in 1928. The introduction of retail branding reassured consumers that Marks & Spencer products had a specific quality guarantee. The company grew at a rapid rate, opening its flagship Marble Arch store in Oxford Street, London, in 1930.

One of Marks & Spencer's aims was to take care of its staff as well as its consumers. It set up an in-company Welfare Department in the early 1930s. After the Second World War - during which over a hundred stores were damaged - the company underwent a period of rapid expansion.

In 1975 it opened its first European store on Boulevard Haussmann in Paris. In the UK, further expansion in the 1980s, led to the opening of the first Marks & Spencer edge-of-town store at the Metro Centre, Gateshead. The establishment of St Michael Financial Services led to the launch of the Marks & Spencer Chargecard in 1985 and by 1988, Marks & Spencer Financial Services moved into the black, one year earlier than forecast.

St Michael FRUIT

I ♥ M&S

MARKS & SPENCER *Makes Ordinary, Extraordinary.*

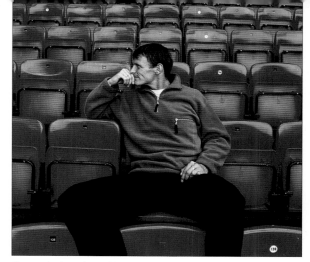

MARKS & SPENCER
FOOTWEAR

CLASSICS ARE BLACK

MARKS & SPENCER
COSMETICS

The Product

Marks & Spencer is perhaps most famous for its underwear. It has a 35% share of the UK ladies' lingerie and men's underwear market.

It is also recognised as a major supplier of quality ladieswear. In 1996 it reorganised 170 stores and split ladieswear into formal and casual ranges including accessories to more accurately reflect the way that women shop - tailored suits are next to blouses, jeans next to casual tops. The result is increased clarity and more multiple purchases.

Marks & Spencer is the UK's second largest jeans brand for women. One in ten pairs of all shoes is bought at Marks & Spencer and ten million blouses are sold every year. In the menswear sector one in four men's suits sold in Britain is from Marks & Spencer and the company sells four million ties every year.

Since its launch, the company has branched out from clothing into food. Today, M&S accounts for over 50% of the chilled ready meal market, making it the market leader and is the UK's biggest supplier of sandwiches. The company also sells a range of toiletries and cosmetics, gift items and stationery as well as home furnishings from sofas to saucepans. Its wedding list service is now the UK's largest own-brand, bridal gift service.

Financial services is one of the fastest growing areas of Marks & Spencer's business. In 1996/97 the number of Chargecard account holders increased by 17% to 4.5 million. Along with account cards, Marks & Spencer Financial Services offers personal loans, unit trusts and PEPs, and a range of life and pension plans.

Recent Developments

The last decade has seen rapid international expansion - 1988 proved a key year in the company's foreign fortunes, with the acquisition of Brooks Brothers, America's longest established clothing company; the Kings Super Markets 16-strong chain of quality stores based in the United States; and expansion into Hong Kong. The company owns stores in France, Belgium, the Netherlands and the Republic of Ireland. It also has franchised businesses in a number of countries including Austria, Hungary and Israel and is looking to move into central Europe, the eastern Mediterranean and elsewhere in the Middle East.

Marks & Spencer Home Delivery has grown into an £85 million business. It offers everything from flowers to school uniforms and is expanding into mail order adult clothing catalogues for those consumers who prefer to buy from home.

Promotion

The St Michael trademark was introduced in 1928 by Simon Marks. He felt that a standard brand applied to all the company's goods would imbue them with a 'seal of authority'.

Over the years Marks & Spencer has advertised less than most retail brands.

Even during the 1950s, when advertising was becoming fashionable, Marks & Spencer was reluctant to use advertising to increase sales.

Today, the company publishes a successful customer magazine - two million copies are printed four times a year - targeting upmarket, ABC women. Other promotional activities include window displays, in-store posters and point of sale materials. Recent advertising campaigns include an awareness-raising initiative designed to boost public perceptions of M&S's quality ranges of footwear, cosmetics and jeans through selective executions in women's magazines and weekend review sections of the national press.

Its steady progress can be attributed to its image as a quality brand. Store and product presentation and service have always been of a high standard and the St Michael guaranteed refund is intended to reassure customers.

MARKS' PENNY BAZAAR

Brand Values

Simon Marks and Israel Sieff drew up six basic principles for the company: to offer customers a selective range of high quality goods under the St Michael brand name; to encourage suppliers to make use of the latest technology to ensure goods were as high a quality as possible; to cooperate with suppliers and enforce quality throughout; to expand display space and offer pleasant, convenient surroundings; to simplify operating procedures and finally, to foster good relations with customers, suppliers and staff.

These tenets form the backbone of the Marks & Spencer image. The St Michael brand is a guarantee of quality at affordable prices.

The Market

The alcoholic drinks market is highly competitive, constantly changing and evolving as brewers fight to increase their share of a relatively fixed volume of sales by introducing new products and product variations. The UK lager market has traditionally split into two parts: standard and premium, according to price differences and alcohol content. Standard lager sales have slightly declined in recent years while premium lagers have enjoyed the fastest growth. Premium lager now accounts for over 35% of all lager sold in the UK. Stella Artois, the leading premium lager, is largely responsible for driving the growth of the sector and is now the strongest beer brand in the UK.

Achievements

The strength of the Stella Artois brand and the quality of the product have enabled Stella Artois not only to maintain its dominant market position but to achieve a rate of growth that far outstrips its competitors, increasing its premium lager market share to over 20%.

Already the UK's leading premium lager, the brand has grown steadily throughout the 1990s despite being consistently outspent in advertising terms by rival brands, such as Budweiser and Holsten.

In the last few years, the rate of Stella's growth has dramatically accelerated. At the end of the financial year ending February 1998, sales of Stella Artois had increased by 30% year on year, bringing total sales for 1997/8 to more than 1.3 million barrels. In the take-home market alone, which accounts for less than a third of Stella's total sales, this growth was enough to make Stella the most valuable brand, with sales of £165 million, beating its closest beer rival, Carling Black Label, as well as the

largest spirits brands, such as Bell's whisky (Source: AC Nielsen, MAT to February 1998).

Among all lager drinkers, the brand today enjoys spontaneous brand awareness of 46% and spontaneous ad awareness of 16%. In key brand affinity scores, Stella beats all other lagers, with 30% of all lager drinkers claiming to drink it regularly, 14% drinking it most often, and 15% citing it as the brand they like best. Across all ages, more people cite it as the brand that is most 'for someone like me' than any other lager (Whitbread's lager Image and Awareness survey, September to December 1997 and Millward Brown, March-April 1998).

History

Stella Artois' origins date back to 1366 and a small brewer called Den Horen (The Horn) in Leuven, Belgium. Sebastien Artois was appointed master brewer there in 1708 and bought the brewery in 1717. By 1800 Den Horen had become the largest brewery in the French-speaking world and in 1892, the Artois brewery started experimenting with fermenting yeast. By 1926, the recipe for Stella Artois had been perfected. Stella Artois was originally brewed as a Christmas beer named after the brewery's owner. The recipe has remained unchanged since then although the product is now widely consumed all year round.

The brand first entered the UK in bottles in 1937. In 1976, with demand for the brand growing fast, Whitbread was granted permission to brew Stella Artois under Licence in the UK and production began at its Luton brewery. In 1979 Stella Artois took a leading role in the development of sports sponsorship when it sponsored the Stella Artois Grass Court Championships for the first time. The event has become a highlight of the sporting summer, attracting top names from the world of tennis and in June 1998, the brand celebrated the 20th Stella Artois tournament at Queen's Club, London.

Stella Artois' first foray into television advertising was in 1986 with the introduction of a small-scale regional test on HTV. This was followed in June 1990 with the launch of its first major TV commerical, 'Jacques' in the TVS and HTV regions and subsequently in other regions including London, a key area for premium lager sales. The campaign was also extended into cinemas, the precursor for forthcoming Stella Artois successes on the wide screen. In answer to the growing trend towards bulk packs, Stella Artois launched a 12-can multipack in 1988 and in 1991 brand appeal was further broadened by the introduction of Stella Artois in 330ml non returnable bottles in the take home trade for the first time.

The Product

Stella Artois is an authentic, distinctive continental-style premium lager brewed to 5.2% alcohol by volume. Only the finest ingredients are used in the brewing process. These include the female Saaz hops; rare two row malting barley and the original Stella Artois yeast. Stella Artois comes in draught form and is available in

pubs and clubs. It is also available in cans from specialist off licences and supermarkets. Two sizes of bottle are available - the 33cl bottle and continental-style 'stubby' 25cl bottle.

Recent Developments

Stella has managed to increase its momentum without making any significant changes to the product or the way it is presented. The beer itself remains unchanged and in a market crowded by hype, the only significant new packaging formats have been non-returnable bottles launched in six packs, and most successfully, the 25cl 'stubby', which enhances the brand's genuinely continental image and has fared particularly well with take-home drinkers. The most recent new packaging initiative in the take home market is the embossed Stella can. Launched in September 1998, its aim is to reinforce Stella's quality credentials and impact on shelf.

Promotion

The "Reassuringly Expensive" advertising campaign has run now for over two decades and is one of the best known in the UK's advertising history. Throughout the 1980s, London agency Lowe Howard-Spink developed a press campaign which positioned the brand

clearly as the UK's most exclusive lager.
In the early nineties, as premium lager
moved mainstream, the campaign transferred
to television. The subsequent ads have won
numerous awards and have played a
fundamental role in the success of the brand.

The latest execution 'Last Orders', debuted
in UK cinemas in July 1998 before rolling out
onto TV. The ad remains in the established
timeless, Provencale setting and features an old
man, apparently dying, who requests a pint of
Stella as his final wish. When his son succumbs
to temptation and drinks the pint instead, then
setting up the local priest as the culprit, the old
man's reaction betrays the fact that he's in much

better shape than we first thought. Some
people, it seems, will do anything for a pint
of Stella Artois.

During 1997 Stella invested heavily in a
programme of film-related promotional activity,
including advertising, broadcast sponsorship of

films on Channel 4
and Channel 5, a
national promotion
with video chain
Blockbuster and a
series of free outdoor
screenings of movie
classics throughout
the summer.

In 1998 the
programme was
refined and the
positive association
between Stella Artois
and quality cinema was
strengthened. The
activity kicked off when
Stella announced a
themed film deal with
EMAP Media, spanning
both broadcast and
consumer press.
Among other activities,

a more extensive sponsorship of Channel 4's
film output was undertaken. The successful
outdoor movie screenings were repeated
and this was complemented by a more
selective revival of 'art house' films in
independent cinemas.

Stella Artois is an active, yet highly
individual sponsor. In August 1997 it
sponsored The Assembly Rooms, the focal
fringe venue for the Edinburgh Fringe Festival,
for the sixth year running. In 1998, to underpin
Stella's links with quality film, the brand
supported events within the Edinburgh Film
Festival. The association underlines a consistent
strategy of associating the brand with cutting
edge entertainment and star names. This also
extends into sport where, as a long-time
sponsor of the Stella Artois Tennis Tournament,
the brand has enjoyed high profile association
with top British tennis players such as
Tim Henman and Greg Rusedski.

Brand Values

Stella Artois is the UK's leading premium beer
brand. As its appeal becomes more mainstream,
its sense of exclusiveness, genuine quality and
continental heritage become even stronger.
The brand therefore manages to hold a position
in the mind of the consumer which is expensive
and premium, at the same time as it is being
drunk by more and more people.
The advertising has capitalised on the brand's
premium ingredients and Belgian brewing
heritage to create a brand which stands apart
from the competition. "Reassuringly Expensive"
has moved from being a symbol of yuppie
excess to being a reassurance of supreme
quality and worth which is stated in the ads
and recognised by the UK lager drinker.

Brewed in UK.

STELLA ARTOIS **Stella Artois. Reassuringly expensive.**

TAMPAX®

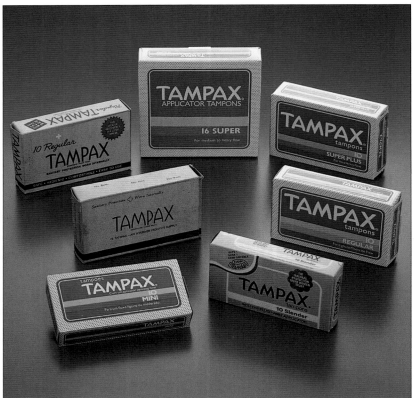

The Market

Tampons are the second largest segment of the UK 'sanpro' market but tampon volume share has declined dramatically. In 1991, tampons accounted for 42% of the market; by 1997 this had dropped to 37% as sanitary towels and pant liners rose in popularity.

The reason for this decline is technological advances in the sanitary towel market. The introduction of ultra thin sanitary towels, such as 'Always Ultra', meant that for the first time there really was an alternative to tampons which met consumer needs for protection, comfort and discretion. Although there remain situations where only a tampon will do, such as swimming, women are now choosing both tampons and towels at different stages of their periods: 54% of UK women now use the two different products. There are approximately 14 million menstruating women in the UK and around 40% of them are tampon users.

Increased consumer awareness of Toxic Shock Syndrome (TSS), an extremely rare but serious disease linked to the over-long use of tampons, has also had an affect on tampon sales.

Achievements

Despite falling sales of tampons, the Tampax brand is the market leader and dominates the UK in terms of volume and value. Tampax has a 55% share of the market by volume compared with Smith & Nephew's 29% share and own label's 16%.

Tampax dominates the applicator sector of the market. The non-applicator, or digital sector, accounts for 37% of the total tampon market and is dominated by Smith & Nephew brand Lil-lets. However Procter & Gamble, the owner of the Tampax brand, has identified the non-applicator sector as an opportunity for incremental business and is now putting greater marketing effort behind its Tampax non-applicator product.

Tampax Satin launch in February 1997, based on a 'comfort' positioning, halted the decline in market size and grew the brand.

History

Although Tampons were first introduced commercially less than 60 years ago, the concept goes back to the Egyptians who used rolls of soft papyrus. Roman women also found their own methods using rolls of wool. Wealthy Byzantine women, meanwhile, used only the finest wool which was specially 'carded, combed and rolled into tampons by Greeks in the Crimea - probably the first commercial tampon production plant.

It wasn't until after the first World War that sanitary pads were first manufactured. Up until that time women improvised with cloth - the idea of a specially designed pad arose from the use of surgical bandages by French nurses. By the 1930s, American doctor Earle C Haas realised that conventional sanitary towels restricted physical exercise because of their bulkiness. With the help of his wife, a nurse, he developed a tampon from compressed surgical cotton with a cord stitched along its length for removal, and with a cardboard applicator for insertion.

Haas obtained a patent for his product in 1933 and not long afterwards stores in America began selling it. Haas subsequently sold his patent to three other Americans - Thomas Casey, Earle Griswold and Ellery Man - who launched an ad campaign for the product which they called Tampax.

As more women in the US tried tampons, word spread about its convenience and sales took off in Europe. A UK company was formed in 1937 although for the first year of its life, tampons were imported from the US and sold by mail order until a British factory was built.

Although women were very pleased with the product, it was not universally applauded. Clergymen denounced tampons claiming that they were agents of defloration and general wickedness. As a result, the government discouraged sales to single women.

As well as applicator Tampax, Hollypax - a non-applicator version - was introduced in the 1930s. It was dropped in 1957 due to declining sales, although around the same time a company called Lilia introduced its own non-applicator tampon called Lil-lets.

During the Second World War, Tampax tampons were rationed and part of the British factory was given over to the production of war materials. However, they were used by women in the forces and as women returned home after the war they told their friends about the product.

Initially, only one absorbency was available but in 1947 another, called Tampax No. 2, was launched. Tampax No. 1 and No.2 were renamed Regular and Super in 1954.

A new factory was built in the UK in 1959 and between 1960 and 1981 it was expanded three times to keep up with demand. All products sold in Europe, the Middle East, Africa, China and Russia are still made in the UK.

Tambrands, the company which manufactured Tampax, was bought in 1997 by Procter & Gamble.

In 1992, a second Tampax tampon called Compak was introduced. It shared the construction of the original Tampax flushable applicator tampons but used a unique plastic applicator which remains compact for carrying around and extends to a standard size applicator when used.

Tampax Non-Applicator (then named Tampets) were introduced in 1994. They were the company's first non-applicator tampon. They have a gently tapered tip, together with a smooth outer cover and indented finger base.

In the same year, the original Tampax tampon was improved with a new, stronger wrapper so that it could be kept safely in a handbag. A stronger cord was stitched along its entire length for security and easy removal.

Tampax tampons are made of soft hygienic materials and the tampons, applicator (if made of cardboard) and wrapper can all be flushed away as they are biodegradable. Plastic applicators must be disposed of in an incinerator or a bin. The disposable applicator tubes are made of spirally-wound strips of paper held together with vegetable-based, water soluble glue.

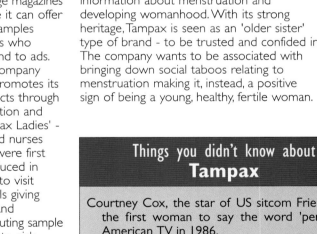

The Product

Tampax are made of cotton or rayon or a mixture of the two. The brand dominates the applicator sector of the market. Applicators are made of cardboard or plastic and some have rounded tips for easier insertion. The market for non-applicator tampons - also known as digital tampons - is dominated by Smith & Nephew's Lil-lets brand.

Tampax are available in a number of different absorbencies - Regular, Super, Super Plus, and Tampax Mini.

Promotion

Tampax advertises heavily both on TV and in the press - it spends £1 million a year in the UK on magazines alone. The company first ran a TV ad campaign in the UK in 1989. Tampax has traditionally been advertised as a generic brand although it has recently started to promote individual products such as Tampax Satin on TV and Tampets and Tampax Compak in the press.

The brand avoids TV to specifically target young teens preferring teenage magazines where it can offer free samples to girls who respond to ads. The company also promotes its products through education and 'Tampax Ladies' - trained nurses who were first introduced in 1956 to visit schools giving talks and distributing sample packs to girls aged between 12 and 13. It is estimated that the 'Tampax Ladies' reach 70% of all UK school girls.

Recent Developments

Tampax Satin were introduced in 1997. These were specially designed for easy insertion with a silky, rounded tip applicator and targeted at women aged 16 to 24. P&G launched Satin to increase tampon use and address consumer concerns over comfort. The launch of Satin was backed by TV and press advertising as well as direct marketing and PR.

Tampax is now available in 120 countries worldwide and P&G says it intends to pursue further sales in developing countries.

Brand Values

Tampax is associated with trust. Indeed, the Tampax advertising slogan throughout the 1960s, 1970s and 1980s was: 'Trust is Tampax'.

Tampax is the innovator and educator in the tampon market. It is the first point of contact for many young women looking for information about menstruation and developing womanhood. With its strong heritage, Tampax is seen as an 'older sister' type of brand - to be trusted and confided in. The company wants to be associated with bringing down social taboos relating to menstruation making it, instead, a positive sign of being a young, healthy, fertile woman.

easy going

Things you didn't know about Tampax

Courtney Cox, the star of US sitcom Friends was the first woman to say the word 'period' on American TV in 1986.

TV advertising in the UK was not allowed for feminine protection products until the late 1980s - even now it is not allowed on during the day in school holidays or before the 9pm watershed.

An estimated 70% of UK tampon users never switch brands.

VAT is charged on feminine protection products at 17.5%.

Up until the early 1970s, pressure from the church forced Tampax to carry a warning on its packaging that unmarried women should not use the product without the advice of their doctor.

AGB data shows that 3% of feminine protection products are now bought by a male partner doing a main shop.

The 'Tampax Ladies' - nurses who visit schools and provide information and advice were first introduced in 1948. They now visit schools from New Zealand to China.

TESCO
Every little helps.

The Market

The British grocery retail sector is among the most competitive in the world. A core of four brands battle for market share and customer loyalty and one of the key determining factors in where consumers choose to shop is price.

Tesco has a continuing policy of keeping prices low and is currently Britain's largest grocery retailer. It has 588 stores throughout Britain, 76 in Ireland, 42 in Hungary, 31 in Poland and 13 in the Czech Republic and Slovakia. In addition, it has recently purchased the Lotus chain of supermarkets in Thailand.

In the early nineties, Tesco began eroding Sainsbury's pre-eminent position and by 1996 consumer research showed that Tesco had a better overall image than Sainsbury, driven by the strength of its customer service, prices and value for money.

Achievements

In the 1970s, Tesco was associated with a 'Pile it high sell it cheap' philosophy. It pioneered the development of superstores and in the 1980s began investing heavily in the format. By 1986, its turnover was £3.5 billion and operating profit was £145 million. However, there was a fundamental weakness in the company - the strength of the Tesco brand itself. Consumer research showed that rival Sainsbury's had a better image than Tesco on quality, value for money, reputation and customer service and that its traditional strength - price - was being eroded. The brand's main problem was that consumers didn't know what Tesco stood for: superstores or old High Street stores; low prices or quality; food stores or 'Home and Wear'. There was no overall identity to pull the diverse images of Tesco together.

The company set about transforming the brand through a range of marketing and service initiatives which improved the product offering and ensured customer loyalty. These included adding new store formats such as Tesco Metro for urban shoppers, the introduction of the Tesco Clubcard - the first national loyalty card in the grocery sector; expanding the range of products available and improving customer service. Tesco Clubcard increased the loyalty of existing shoppers and attracted new shoppers and as a result Tesco became market leader in terms of market share, customer loyalty and market penetration.

These changes significantly increased Tesco's trading performance. Turnover increased from £3.5 billion in 1986 to £17.8 billion in 1998 and market share increased from 13.4% of the core grocery market to 21.5% over the same period. This is the highest market share Tesco - or any other supermarket - has ever achieved on AGB's measure of the packaged grocery market, having overtaken Sainsbury in 1995 to become Britain's largest supermarket group.

The company now plans to further develop the Tesco brand into new markets in Europe and beyond.

History

Tesco was founded by Jack Cohen in 1919. After serving in the Royal Flying Corps during the First World War, 21 year-old Cohen invested his serviceman's gratuity of £30 in NAAFI surplus groceries to sell from a stall in the East End of London.

Cohen went on to trade successfully in a number of London markets and also started selling wholesale goods to market traders. By the late 1920s he was switching his attention from market stalls to open fronted shops on the high street and in 1929 the name Tesco first appeared above a lock up shop in Edgware, north London. Cohen began to expand his business empire and by 1939 there were 100 branches of Tesco. After the war, the company floated on the Stock Exchange with a share price of 15 shillings and Cohen began to acquire a string of other companies.

In 1960, Tesco began selling clothing and household goods and by 1968 it opened Britain's first superstore in Crawley, Sussex selling both food and non-food products. Throughout the decade it also introduced 'Green Shield Stamps' which consumers could collect and redeem against a range of household goods. These were replaced in 1977 by a price cutting campaign called 'Checkout at Tesco.'

In 1982, Tesco celebrated its 50th anniversary as a private listed company and raised £500,000 for charity. In the same year it introduced the first computerised checkouts. A year later Tesco became Tesco Plc and in 1985 a rights issue was launched to raise £145 million for a superstore development programme. This was followed by a £500 million investment programme to build 29 new stores and provide 10,000 new jobs.

The company became Britain's biggest independent petrol retailer in 1991 and expanded its store format by launching Tesco Metro in London's Covent Garden. By 1997, the company won 'Retailer of the Year ' award and was voted the UK's 'Most Parent-Friendly Supermarket' by Great Ormond Street Hospital's 'Tommy's Campaign' award scheme. It also branched out into financial services with

every
1/3 OFF ALL FROZEN PIZZAS AT TESCO
Make sure you get a slice of the action at Tesco. From today, you'll find one third off all frozen pizzas for the next week. Top that.
little helps
UNBEATABLE VALUE
TESCO

WE SCAN EVERYONE ELSE'S PRICES BEFORE YOU SCAN OURS, BECAUSE *Every little helps.*

DEMON PIES.
TESCO VALUE PORK PIE
29p.
SEE INSTORE FOR DETAILS AND PRODUCTS UNDER OUR UNBEATABLE VALUE GUARANTEE. EXCLUDES EXPRESS
TESCO ⊠ UNBEATABLE VALUE
EVERY LITTLE HELPS

the introduction of the Tesco Visa card and its first in-store bank branch.

The Product

Tesco has 588 stores across the UK and operates a number of different formats from superstores to Tesco Express.

The launch of Tesco Metro stores in 1992 and Tesco Express stores in 1994 took supermarket shopping into a new era by focusing on fresh food. Metro stores are seen by consumers as upmarket, stylish and modern. They offer a diverse range of premium, exotic and luxury foods alongside Tesco's traditional value for money image. Express stores provide consumers with a range of goods quickly and conveniently but maintain the low prices Tesco offers at its superstores.

Tesco has built its reputation on giving consumers value for money. It has introduced 'New Deal Pricing' and 'Value Lines' - the first economy own label range launched by any supermarket in the 1990s. In every store there are also around 1,000 products which are on special price promotion at any one time.

The company is continually expanding its product range and in 1997 launched 2,500 new own brand lines. It has redesigned and expanded its fresh food counters and an increasing number of stores offer fish, hot chicken and meat counters. Its non-food product range has expanded and includes not only clothing but also stationery books, videos, CDs and computer software.

Tesco launched the first national loyalty card in the grocery sector in 1995 to reward loyal customers. There are now more than 10 million Clubcard holders of which 8.5 million use it on a regular basis. Every quarter, Tesco mails its Clubcard members with reward vouchers - and to date, has given back a total of £300 million. Over 25,000 vegetarians and diabetics have registered their dietary requirements with the Clubcard Help-Line and receive special product coupons accurately targetted to their needs. Club members have also been offered a range of additional benefits since the launch of the scheme - ranging from special deals on holidays to earning points in B&Q and on gas and electricity bills with ENERGi from Norweb.

In 1996, the company branched out into the financial services market with the launch of Clubcard Plus a savings account which allows customers to pay for their shopping and offers a competitive interest rate.

Recent Developments

Tesco is keen to develop a relationship with parents and children and installed baby care facilities in store in late 1993. It also removed sweets from checkouts, launched a Tesco creche in Watford three years later and introduced Tesco Baby Club which offers information, expertise and money saving vouchers through a series of magazines and special offers.

Tesco Direct was launched nationally in 1995 to offer customers the added flexibility and convenience of home delivery on a small range of products including wine, flowers and hampers.

Tesco recently introduced a range of customer service initiatives. Consumers told the company that they wanted more checkouts, less hassle and shorter queues - in response Tesco launched 'one in front' where if there is more than one person in the queue, Tesco opens another checkout. 'Customer Assistants' were introduced in 1996 to help customers with bag packing. In addition, major irritants such as revolving entrance doors were removed.

By the end of 1997, Tesco's long-running 'Computers for Schools' scheme had provided 29,000 computers to schools - equating to one computer for every school in England, Scotland and Wales.

Promotion

Between 1990 and 1992, Tesco ran a high profile advertising campaign starring Dudley Moore as the 'Man from Tesco' on a worldwide search for the best quality products. It was unlike any other supermarket advertising - engaging, humorous and charming - designed to gain the emotional high-ground of quality in consumers' minds.

By the mid-Nineties, however, Tesco had to adapt to new market realities shaped by the recession, the success of discounters and the improvement of its rivals advertising campaigns. In 1992, a strategy review suggested a new direction focusing on a new shopping deal: quality + price AND service = value. The notion was encapsulated in a new marketing slogan: "Every little helps".

Tesco has run a substantial TV campaign promoting its "Every Little Helps" strategy. Its 'No Quibble Guarantee' - if consumers are not happy with any product bought at Tesco they will be given a refund or exchange - is illustrated in a TV commercial by a shopper who exchanges a trout because it looks miserable. The Dotty campaign, starring Prunella Scales as 'Mother' and Jane Horrocks as her long-suffering daughter, has been highly successful. In research for the company, the Dotty ads regularly receive 90% prompted recognition. After just one burst, Dotty came seventh in a survey of memorable celebrity advertising, achieving 29% recall (Planning Partnership/Daily Mirror).

Dotty is designed to make customers feel good about Tesco. She constantly puts Tesco to the test - an idea inspired by the company's unfailing commitment to staff delivering outstanding customer service. Without this commitment there would be no Dotty campaigns and consumers would not think so highly of the brand. Today, Tesco claims its advertising is more effective and efficient than campaigns run by its competitors, some of whom spend considerably more on advertising. The Tesco ads' humour makes people remember both the ad and the message, qualitative research shows. And it still feels fresh and new - most people think it's only been around a year or so when

in fact it was launched in May 1995. So far, there have been more than 15 commercials in the three year campaign.

Tesco has also launched a Clubcard magazine which is sent to four million customers every quarter. It comes in five different editions representing the different lifestyles of different groups of Tesco consumers from new mothers to students, to ensure that information is up to date and relevant to all customers no matter who they are. In 1996, Tesco used 5,000 variations of communication tailored to people's lifestyles and shopping habits.

Brand Values

Once known for its 'pile it high, sell it cheap' approach, Tesco still has a reputation for value for money but the brand is now also highly regarded for the standard of its customer service and the quality and breadth of its product range.

THE NATIONAL LOTTERY™

The Market

The launch of The National Lottery on November 14 1994 signified a radical transformation in the nature and size of the UK gaming industry. Overnight, gaming was transformed into a part of everyday life for a large proportion of the population. The lottery was positioned as a 'harmless flutter' which could be enjoyed by all adults in the UK.

The National Lottery has undoubtedly impacted upon other areas of the gaming market. Whilst it has taken market share away from its competitors, including bingo and pools operators, it has also been instrumental in increasing the size of the gaming market as a whole. The UK gaming market is now estimated to be worth over £40 billion a year. The National Lottery occupies around 13% of the market, but is responsible for a substantial 58% of all monies raised by the gaming industry for Good Causes and government taxes.

Achievements

The National Lottery is a massive success. In just three years both The National Lottery On-line game (the technical term for the Saturday and Wednesday draws) and Instants games have become an integral part of everyday life, drastically altering people's perceptions of gaming and creating a new and powerful structure for raising money for good causes around the country.

Amazingly it took only 18 months after launch for Camelot to establish the world's most efficient lottery and the UK's biggest consumer brand, with sales by March 1998 totalling over £13 billion. Indeed, The Henley Centre concluded after just 14 weeks that The National Lottery represented "the most dramatic product launch in British history". The Lottery quickly became a national institution with over 60% of the country playing regularly. It is estimated that over 90% of the UK adult population have played at least once. The Lottery has created over 500 millionaires, with total prize money for all lottery winners amounting to over £6 billion.

By the end of its first week, The National Lottery had raised £12 million for the five Good Causes chosen by parliament - Sports, Arts, Heritage, Charities and the Millennium.

The National Lottery raises more for Good Causes and government than any other lottery in the world, with an average weekly contribution of £28 million. To date, over £5 billion has been raised for the Good Causes.

Before the launch of National Lottery Instants, the annual UK scratchcard market was worth £44 million. It took only 13 days for Instants sales to equal this figure. With a market share of approximately 90%, Instants is now by far the UK's largest impulse brand. In 1996 sales totalled £900 million, which was larger than the sales of Coca-Cola, Kit-Kat and Mars Bars combined. The level of interest in Instants is maintained by launching new Instants games regularly.

History

In March 1992 John Major's government proposed the creation of a UK National Lottery. The purpose of the Lottery was to provide designated 'good causes' in the UK with a huge injection of funds. With this objective in mind, the Government put the opportunity to operate the UK Lottery out to tender. Eight organisations applied and in May 1994, after a lengthy review of all applications, the Government announced that Camelot Group plc had won the tender and would run the Lottery for its initial seven-year licence. Camelot Group plc was a consortium set up by five separate companies - Cadbury Schweppes, De La Rue, GTECH, Racal Electronics and ICL. Each company brought to the consortium an area of expertise pivotal to the successful running of The National Lottery.

Winning the licence was only the first step in what was to be a very long road. The newly-formed company had just 24 weeks to set up the Lottery from scratch. Camelot embarked on this challenge with the knowledge that if they were not ready by November 14 1994, they would be fined £1 million for each and every day they were late.

Camelot faced three major hurdles to launch the Lottery: technical requirements, establishing a retailer network and communications strategy.

Camelot created the largest communications network in the UK, equivalent to the four biggest high street banks combined. The network was capable of processing up to 400,000 transactions per minute. The software used equated to 200 person years of software development time.

Retailers needed to have terminals installed. Over 10,000 retailers were selected by Camelot to have terminals installed in their premises; these included multiple retailers,

independent retailers, forecourt operators, off-licences and Post Offices. Over 10,000 terminals were built and installed by the launch date. At launch at least 93% of the UK population lived or worked within two miles of a lottery outlet. Each of the 10,000 retailers had to have trained operators; this required 80,000 individuals to be trained between September and October 1994. Camelot set up ten regional centres in order to train retailers, and after launch to act as payment centres for major winners.

Getting the communications and education right at launch was essential: the public had to understand the brand, believe in the brand, and be inspired to go forth and purchase National Lottery tickets. The National Lottery was launched off the back of the now famous advertising campaign featuring the slogan "It Could Be You" and the 'Hand of Good Fortune' which was the random hand of luck that pointed out winners and reaffirmed the belief that anyone could win.

Camelot was up and running ready for the launch on the designated date. The rest is history.

The Product

The National Lottery in its present form consists of two brands - the On-line game (twice weekly draw) and Instants (scratchcards).

The On-line game mechanic involves choosing six numbers from 1 to 49. Players then decide which draw they would like to enter, Wednesday or Saturday.

Each line of numbers for each draw costs £1. Twice weekly the lottery balls are drawn randomly on The National Lottery show produced and broadcast by the BBC.

IT COULD BE YOUR WEEK.

IT COULD BE YOU.

THE NATIONAL LOTTERY

The first ever show attracted over 22 million viewers. If a player matches three or more numbers they win a prize. Players can win from £10 to tens of millions of pounds.

In addition to this basic game, the On-line game also gives players two other options of how to play the game: 'Lucky Dip', which is a set of six numbers chosen randomly by the terminal and 'Multidraw', where Players can buy tickets for up to 16 draws or eight weeks in advance.

If nobody wins the draw jackpot, the jackpot rolls over to the next consecutive draw. The draw can rollover a maximum of three times. If there is no jackpot winner on the fourth rollover draw, the jackpot is shared between those who have matched five numbers plus the bonus ball. The jackpot has rolled over many times, including three double rollovers but as yet there has never been a triple rollover.

From time to time the jackpot is boosted to increase player interest. These 'Superdraws' are nearly always themed, for example the 'Christmas Superdraw' in 1997, which had a guaranteed minimum jackpot of £25 million.

National Lottery Instants was launched in March 1996 and is now the biggest impulse brand in the UK. It consists of a variety of themed cards, with different prize levels and odds of winning. All Instants games are easy to play, whether it's 'Match three like amounts', 'Beat the score', or 'Three in a row'. Players simply scratch off the latex play area to find out if they have won instantly. Prizes range from £1 up to £100,000.

Recent Developments

On February 5 1997, a second On-line draw was launched: Wednesdays would never be the

PLAY IN ADVANCE AND EVEN ON HOLIDAY IT COULD BE YOU.

THE NATIONAL LOTTERY

same again! The second draw followed the same game style as the Saturday draw. The first eight weeks of the midweek draw saw total sales rise by 28%. Sales of the Wednesday draw are approximately £29 million a week.

An exciting new game was launched from Instants on February 17 1998. 'TV Dreams' offered a departure from the regular scratchcard format, offering the player three ways to win - an instant cash prize, the opportunity to play at home by matching numbers on the ticket with those drawn on a TV Show, and the opportunity to take part in a television show called 'The National Lottery Big Ticket'.

Camelot has emphasised the importance of new media in its marketing mix by investing in an Internet site - www.national-lottery.co.uk. The site provides an important source of information for all aspects of National Lottery games using the latest software for ease of explanation. The site was designed to reflect and build the brand values of both On-line and Instants. Banner advertising was used to increase interest in the site, which has received praise from many independent bodies for its content and design.

Promotion

Of all the advertising campaigns of the 1990s, few will be remembered as well, or will have created such excitement as, the "It Could Be You"

campaign created by Saatchi & Saatchi. The Hand of Good Fortune image conveyed the central idea, based around the key consumer insight that chance was the most motivating factor about the lottery for the British population. The hand, with its magical grandeur, captured the hearts and minds of the nation.

The launch saw a marketing campaign on an unprecedented scale with over £39 million being spent on television, radio, poster, press, point of sale and direct mail packs. By November 19 1994 approximately 40 million adults had seen the commercial at least 13 times. The direct mail push was the largest recorded with 21.8 million homes receiving educational leaflets on all aspects of The National Lottery game.

The launch of The National Lottery was a resounding success. Indeed, Marketing magazine concluded: "The National Lottery took the country by storm in 1995... it is by far the leading brand in both Adwatch of the year tables - the highest total recall during the year and the highest single awareness figure recorded".

Professor Barwise, Director of the Centre of

Marketing at the London Business School, who led an independent audit looking at the Lottery, concluded: "The Launch of the National Lottery has been a clear marketing success. I believe this has not been a matter of mere good luck, but instead reflects the high quality of marketing analysis and planning in the successful application".

In February 1997, the Lottery embarked on its most ambitious project since the launch when it succeeded in rejuvenating the middle of the British week by transforming dull Wednesday into exciting 'Winsday'. The Lottery also regularly uses tactical ads to tell the public about Rollovers and Superdraws.

Instants, launched on March 21 1995, positioned itself as the impulse brand of the 1990s. The launch campaign centred around the line "Forget it all for an Instants". The advertising campaign portrayed the Instants brand as a harmless flutter to take the player away from everyday routine for an instant.

Brand Values

The National Lottery has become part of the fabric of British daily life - the brand is trusted, loved and respected. The random and chance elements of the On-line game - where lives can be transformed by winning - gives the brand a great magical quality. The National Lottery makes dreams come true.

The Instants brand is light-hearted - it wants to release people's playfulness. It gives the opportunity for people to have a break from normal mundane everyday things and have fun, instantly.

The National Lottery and Cross Fingers logo and the Instants logo are trademarks of the Secretary of State for Culture, Media and Sport. It Could Be You, The Hand of Good Fortune, Winsday, Lucky Dip, TV Dreams and If You're Game We Are are trademarks of Camelot Group plc.

The Market

The UK is possibly the most competitive and dynamic newspaper market in the world. It also has the most national newspapers with ten produced each day of the week. An estimated 57% of the population read a national newspaper every day and 63% on Sundays and that doesn't include the country's 1,952 regional, weekly and free papers. Newspapers enjoy greater penetration than any other print medium - on a weekday this equates to over 26 million readers. The average British adult spends 28 minutes each day reading newspapers.

Achievements

Rupert Murdoch bought the ailing Sun in 1969 for £600,00. It sold less than 800,000 copies a day at a time when its main rival, the Daily Mirror, sold 4,250,000. Through a combination of punchy, hard-hitting news coverage and a strong sense of humour, The Sun overtook the Mirror in 1978 to become Britain's best selling daily newspaper as circulation passed the four million mark. Today, it remains the biggest selling English language newspaper in the world with sales of around 3.8 million copies.

History

The modern Sun was born in 1969 but its pedigree dates back to 1911 when trade unionists produced a strike sheet called the Daily Herald. By 1933 this had become the world's biggest selling newspaper with a circulation of two million copies per day.

However, by the 1960s the Daily Herald was in serious difficulties, its columns were filled with dry-as-dust trade union reports and readers deserted in droves. In 1964 its owners, the International Publishing Corporation, decided to kill off the Herald and launch a new paper called The Sun. This was aimed at the affluent young and the graduates emerging from the red-brick universities and technology colleges. The target circulation was two million but by the middle of 1969 sales had slumped to 850,000 and the paper was losing a lot of money. By July 1969 IPC began negotiations with Rupert Murdoch and sold him the title for £600,000.

The new-look Sun became an easy-to-read tabloid and promised to be a fresh, lively, campaigning paper. The first issue sold more than one million copies. Within a year, sales had doubled and after four years circulation reached three million. In 1970, the first topless Page Three girl appeared. In 1983 the most famous Page Three girl of all, Samantha Fox, first showed her assets.

The Sun moved to Wapping with other News International titles in 1986 and by 1990, full colour printing and on screen page make-up enabled The Sun to publish daily supplements on sport, women's interests, food, TV listings plus regular pull outs on do-it-yourself, homes, gardening and a Saturday comic.

In 1993, The Sun reduced its cover price to boost circulation and a year later - having achieved its aim - put the price back up again.

The Product

Love it or loath it, The Sun is indisputably one of the biggest newspaper success stories of the twentieth century. Outrageous, hard-hitting, sometimes shocking but always entertaining, it is essential daily reading for 10 million people.

The motto it carries under the masthead -"Dedicated to the People of Britain"- encapsulates the ethos which makes it so successful. It understands the issues that concern the working men and women of Britain and speaks their language.

Its terse, tight style is widely recognised as prose to be applauded. Foreign Office staff were shown examples of how complex issues were shown simply and clearly in The Sun and were urged to emulate the newspaper's crispness in the daily dispatches they sent in. The Department of Social Security has called The Sun for help with phrasing in government leaflets.

The Sun's trademark is its sense of humour. No one can forget the 'Freddie Starr ate my Hamster' front page and around the world. The Sun is also synonymous with Page Three.

Special regional editions have successfully exploited niche markets in Scotland, Ireland and Tenerife, offering coverage of local news and with local advertising, while maintaining the essence of the editorial product.

Recent Developments

The Sun swapped political allegiance by backing Tony Blair and the Labour Party at the 1997 General Election.

As The Sun's editorial message was more clearly focused on the concerns of the ordinary man and woman in the street, the Conservative government's policies on Europe, the economy and law and order increasingly came under attack and The Sun urged readers to vote for Blair in the May election.

The Sun has discovered a new Page Three girl Melinda Messenger who is dubbed The Sun's 'Girl for the Millennium.'

Two Sun photographers won top prizes at the 1996 British Picture Editors' Awards and The Sun's political editor Trevor Kavanagh was named 'Journalist of the Year' in the 1997 British Press Awards.

Promotion

The Sun has created and maintained its market share over the years through fresh, innovative marketing activity designed to recruit new readers and retain existing ones.

In the early 1980s it was the first paper to introduce £1 million bingo and it then ran a highly successful 'France for a pound' promotion. In the 1990s it developed a constant stream of new promotions to reflect the needs and motivations of its readers: holidays for £8.50; games linked directly to television programmes such as Bruce Forsyth's 'Play Your Cards Right', and Nicky Campbell's 'Wheel of Fortune', Scratchcards and £29 air fares with Ryanair to Ireland and Scotland.

The recession that hit the UK so severely in the early 1990s had a severe impact on the popular tabloid market. As the economy improved, publishers found readers had got out of the habit of regularly buying newspapers. Drastic action was called for, so The Sun cut its price from 25p to 20p and sales increased by over 750,000 copies a day - an uplift of almost 25%.

Big in-paper promotions have always been supported by heavy TV expenditure. In the 1980s The Sun used a fast moving, fast talking style which set the tone for TV advertising for tabloid papers during that period. In 1993, the paper adopted a new style where the promotional idea was strongly linked to one of The Sun's core values - a sense of fun. Research indicated that the slogan 'No Sun, No Fun', audibly reinforced with a riff from James Brown, was quickly picked up by the target market.

Following the election of the new Labour government The Sun ran a new ad campaign in the Spring of 1998 with the slogan 'Dedicated to the People of Britain.' It also ran a large scale branding campaign to pull in new readers.

Brand Values

The Sun is a newspaper with attitude. It is the only paper on the market on which opinion is so deeply divided - you either love it or you hate it. The paper arms its readers with the same information as its key competitors - but does so in a humorous and lively manner.

It's young modern and in tune with current trends, but it has its serious side too. Its reputation for sports coverage is second to none. It campaigns tenaciously for the things it believes in, or doesn't (such as the single European currency) and it aims to react with speed and sensitivity to national tragedies such as the death of Diana, Princess of Wales and Dunblane.

Things you didn't know about The Sun

The Sun has over 10 million readers every day - equivalent to the population of Belgium, or Chicago, Stockholm, Amsterdam, Munich, Brussels and Rome put together.

Sun readers earn between them double the GDP of New Zealand.

Every year The Sun uses 88,970 549 kilometres of paper - enough to go to the moon and back, ten times.

The Sun's first 'Lotto' game in March 1988 is in the Guinness Book of Records for the largest number of entrants - 4,305,162 - in a newspaper competition.

Letters page editor Sue Cook has to deal with up to 3,000 letters a week and agony aunt Deirdre Sanders replies to 1,100 a week on average, though her biggest haul was 5,000 in a single week.

The Sun was the first paper to give away a £1million bingo prize. The second £1 million winner collected the prize as a result of fraud and ended up in a law case.

Thomas Cook

The Market

Throughout the 1990s, travellers have become increasingly adventurous and sophisticated in their requirements and are looking for more convenient ways to book their holidays. Thomas Cook occupies a unique niche in the travel industry acting as a tour operator, a travel agent and a provider of financial services such as travel insurance and travellers cheques.

Achievements

Thomas Cook is one of the most widely recognised Travel and Financial Services brands in the world. It has over 1,400 wholly-owned and representative offices in around 100 countries. It also owns the world's largest network of foreign exchange bureaux and is the world's largest supplier of travellers cheques outside the US, with annual sales of over $16 billion and a global market share of around 30%.

History

In 1841, a 33 year-old printer called Thomas Cook attended a meeting of the Leicester Temperance Society which was keen to rid Victorian Britain of its social ills, particularly alcohol. Cook had the bright idea of organising a trip on the recently introduced railway line between Leicester and Loughborough to promote the Society's work. He organised the trip for 570 people and the price of one shilling

included sandwiches, dancing, games and an accompanying brass band.

It was such a success that Cook began organising other tours to places such as Liverpool and also started arranging accommodation for his 'tourists'.

In 1851, Cook took 165,000 people from the Midlands to the Great Exhibition held at Crystal Palace and continued to expand his business across Britain. However, he knew that he had to crack Europe and so organised his first trip to the Continent, taking a party down the Rhine to Strasbourg. Trips to Switzerland and Italy soon followed.

At around the same time Cook launched two revolutionary new systems. One was the hotel coupon which enabled travellers to pay for hotel accommodation with the use of a printed piece of paper rather than money. The other was the first travellers cheque which he called a 'circular note' and which allowed travellers to obtain local currency.

In the 1860s, Cook expanded his empire to Egypt and built a fleet of luxury liners to take tourists down the Nile. The opening of the Suez Canal in 1872 allowed him to offer his first

trip around the world. It lasted 200 days and took in America, Japan, China and India.

Cook's son, John Mason Cook, took over the business in 1879 and further expanded it to help merchants and government officials - the business travellers of their day - to reach their destinations. In 1884, he organised a relief operation to rescue Major General Charles Gordon from Khartoum and arranged for the movement of 18,000 troops and 130,000 tons of stores. But despite his efforts Khartoum fell.

Both Thomas Cook and his son died in the 1890s and the business was taken over by Cook's grandsons who sold the business in 1928 to rival firm Des Wagons-Lit et des Grands Express Europeans.

During the Second World War, Thomas Cook's headquarters ran an enemy mail department through which people behind enemy lines could communicate with friends and relatives. It was also involved in the evacuation of children from major cities.

The post-war period was characterised by the growth of the travel market and the rise of cheap air travel. This enabled mass tourism for the first time and Thomas Cook began providing package holidays.

In 1972, Thomas Cook became part of the Midland Bank Group. In 1995, Thomas Cook was bought by Westdeutsche Landesbank, Germany's third largest bank.

The Product

Thomas Cook has 385 high street shops in the UK and Ireland which offer a range of package holidays as well as organising independent travel

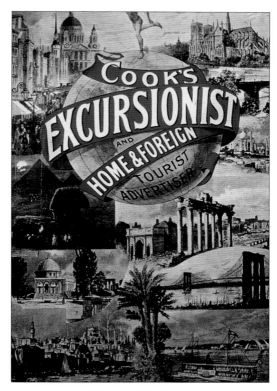

arrangements. Thomas Cook bureaux de change provide over 100 different international currencies and handle 14 different types of travellers cheques.

As well as being one of the leading travel agencies in the UK, Thomas Cook has major retail businesses in Australia, New Zealand, Canada, Hong Kong, Mexico and Egypt. It also owns major tour operators in the UK: Sunworld, the UK and Ireland's fourth largest short-haul tour operator and charter airline company; Thomas Cook Holidays, the company's long-haul operator; and European short breaks specialist, Time Off.

The company has over 600 foreign exchange bureaux in the UK and a network of over 1000 bureaux worldwide, including 164 bureaux at 48 international airports. These bureaux have access to over 100 different foreign currencies, many of which are available on demand.

Thomas Cook is the world's largest supplier of travellers cheques outside the US and generates over $16 billion a year through its relationships with MasterCard, Euro Travellers Cheques International and Visa.

Through its commercial foreign exchange activities, Thomas Cook provides international payment services to over 7,000 corporate customers who transact business overseas.

Direct Mail fully supporting the change in strategic direction and features an impactful cartoon style in bright eye-catching colours with strong price messages.

Over the years, customers have come to expect good service from Thomas Cook but customer research showed in previous years that customers incorrectly assume this is at a premium price, therefore the emphasis has moved to price competitiveness - an approach which in many ways reflects the increasingly aggressive attitude taken on price and discounting by the travel industry in general.

The nice surprise is the prices

The cartoon style combined with great prices effectively communicates both national and tactical campaigns highlighting the best deals and a more approachable image on the high street for all holiday products. A new advertising strapline of 'The nice surprise is the prices' reinforces the strong price competitiveness of Thomas Cook on the High Street.

Thomas Cook is also the brand leader in the retail Foreign Exchange market in the UK. The foreign exchange communication strategy centres around providing a high level of service and the advice and information that many customers require when purchasing holiday money.

Television advertising is used as much as the main medium to play out this strategy with a summer campaign promoting the two key service propositions - commission-free buy back of unused holiday money and free currency 'wise guides' and converters. Another major feature of the foreign exchange customer proposition is the introduction of commission-free 'sale days' which have been highly successful, both from an advertising and sales perspective. On these occasions, national press and local branch point of purchase material, as well as local activities, are used as the advertising medium.

Recent Developments

In July 1996 the Group acquired Sunworld, the UK and Ireland's fourth largest short haul operator and charter airline.

In the last two years Thomas Cook has made considerable investment in Thomas Cook Direct, the company's holiday booking service by phone, which is available in the UK, Canada and Australia. It has also launched Thomas Cook Online, the UK's transactional internet site; and the launch of the internet's first interactive commercial foreign exchange web site in North America.

In 1998, the Group launched Global Services. The Global Services business offers a complete package of traveller services for leisure and business travellers wherever they are in the world, with a range of travel, financial, emergency, assistance and other special services 24 hours a day, 365 days a year, in more than 30 languages.

Brand Values

Thomas Cook's mission is to provide exceptional service from exceptional people. It is recognised for the consistent quality of its service around the world and it invests heavily in its most important asset - its staff. The company's philosophy is that the customer comes first and all company policies are formulated with customer service in mind. International customer research continually shows that the Thomas Cook brand is the most recognised and respected name in travel and is associated with values such as trust and security.

Photo: A.T.C

Promotion

Thomas Cook Retail has implemented some major changes in its travel advertising strategy over the last two years which have seen Thomas Cook position itself as a 21st Century company with a more up to date, fun and innovative approach to travel. Integrated campaigns see TV, National Press, Point of Purchase material and

The Market

Virgin's market is as diverse as its product range. The company says that its target markets are often those where the customer has been consistently ripped off or under served, where confusion reigns and the competition is complacent. Virgin is a unique entity and as such has no single rival because it operates in music and entertainment, retail, travel and financial services.

There are now twelve main divisions and investments of the Virgin Group: V Entertainment Group, Virgin Retail, Virgin Travel, Voyager Investments, Virgin Hotels, Ginger Media Group (including Virgin Radio), Virgin Entertainment Group, Virgin Direct, Victory Corporation, Virgin Rail Group, Virgin Express Plc and Virgin Trading. All operate autonomously and the level of Virgin's shareholding varies.

Achievements

According to a recent survey (NOP), 96% of British consumers have heard of Virgin and 95% can correctly name Richard Branson as its founder - not bad for a company which started life in a public phone box. In his teens, Branson set up a student magazine and a small mail order record business which has since grown into a multi-million pound empire and now encompasses airlines, weddings, financial services and cosmetics.

The interests of the group include retailing, the Internet, book and software publishing, travel, hotels and cinemas, through over 100 companies and in 23 countries.

Virgin is one of the UK's largest groups and has achieved organic growth from sales turnover in 1983 of £50 million to more than £2.3 billion in 1997 (excluding Virgin Music).

Virgin Direct took £33 million of funds under management in its first month. Virgin Cola sold £50,000-worth of the product in its first three months with just four employees. Yet the company insists it does not wildly speculate on new ventures. The focus, instead, is on building businesses that can generate their own organic growth.

History

Richard Branson started his business empire with the launch of 'Student' magazine in 1968. The first business to bear the Virgin name was Virgin Music which was set up in 1973 by Branson and his cousin, Simon Draper, neither of whom knew much about the music business (or, indeed, any other business at that time). From a small mail order operation, Virgin Music grew to become the largest independent UK record company and the sixth largest record company in the world, signing acts such as Mike Oldfield, Culture Club and the Sex Pistols. Branson sold the company to Thorn EMI in 1992 to free funds to invest more in Virgin Atlantic.

As Virgin Music became increasingly successful, it started to diversify. In 1983, it began to distribute films and videos through Virgin Vision and Virgin Games, a computer games software publisher, was launched. The group's combined pre-tax profit climbed to £2 million on a turnover of just under £50 million. But in 1984, it took perhaps its biggest gamble when it launched Virgin Atlantic Airways offering a higher level of service at competitive prices. Virgin Holidays was introduced shortly afterwards. By 1989 the airline announced pre-tax profits of £10 million and has continued to expand and add further routes.

Two years later Virgin Retail Group and WH Smith announced a joint venture to develop the Virgin Megastore business in the UK and open stores in Spain, the Netherlands, Australia and the US. By 1994, Virgin Retail had acquired the Our Price chain in the UK and Ireland and Virgin Retail became the UK's largest music retailer.

Branson then decided to take on the financial services sector and provide consumers with no-nonsense financial packages, cutting out sales people and their commission.

1996 proved to be a busy year for the group. Virgin Travel Group acquired Euro Belgian Airlines, renamed it Virgin Express and began to operate a low cost, no frills service to a number of European cities. The V2 Music label and music publishing company was launched and Virgin Net was set up to enable users to get the most out of the Internet. Virgin Bride opened its doors for business and the group was awarded the Cross Country trains passenger rail franchise.

A year later Virgin Vie, a cosmetics and beauty care company, opened its first four stores. Meanwhile, Chris Evans's Ginger Productions acquired Virgin Radio for £85 million. Virgin has a 20% stake in the company and Branson sits on its board.

The Product

Virgin is perhaps most closely associated with its airline Virgin Atlantic but the company also operates Virgin Express - scheduled flights at 'no nonsense prices' between major European cities including Brussels, Milan, Madrid and Copenhagen.

However, the group's product range is extremely broad and includes everything from insurance to cola.

Virgin has a range of media and entertainment interests. Its most public face is the Virgin Megastore empire which stretches from London to Las Vegas offering consumers a wide range of music, CDs and videos. The Paris Megastore is the second most visited tourist attraction after the Eiffel Tower. The company says that in some countries where it opens new Megastores, consumers already know the Virgin name, but in other places the Megastore may be the only Virgin presence - so it has to be aware of how the brand name is perceived and adapt to local cultures.

Virgin Publishing was launched in 1991 and has become one of the major forces in British publishing, producing around 200 new books each year. Its two paperback imprints Nexus and Black Lace between them hold around 70% of the UK market for erotic fiction.

Virgin Radio was launched nationally on AM in 1993. It was awarded a London FM licence in 1994. In 1997 the two stations were listened to by over four million people a week. The same year, DJ Chris Evans took over the breakfast slot and liked the station so much that he bought it for £85 million. Virgin Radio is still managed by key Virgin staff and the company retains a 20% stake. The company has a further hold on the music industry through V2, an independent record label, whose signings include up and coming bands The Stereophonics and Mandalay. V2 has wholly-owned affiliates in a number of countries including the US, France and Germany.

Virgin is also involved with new media and set up Virgin Net as a joint venture with International CableTel. It claims that it is the first consumer service provider to offer a full Internet service to both complete beginners and experienced users.

Virgin Cinemas, which the Virgin Group bought from MGM in 1995, claims to provide the last word in customer-focused entertainment. In Virgin's Premier Screens film fans enjoy large seats - you would have to be 6'10" for your knees to touch the seat in front - and can order from a food and drink menu from their seats. Virgin plans to develop the chain over the next five years and open new 'Megaplex' sites around the UK.

The company took the financial services industry by storm by launching Virgin Direct, which offers customers investment and insurance products but without having to pay commission to salesmen or middlemen. It has attracted over 200,000 customers who have invested over £1 billion since its launch in 1995 and has recently introduced new products such as the Virgin One Account - a flexible mortgage and bank account.

In 1994, Richard Branson decided to give Coca-Cola and Pepsi a run for their money by introducing Virgin Cola under a joint venture with soft drink company COTT. Virgin subsequently bought out COTT in 1998. The brand is available in Asda, Safeway and Woolworths amongst others and has now been launched in Japan, France, South Africa and Belgium.

Virgin Bride was set up to offer the happy couple everything they need for the big day - from the confetti to dress and even honeymoon destination, all under one roof.

For those who want to get away from it all, Virgin offers a string of 40 hotels in Europe. Each has a strong individual character but all share similar standards of service and quality and if a desert island is your idea of paradise then you can hire Richard Branson's Caribbean hideaway, Necker Island. The company also runs the Virgin Airship and Balloon Company which is the world's biggest operator of commercial airships and balloons.

Promotion

One of the results of Richard Branson and his products' ubiquity is that the company doesn't need to spend much on advertising - its ad budgets have always been and remain minimal. Virgin Direct found that word of mouth supported by small public relations campaigns was 30 times as effective as the small amount spent on advertising.

Virgin Cola provides a perfect example of where PR has been used to its full potential. In the UK Pamela Anderson proved to be a magnet to the media. In addition, other activities included a ground-breaking promotional give-away in The Sun newspaper in which Virgin gave away a stake in the fortunes of the company. The promotion gained over £2 million worth of in-depth exposure both in terms of the in-paper support and The Sun's TV advertising.

Recent Developments

Cosmetics and toiletries company Virgin Vie was launched in October 1997 to offer a premium quality range of 5,000 products for men and women. It sells the products via direct mail as well as in high street Virgin Vie stores.

The company has also expanded into the general clothing market and launched the Virgin Clothing Company in August 1998. Inspired by the desire to deliver a range of clothing and footwear to serve the needs of urban style conscious people, Virgin says it will offer one of the most varied fashion ranges to be distributed around top independent fashion retailers and department stores across Britain.

Brand Values

The strength of Virgin lies in its brand name which embodies value for money, quality, service, fun and innovation. The launch of each new Virgin product comes with a promise to deliver these values and the company's skill has been in spotting opportunities and leveraging the brand into other areas.

virgin atlantic

The Market

The international airline industry is highly profitable and increasingly competitive. Following a difficult period at the start of the 1990s, the industry is now set for increased growth as new markets in the Pacific Rim, India and China open up for business. Even so, transatlantic and European routes are still enormously important markets for airlines to operate in, particularly in the field of business travel. To survive, airline companies have been forced to focus on capturing the market with an improved range of services.

Achievements

Virgin Atlantic Airways is one of the most forward-thinking companies of our times. Since its launch in 1984, it has become Britain's second largest long haul airline and has succeeded in breaking British Airways' monopoly on transatlantic routes, with a 25% market share.

Within the industry, Virgin Atlantic has set new standards for customer care. It has introduced a number of innovative products which other airlines are striving to emulate. It was the first airline to offer just two flight

carrier of frequent fliers, according to TDI research. Virgin Atlantic's own in-flight surveys reveal that 91% of passengers in Upper Class would fly with Virgin Atlantic again and would recommend the service to others.

The company's achievements have been recognised by a number of prestigious award schemes. It has been voted 'Airline of the Year' four times by the readers of Executive Travel, 'Best Transatlantic Airline' by Travel Weekly and Travel Trade Gazette for seven years running, and was elected as 'Brand of the Year - Service' at the ITV Marketing Awards in 1992. Its Upper Class service has been voted 'Best Business Class' no less than eight times by Executive Travel and seven times by the readers of Business Traveller. Holiday Which? also voted Virgin Atlantic the best British airline for the second time in 1997.

As a result, Virgin Travel Group has enjoyed considerable financial success with a turnover of £785 million for 1996/1997. In 1996 the airline carried 2.3 million passengers (Source: CAA Annual and Monthly Operating & Traffic Statistics).

The company was set up in 1984 based on an idea from an Anglo-US lawyer called Randolph Fields. Within three months the airline began to lease its planes and started up its first operation from the UK to New York (Newark). From the outset, Virgin Atlantic's mission was to provide the highest level of service at excellent value for money for all classes of air travellers.

The airline's transatlantic routes expanded rapidly taking in Miami (1985), Orlando (1986), New York JFK (1989), Los Angeles (1990), and Boston (1991). This was followed by flights to Tokyo, Athens, Hong Kong, San Francisco, Washington and Johannesburg, followed by the formation of the Asia Pacific Partnership with Malaysia Airlines and Ansett Australia.

More recently, Virgin Atlantic has launched a daily service to Johannesburg and second daily services to Los Angeles and Orlando. The company has also commenced a new codeshare agreement with Continental Airlines which affects all Virgin's transatlantic services and enables Virgin to offer its passengers the flexibility of six London to New York flights every day by selling seats on Continental's Gatwick-Newark services.

Virgin Atlantic has introduced a string of industry 'firsts' including individual TV screens for all passengers and child safety seats supplied on request. Another safety feature is the introduction of on-board automatic defibrillators and staff trained to handle passengers with cardiac problems. Virgin Atlantic's Upper Class

classes, Economy (a choice of Premium Economy and Economy) and Upper Class, a first class service at a business class fare, abandoning the three tier structure used by other airlines.

Renowned for its consideration of all passenger needs, both in-flight and at the airline's airport facilities, it is the preferred

History

At the start of the 1980s, putting the customer first was not the airline industry's top priority - ferrying passengers from A to B was paramount. Virgin Atlantic changed this by emphasising its commitment to customer care and value for money.

Free wheel drive.

was also the first to offer a sleeper service with flexible meal options, which is known as the 'Snooze Service'.

The Product

Virgin Travel Group consists of Virgin Atlantic Airways, Virgin Holidays - which sells 220,000 long-haul holidays every year - and Virgin Aviation Services.

The principal subsidiary, Virgin Atlantic Airways Ltd, is based at Heathrow, Gatwick and Manchester and carries over two million passengers a year. Virgin Atlantic operates departure lounges at Heathrow - the flagship, The Clubhouse, Gatwick, New York (JFK and Newark), Boston, Washington and Johannesburg and provides lounge facilities at each of its gateways.

Virgin's Upper Class has changed the face of business travel by supplying a chauffeur-driven car to collect passengers from their point of origin and transfer them to their final destination, both on the outbound journey and return. Upper Class passengers can also take advantage of a first class baggage allowance, separate check-in plus a 'Drive Thru' check-in service at Heathrow, Gatwick and Newark and all the amenities of the award-winning Clubhouse at Heathrow or Gatwick prior to departure. Once onboard, passengers can enjoy 55-60" seat pitch, a first class sleeper seat, an onboard bar and a lounge to relax in.

Virgin Atlantic also operates Virgin Freeway, one of the most generous frequent flyer programmes available. It was the first programme to offer Freeway miles for travel in all classes. After a first Upper Class round trip, a Freeway member will earn enough miles for two return flights between London and Europe. Miles can also be earned with Virgin's partner airlines - SAS, Austrian Airlines, Air New Zealand and British Midland. American Express Cardmembers who are in its Membership Rewards Programme, can transfer points from the Card to Freeway Miles so that they can take advantage of the many Virgin Freeway rewards, ranging from flights to a Kenyan safari.

Virgin Atlantic was the first airline to recognise the different needs of economy travellers so it introduced a special service - Premium Economy. Premium Economy offers facilities and service more comparable to a traditional short-haul business class. Passengers have separate check-in, a separate cabin onboard, and a more comfortable seat with 38" seat pitch. They also have priority meal service, priority duty free, priority baggage handling, complimentary pre-take-off drinks and newspapers, for the price of a fully flexible ticket.

Virgin Atlantic's Economy service is the first to provide every passenger with a seatback TV screen providing a selection of up to 45 channels of movies, comedy, news, music and drama, Nintendo and classic PC games. They also receive an amenity kit which includes a headset to keep after the flight, complimentary drinks, and a choice of three entrées with meals.

Recent Developments

In recent years, Virgin Atlantic has gone from strength to strength, extending its network of routes around the world and capturing market share from the leading players in the industry. A partnership agreement was signed with Malaysia Airlines in 1995 to provide a double daily scheduled service from London to Kuala Lumpur and a daily service onward to Australia. Virgin Atlantic also operates a codeshare partnership with Continental Airlines on all Virgin Atlantic's flights to and from the US.

Virgin Atlantic is the launch customer of Airbus' new A340-600 due for delivery in 2002.

Promotion

The greatest advertisement for Virgin is probably Richard Branson. Virgin's brand values emanate from his personality. Branson is often perceived as the consumer's hero, an entrepreneur operating in a style all of his own.

In addition to his status as one of Britain's most admired businessmen, Branson's daredevil antics, such as ballooning across the Atlantic, have given the Virgin brand additional publicity. He also keeps a shrewd eye on promotional opportunities. When he heard of British Airways' decision to remove the Union Jack from their plane exteriors, for example, he capitalised on the change by introducing the Union Jack onto Virgin planes.

Virgin Atlantic has proved an astute advertiser over the years. Its logo is highlighted on all its goods and services and is a highly protected property. Virgin Atlantic has implemented an integrated media strategy to promote its brands, including television, newspapers, posters, promotions and direct mail.

The most recent TV and cinema advertising campaign featuring the 'Grim Reaper' is aimed at independent younger travellers and promotes the experience of flying Virgin and living life to the full. It has won numerous marketing awards and creative accolades for being a very 'non airline' airline ad. Awards won include a Golden Lion in the Travel, Transport and Tourism category at the Cannes International Advertising Festival; a Silver in the British TV Advertising Awards, a Solis award for Travel & Air Transport TV at the International Tourism & Leisure Festival. It was also the winner of the Travel

category in the London International Advertising Awards.

In addition, a selection of strip advertisements, emphasising Virgin Atlantic's Upper Class services and comfortable facilities, have featured in the UK press and have won several leading marketing awards.

In 1997 Virgin Atlantic countered BA's and Sainsbury's half price flights promotion by taking full page ads in the national press over a four day period with a less restricted offer. It resulted in over £3 million worth of bookings.

The company also ran a 'route network' outdoor ad campaign utilising 96 sheet posters and London taxi sides in one month bursts per quarter over 12 months. This boosted awareness of routes flown by Virgin by up to 19%.

Brand Values

Virgin Atlantic strives to provide the best possible service at the best possible value.

It is a distinctive, fun-loving and innovative brand which is admired for its intelligence and integrity. Judging from the results of a poll conducted by research agency NOP, the public also associates it with friendliness and high quality.

The Market

Visa is the leading financial services brand in the world according to Interbrand. At the end of 1997, more than 640 million Visa cards had been issued worldwide. The market for general purpose cards which includes Amex, JCB, Mastercard and Diners Club totalled $US 2.0 trillion in 1997, with 1.2 billion cards in circulation. Visa cards are the most widely-held and most widely used cards around the globe - the closest thing to a universal currency. Visa's declared aim is to replace traditional cash and cheques as preferred forms of payment. In fact, in the year ending December 1997, Visa International's EU Region's cardholder spending increased by 24 per cent to $392.2 billion whilst Visa's worldwide sales totalled a staggering $US 1.2 trillion.

Achievements

Over the last 20 years, consumer preference for Visa has begun to change payment habits. As a payment method, the Visa brand reassures consumers that they have a payment facility that enables them to purchase anything - from everyday groceries to TV sets or an annual holiday.

Visa's global computer and telecommunications network, VisaNet, is the world's leading consumer payment processing system. VisaNet provides electronic authorisation and transmits clearing and settlement data for member financial institutions around the world. It handled more than 18 billion transactions in the year ending December 1997 - and at peak processed 2400 transactions a second.

History

Visa traces its history back to 1958 when the Bank of America started its BankAmericard program. In the mid-1960s, the Bank of America began to license banks in the US to issue its Blue, White and Gold BankAmericard.

In 1970, US banks issuing BankAmericard formed a new membership corporation, National BankAmericard Inc, which they owned, to administer the program in the US.

In 1974, an international company, IBANCO Ltd, was formed by Bank of America's International licensees to administer the programme outside the US. The Blue, White and Gold system took on a single international identity in 1977 and adopted the name 'Visa'. It was the first common identity for multi-bank recognition, acceptance and interchange of value. IBANCO Ltd became Visa International Inc and National BankAmericard Inc became Visa USA Inc.

Visa International is a membership organisation of 21,000 financial institutions worldwide, providing the products and systems which make up one of the world's leading brands. Visa International's declared aim is to help its member financial institutions enhance their competitive strengths by: being the overwhelmingly preferred payment brand; by offering a broad range of product functions; by providing the best global system of information interchange in the world and by positioning Visa to be a major player in setting the standards and rules in a transitional environment - for example, as the European single currency is introduced.

Visa International's global strategy is determined by its international board whose members are drawn from six autonomous regional boards. The six regions are Asia Pacific, Canada, Central and Eastern Europe, Middle East and Africa (CEMEA), the European Union, Latin America and the US.

Financial institutions, such as banks and savings banks, are eligible for Visa membership if they are organised under banking law and recognised by their national central banks as offering accounts from which any or all of the money on deposit can be withdrawn on demand. Member institutions can issue Visa cards to their customers,

making their own decisions about pricing and marketing and signing up and providing services to merchants (eg retailers, hotels) to accept Visa cards.

The Product

Visa cards are accepted at over 15 million locations worldwide. More than 178,300 ATM dispensers in Europe now accept Visa and over 400,000 worldwide.

Recent Developments

In 1995, Visa International formed two new regions: Visa EU - a European Union region covering existing EU members, the European Free Trade Area, Turkey, Israel, Cyprus and Malta - and Visa's Central and Eastern Europe Middle East and Africa region. Visa EU gives Visa members in these well-established markets the group strength to play a major role in building the European payments system. In 1997, the number of Visa EU cardholders increased by 15% to 117.9 million.

Visa Cash, Visa's chip card alternative to small change, was first used publicly in 1995. The product has been widely tested around the world, both as an addition to existing Visa cards and as a stand alone card. Cardholders can replenish the value on their cards by transferring money either from their bank account or credit

One of the most recognised and emotive symbols in the world, the Olympic Rings, provides the greatest brand enhancement opportunity associated with any sporting or cultural event. Through Visa's sponsorship, Visa Members can directly harness this power as well as the prestige and goodwill associated with the games to enhance their own brand image through local marketing campaigns. Members are able to create their own unique Olympic Visa card, for example.

Visa's past Olympic partnership has included three Olympic Summer Games (Seoul, Barcelona and Atlanta) and four Olympic Winter Games (Calgary, Albertville, Lillehammer and Nagano). Since 1986, Visa Members have issued more than 15 million Olympic-themed Visa cards worldwide. Visa and its Members have made significant financial contributions to Olympic hopefuls as well, providing nearly £10 million pounds to Olympic teams worldwide. These donations help athletes receive better training opportunities and facilities.

The Atlanta Olympic Games in 1996 generated positive results for many Visa Members. In February 1998, Visa was once again at the Olympics in Nagano, Japan. Visa and its Members developed a range of Olympic-themed promotions, competitions and incentive programmes to drive specific business objectives.

Visa will also be in Sydney for the Millenium Games in September 2000. The event is already on track for attracting intense media coverage as well as considerable interest from an enthusiastic worldwide public, enticed by the dual appeal of the historic games and a popular destination.

In 1996, Visa launched a new international advertising campaign in 11 countries in Europe. The executional idea shows the 'Visa Family' using their Visa card in everyday situations using scenarios based on family life. It therefore encourages consumers to think about using Visa whenever they are making a payment; feel that with Visa they are in control; and extend the habit and use Visa as an automatic choice.

It is a promotional vehicle that has proved popular amongst consumers, and has delivered in terms of increasing consumer awareness and preference for Visa. In six markets across Europe where the effectiveness of the Visa Family was researched, both brand awareness and preference for Visa increased significantly.

Visa has also been able to prove that integrated brand communications are actually driving usage of Visa cards across Europe. An econometric model has been developed that isolates the factors influencing card usage - for example economic factors, advertising and new card issuance - and quantifies their effect.

This has shown that in 1996, an extra 2.2 transactions per card (in Italy, where the model was initially run) are directly attributable to Visa's advertising.

Visa is advertised throughout Europe under the campaign strapline: "Making life easier".

Brand Values

Visa is the leading financial services brand in the world - a brand that stands not just for the quality of its product but the levels of service experienced by its customers. Visa has the highest awareness and consumer preference of any major payment brand both globally and within the EU region, according to research commissioned by Visa.

card at special loading machines in shopping centres, car parks and bank branches. There are now more than eight million Visa Cash cards in use in over 20 countries around the world.

Visa is also leading the way in facilitating chip card payments on the Internet and in introducing security protocols to make the Internet safe for payment cards.

Promotion

Visa supports its brand through a range of advertising, sponsorship and promotional activities of which the most prestigious is its association with the Olympic Games. The Olympics is the world's biggest and best known sporting event which regularly attracts a cumulative global TV audience of more than 20 billion with a broader demographic appeal than any other sporting event. The Olympic Games provide Visa with a powerful marketing platform on which a broad range of activities are built, including advertising and promotions run globally, regionally and nationally.

Visa is one of just 11 worldwide companies to participate in The Olympic Partner Programme, alongside Coca-Cola, IBM, Kodak, Panasonic and McDonald's. These companies know that consumers trust organisations that sponsor the Olympics and equate this sponsorship with industry leadership and excellence. For Visa, the Olympics deliver not only strong image benefits but also significant financial rewards in terms of increased Visa card transaction volume. The association also provides a showcase for Visa's products and services.

WORLDWIDE PARTNER

The Market

The savoury snacks market is dominated by potato crisps, which represent over 55% of volume while other savoury snacks, nuts, corn products and baked snacks make up the remainder. They are an integral part of everyday life in Britain - an astonishing 1.8 million bags are eaten every hour.

Small wonder, then, that the market is growing at an average of 5% per year.

Achievements

Walkers Snack Foods dominates the £2.2 billion pound salty snack business - with over 40% market share - through a combination of product quality, clear branding and strong advertising. Its brands include Doritos, Quavers, Monster Munch and French Fries and, of course, Walkers Crisps - the UK's favourite food brand and the country's second favourite FMCG brand after Coca-Cola (Marketing Week/AC Nielsen, June 1997).

The secret to Walkers' success is superior quality - every bag, every bite. To maintain this level of quality, a dedicated team ensures that not only are Walkers crisps golden in colour, but that the potatoes are the right size and freshness. Every year, Walkers invests millions of pounds in technology. The company is responsible for a number of innovations. It was the first brand to move into foil packaging and to introduce a process known as 'locked in freshness' to ensure that the crisps taste even fresher. Walkers consistently beats its nearest competitors 60:40 in taste challenges. The Walkers manufacturing system is accredited under ISO 9002 and audited by Lloyds Register Quality Assurance.

The well-known advertisements featuring Gary Lineker, first aired in January 1995, have proven to be amongst its most memorable work in recent years. This campaign also helped Walkers Crisps win the ITV/Marketing Week Brand of the Year award in both 1995 and 1996.

History

Crisps were invented in 1853 by a chef at the Moonlake Hotel in Sarasota Springs in the US. They reached Britain some years later when Frank Smith, a grocery shop manager, started the first commercial production. Smith heard about a new way of cooking potatoes in the early 1900s and began experimenting with different slice thicknesses and frying times. He opened his first business in 1920 in a north London garage, distributing his product in open grease proofed bags by cycling around the neighbourhood. When he discovered that his customers liked salt on their crisps he began adding it in a twist of blue paper. Crisps had arrived in Britain!

Walkers' involvement with crisps began later. In the 1880s, one Henry Walker opened a pork butchery business in Leicester. The firm flourished but the Second World War brought problems for Walkers due to food shortages and rationing. By 1948, Walker's shops were sold out by 10.00am each day, and the company was looking for something else for its workforce to do. It finally selected crisps, which were very popular with the public and not subject to rationing. At first, potatoes were cut by hand, fried in a small chip shop fryer and salt was sprinkled on top. Business boomed, and automation followed in the 1950s.

Walkers is part of the PepsiCo organisation and employs over 4,000 people in the UK alone. Today, Walkers Crisps are still made in Leicester but rapid growth has meant that further factories have opened in Peterlee in the north east and Swansea in Wales. Walkers celebrated its 50th anniversary in 1998.

The Product

Crisps are better for us than we may imagine. Research by the Department of Nutrition and Food Services at King's College London found that crisps are high in carbohydrate and dietary fibre, the vegetable oil is high in polyunsaturates and there are significant amounts of protein. The fat they contain is vegetable oil, with no cholesterol and relatively low levels of saturated fat.

Walkers Crisps are available in thirteen different flavours. The company also makes Walkers Crinkles and H Walker Originals.

Recent Developments

Walkers has introduced new products and variants to constantly support the brand. In 1997, Walkers introduced its new lower fat crisps, Walkers Lites. Lites were launched in response to a growing trend among UK consumers for healthier eating. Positioned as 'better for you crisps', these have 25% less fat than the standard variety. The company's unique technology means that Walkers Lites are lighter and tastier than other low fat crisps already on the market.

Other developments include the launch of two new flavours, Barbecue and Cheese and Chives crisps.

However, Walkers Snack Foods has not simply concentrated on potatoes. Walkers Doritos were launched in May 1994 and within a year had quadrupled the size of the UK corn snack market. Doritos are available in three flavours - Tangy Cheese, Cool Original and Sizzlin' Barbecue. 1997 saw the national launch of French Fries.

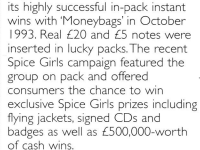

Television's London Tonight.

Product promotions are also important. Walkers first launched its highly successful in-pack instant wins with 'Moneybags' in October 1993. Real £20 and £5 notes were inserted in lucky packs. The recent Spice Girls campaign featured the group on pack and offered consumers the chance to win exclusive Spice Girls prizes including flying jackets, signed CDs and badges as well as £500,000-worth of cash wins.

Savoury snacks are often an impulse buy, so good in-store merchandising is essential. All Walkers consumer activities are supported by point of sale material to reinforce all other forms of communication used.

Walkers also invests money in the category as a whole, working alongside retailers of all sizes to ensure snacks gain the visibility needed to drive sales.

Brand Values

Walkers Crisps are a simple pleasure in life which everyone can enjoy. They are Britain's best-loved crisps. Although producing really fresh, good quality crisps is very important, Walkers doesn't take itself too seriously - the company believes crisps should be fun!

Promotion

To continue growing a brand the size of Walkers at its current rate requires massive investment and continuous innovation. This commitment is demonstrated by the hugely successful Gary Lineker TV advertising campaign.

The 'No More Mr Nice Guy' ads feature the famous football star turned presenter in a new guise. Walkers' choice of Gary Lineker - an ex-Leicester City player as well as one of Britain's favourite celebrities - ties in with Walkers 'favourite brand' status, its Leicester-based heritage and its sponsorship of Leicester City Football Club. One recent commercial in the series featured successful girl band The Spice Girls eating Walkers Crisps.

TV is an important medium for Walkers' mass market communications. The company supports its above the line advertising, however, with a variety of other activities to reach the broadest possible audience. One of Walkers' declared objectives is to grow the total salty snacks market. To achieve this, Walkers works hard to create 'product news'. New flavours and new products - such as Cheese & Chives

and Walkers Lites - add interest and variety for the consumer.

PR is another important activity. Celebrities such as Gary Lineker and the Spice Girls generate additional media interest. The Salt and Lineker campaign in 1996 featuring Paul Gascoigne won the Consumer PR Campaign award for 1997. The launch of Walkers Barbecue flavour scored a PR first when it prompted articles on the front and back pages of The Sun on two consecutive days. The Spice Girls instant win promotion in 1997 generated the highest ever number of PR TV appearances, including Channel 4's The Big Breakfast and Carlton

Things you didn't know about Walkers

Crisps were invented by a chef called George Crum.

Walkers Crisps are Britain's most popular food brand.

10.5 million packets of Walkers Crisps are sold everyday.

There are 13 different Walkers Crisps flavours.

Gary Lineker's favourite flavour is Salt & Vinegar.

Research shows that when asked about crisps, Walkers Crisps is the first name consumers have in mind.

More people have tried Walkers Crisps than any other brand of crisps or snacks (90% adults and 80% children- Millward Brown International).

Walkers Crisps can be bought in more than 400,000 outlets throughout the UK.

A packet of Walkers Crisps contains more Vitamin C than an apple.

WEDGWOOD
ENGLAND 1759

The Market

The market for premium china and crystal is highly competitive. Wedgwood and its rivals, including Royal Doulton and Royal Copenhagen, all target affluent upmarket consumers who appreciate the finer things in life. Wedgwood has a long history of providing consumers with dinner services and ornamental ware but has now repositioned itself as a supplier of a wide range of luxury goods from china and crystal to linens and gourmet foods. It therefore also competes with brands such as Ralph Lauren Homeware and Mulberry.

Wedgwood, together with its sister companies Waterford Crystal and now Rosenthal, is part of the largest premium ceramics and crystal company in the world with a strong presence in the major trading blocs.

Achievements

Building on a long tradition of designing and producing quality products, Wedgwood, Waterford Crystal and Rosenthal now form part of an international business selling world class luxury goods. Both Waterford and Wedgwood have expanded into new categories while taking market share from competitors through their strength in design, quality and distribution.

1997 was a record year for the company. Sales increased by 11% to £417.2 million - an all time high. The crystal market is particularly strong in North America where Waterford increased its market share from 40% in 1996 to 43% in 1997. The US market produced double digit growth, with a 17% sales increase year on year. In Japan, meanwhile, Wedgwood sales were up by 8% in the same period, despite the difficult trading conditions in Asia Pacific.

The company has also made inroads into new market sectors, including writing instruments, cutlery, linens and lightingware.

History

Wedgwood was founded by Josiah Wedgwood, 'Father of English Potters', in 1759. His first big success - and perhaps the greatest contribution to the British pottery industry - was to perfect the production and glazing of the first cream-coloured earthenware. Later called Queen's Ware by Royal assent of Queen Charlotte in 1765, this versatile, accessible earthenware put fine, beautiful tableware within reach of a much wider range of consumers. Wedgwood's most famous commission in Queen's Ware was a 952 piece dinner and dessert service for Empress Catherine the Great of Russia which featured free-hand paintings of 1,244 different English scenes.

Although Wedgwood manufactured ornamental ware such as vases, by 1768 he had developed a fine-grained, black stone ware body which he christened 'Black Basalt'. This was highly suitable for producing prestige wares and has been popular through three centuries. It is used for vases, busts and cameos.

After years of searching for the right ingredients and several thousand experiments, Wedgwood created Jasper - a stone ware body which could be coloured throughout its entire medium. Jasper was prized by Wedgwood above all his creations and until his death in 1795, he devoted much of his energy to producing a range of pieces from cameos to portrait medallions to chessmen and candlesticks in many different colours.

Jasper has been produced by Wedgwood in Stoke-on-Trent for more than 200 years and although today's Jasper is produced using streamlined production techniques, in essence the methods used are the same as those developed by Josiah Wedgwood I - with every bas-relief decoration applied by hand.

The Wedgwood factory first produced bone china in the early years of the 19th Century. This contains 51% calcined animal bone plus china stone and china clay. It is the bone, reduced to a fine ash, which gives bone china its whiteness, its translucency and above all its incredible strength. In fact, it is so strong that four coffee cups will support a Rolls-Royce car and a 15.5 ton JCB earth mover could stand on eight coffee cups!

Since the beginning of the twentieth century, bone china has become Wedgwood's main product and in the past thirty years the design and manufacture of bone china has been considerably enhanced and combines the latest in technology with craft skills. In 1986 Wedgwood merged with the Irish crystal producer Waterford and has attracted an ever growing number of customers from overseas with its wider range of products. In 1995, the group acquired English crystal manufacturer Stuart Crystal and, in 1997, took a majority stake in Rosenthal, Germany's premium porcelain brand.

The Product

Wedgwood supplies premium formal tableware, casual tabletop products including crystal, ceramic giftware and what it describes as 'home accessories' - collectibles and figurines. Its target market is affluent, upmarket connoisseurs of the finer things in life.

The strength of the Wedgwood, Waterford and Rosenthal brands, at home and abroad, has enabled the company to pursue developments in product sectors outside the core crystal and ceramics ranges as it moves towards luxury brand status.

The Waterford brand name has now been extended to Waterford writing instruments, crystal lamps, table linen and even a range of crystal ware created by the internationally renowned Irish fashion designer John Rocha. The Wedgwood name, meanwhile, has been applied by licensed manufacturers to leather accessories, silk handkerchiefs and even gourmet foods as the company leverages the brands

WEDGWOOD
ENGLAND 1759

The other side of English elegance

For a brochure and stockists call 0800 317412.

from its traditional business to the broader luxury gift business - particularly in the all important Japanese market.

However, the heart of the Wedgwood business remains fine bone china tableware. Wedgwood currently uses about one hundred different designs to produce its distinctive English ceramic ware - some designs, such as 'Parnassians,' are exclusive to the Japanese market.

Recent Developments

Wedgwood and its allied brands, Waterford and Rosenthal, have moved firmly into the luxury gifts market and have developed a strong market for the brands in Japan, the US and Continental Europe. In Japan, Wedgwood tableware is often given as a prestigious gift and this gift giving phenomenon has opened up new opportunities for the company such as Wedgwood-branded tea, coffee and linen.

The company sells its products through Duty Free outlets around the world. This retail environment allows it to promote brand extensions such as leather goods and gourmet food as well as its classic crystal and china to the gift buying consumer.

Another important area for the company is the growth of 'hotel ware' with a range of products for the world's finest hotels and restaurants.

To keep in contact with existing and potential customers, Wedgwood has launched an Internet site. This provides information on Wedgwood's products and history and the company receives around 30 e-mails a day with requests for brochures and further information. The most commonly visited pages are tableware and gift ideas. The Internet site was redesigned in 1998 to incorporate more information and will be continually updated to encourage people to revisit it on a regular basis.

Wedgwood has established links with Brunel University to further its reputation as a highly innovative company. Brunel is working on studies related to design innovation in corporate situations. Wedgwood's design teams also work with external product

designers to get cross pollination of ideas, experience and work methods.

In spring 1998, Wedgwood announced plans to make its products 'younger and more contemporary' to appeal to a new generation of consumers.

Promotion

In 1997, Wedgwood carried out extensive international consumer research which revealed that consumers' understanding of the brand had not kept pace with the reality of Wedgwood's product offering. Consumers do not associate Wedgwood with its core product range - china tableware. The research did, however, confirm Wedgwood as a household name with clear and strong associations with quality craftsmanship, premium value and a reputation for making 'very beautiful, special' items.

Wedgwood therefore decided to invest in a major new advertising strategy designed to bring consumer attention back to the heart of the Wedgwood brand - Wedgwood premium tableware. The campaign was also designed to surprise consumers with its relevance to contemporary lifestyles. The message was clear: Wedgwood remains as beautiful and special as ever, but that doesn't have to mean it is kept in a cupboard and only used for Sunday best.

Brand Values

Wedgwood is quintessentially English. It has a tradition of innovation quality and craftsmanship and its designs are widely acknowledged as timeless, elegant, classic and understated. The company philosophy is that its products are not only a pleasure to be enjoyed today, but are also a treasure for the future - many consumers buy Wedgwood to be handed down as a family heirloom. It is a premium product and is summed up by Wedgwood as: 'English elegance at home'.

Things you didn't know about
Wedgwood

A cup handler aided by machine can apply up to 1,500 handles a day.

The largest dinner service ever supplied was a 47,000 piece banqueting service delivered to the Kremlin in 1995.

Every second, every hour of every day a Wedgwood cup and saucer is sold somewhere in the world - that's four million a year.

Craftspeople at Wedgwood's Barlaston factory alone produce 300,000 pieces a week - that's 43 million individual pieces per year from the Wedgwood Group factories.

During the Second World War the decoration of ware was banned for the home market so the Wedgwood factory made utility (undecorated) ware and munitions. It continued to produce patterned wares for export to the US however, generating crucial revenue for the company.

The feel of SmartDesign™

The Market

Around 22 million people in the UK regularly wet shave - that's around 70 per cent of all male shavers and twice the number of those who prefer to dry shave regularly. This adds up to an estimated 500 million blades used by British male shavers each year. The women's market, however, is also significant. Today, women have a 12.2% share of the wet shaving market - equivalent to sales of £30 million in 1997.

The UK wet shaving market was worth £249 million in 1997 - up 8.5% on the previous year. Business is split between refill razor blades and disposable razors, worth £165 million and razor handles worth £18 million (in 1997). In addition, sales of shaving preparations were worth £66 million.

A number of key technological developments have shaped the market over recent years. In the 1960s, carbon steel blades were dominant. By the 1970s, however, the first systems products were introduced (razor handles and refill blades). The 1980s was the disposables decade. By the 1990s, however, specialist systems razors dominated and a new category of female specific razors was established.

Achievements

In recent years, Wilkinson Sword's products have won many industry awards including the FHM 'Best Male Grooming Product' in 1995/6 for the FX Performer. The same product was also highly commended in the New Woman 'Best Male Grooming Product' in 1996. Wilkinson Sword was again highly commended in the New Woman Awards for 'Best Beauty Appliance' in 1997 for its Extra II for Women premium twin disposable razor.

Wilkinson Sword is the only UK razor blade manufacturer to achieve the BS5750 quality standard, demonstrating its total commitment to delivering the best possible product to its consumers.

History

Wilkinson Sword's origins date back over 200 years. The company's founder, Henry Nock, set up the business in 1772. An acclaimed gun maker, Nock already had premises in the City of London on Ludgate Street and workshops nearby. In 1804, Wilkinson Sword received the First Royal appointment to HM King George III, as Royal Gun Maker.

James Wilkinson was one of Nock's apprentices and subsequently his partner.

On Nock's death in 1805, Wilkinson inherited the business. His son, Henry Wilkinson, subsequently moved the company to Pall Mall and extended the company's business from bayonet-making to sword-manufacturing. In 1877, the company moved once more - expanding into bigger premises in Chelsea. In 1879, the business was established as a private company called The Wilkinson Sword Co Ltd.

From the 1890s onwards, Wilkinson Sword steadily expanded its product range. By the turn of the century, over 5,000 products were sold from the company's Pall Mall showroom, ranging from bayonets and swords to cut-throat razors and the revolutionary Wilkinson Sword safety razors which were introduced in 1898.

Armaments were a key part of the business during the First World War. Afterwards, however, Wilkinson Sword introduced its first gardening products and resumed razor production which had been halted for the war effort. One of the company's most famous products, the Empire Razor, was launched in 1929.

The Second World War once more shifted the company's focus onto the war effort. Wilkinson Sword manufactured aircraft fire protection systems, commando knives and armoured clothing, including the famous Flak jacket used widely by US Army and Air Force personnel.

An anticipated return to razor production after the war was thwarted temporarily by a brass shortage. To bridge the shortfall, the company expanded its garden tools range before resuming razor production and developing the first stainless steel blade for the double edged market in 1956. This proved a turning point for the company. Building on its success, Wilkinson Sword subsequently focused on razors and worked to extend its product range.

In January 1972 - the company's bicentenary - it received armorial bearings from the Royal College of Arms with the motto 'Semper qualities suprema' ('Always the finest quality').

The Product

In 1970, Wilkinson Sword brought out the world's first fixed geometry systems razor - Bonded. In 1983, it was first again with a disposable razor which had retractable blades. In 1992, Wilkinson Sword launched Protector, the first systems razor to use wire-wrapped blades for enhanced safety and FX Performer - the first razor featuring flexible blades - was introduced in 1995. In 1998, the company unveiled Protector 3D - the first Systems razor offering three dimensional movement thanks to a

unique double-axis which allows the blade cartridge to move back and forth and side to side.

All Wilkinson Sword razor blades are designed to produce a fine quality tip known as the Gothic Arch section which is viewed as stronger and more durable than the more common straight sided shape used by other razor blade manufacturers. The result is prolonged blade life.

Recent Developments

For 200 years, Wilkinson Sword has been associated with the motto: 'The name on the world's finest blades'. This has been an excellent strapline for a manufacturer of such diverse products as ceremonial military swords, garden tools and razor blades. However, by 1997 the company was ready to undertake a global corporate repositioning exercise, which included the modernisation of its strapline to 'the feel of SmartDesign'.

Its new ethos reflects the contemporary properties associated with the company's blade technology and the unique consumer benefits delivered by the products' design. The focus is on the senses - how the razors feel to hold, what the skin looks and feels like once shaved, and the sense of well-being associated with using the product. Wilkinson Sword's 'Smart Design' positioning conveys the ability for its stylishly designed, technologically-advanced products to deliver tangible benefits to both its consumers and trade constituencies.

In April 1998, Wilkinson Sword launched Protector 3D (shown below), a ground-breaking razor guaranteeing a closer and safer shave with less skin irritation. Protector 3D incorporates intelligently designed elements that give the razor added flexibility to hug the contours of the face.

Protector 3D's first dimension is inherent in the current Protector razor - its pivoting blade cartridge. The second dimension is provided by twin blades which move independently to the cartridge. The third dimension is a technological breakthrough in cartridge mobility. Not only does the cartridge

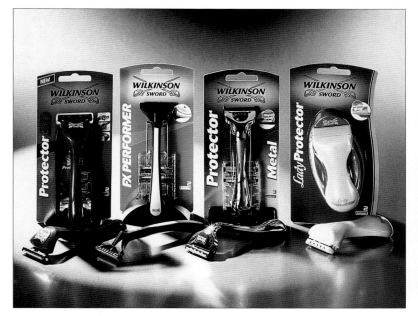

pivot, but it also moves from left to right, ensuring optimum flexibility and closeness to the skin. These three dimensions work in conjunction with 25% thinner guardwires and an enlarged Aquaglide strip to deliver a shave which is both safer, closer and less irritating and ensures that users achieve all this with the minimum number of shaving strokes over the skin.

Another innovation from Wilkinson Sword - FX Performer - incorporates totally flexible blades, a soft Skin Guard™ to stretch the skin and cushion the impact of the blades, and a lubricating strip with vitamin E and Aloe Vera to soothe the skin and reduce razor burn. FX Performer was recently updated and now has an ergonomically designed handle featuring rubber grips to give exceptional handling and control.

In March 1998, Wilkinson Sword launched two ranges of premium toiletries under the Protector and Performer brand names, each one specially formulated for either sensitive or normal/dry skin. The Protector range includes shaving Gel, Foam, After Shave Creme and Deodorant Body Spray while the Performer range of premium toiletries includes a 200ml Gel and 250ml Foam.

Wilkinson Sword's female specific super systems razor - Lady Protector - offers both safety and closeness through its smart design. Lady Protector features unique blade guardwires wrapped around twin blades to reduce the risk of nicks and cuts. The razor also has a pivoting head, ensuring that the blades are always at the best shaving angle to the skin, and an Aquaglide strip to give a smooth shave. Lady Protector Gels, Foams and After Care Creme for both sensitive and dry skin types complete the shaving experience.

Promotion

Wilkinson Sword's products are heavily supported by a range of marketing initiatives. There has been significant investment by the company in its new, innovative systems razors - the FX Performer and Protector 3D - from high impact television advertising campaigns to in-store promotional support via price-marked packs and trial razors.

Wilkinson Sword also places great emphasis on sampling its razors to consumers; an activity that plays a key role in actively communicating the unique benefits of each specific razor. Recent sampling activities have included retailer promotions for FX Performer (with men's fashion retailer, Ciro Citterio) and Lady Protector (with Sock Shop), sampling of Extra II in HMV stores and via sponsorship of the Mike Fab Gere University Tour, and sponsorship of the Youth Clubs UK night club tour where Lady Protector and Protector razors were distributed to members.

Brand Values

As part of the Warner Lambert group of companies, Wilkinson Sword contributes to a global organisation with an $8 billion annual sales turnover. The Group employs 40,000 colleagues worldwide and has an enviable reputation for R&D investment.

Wilkinson Sword manufactures products which are intelligently designed to meet the specific needs of men and women around the world. The brand name has an enviable heritage and is renowned for its focus on design, quality and cutting-edge technology. Wilkinson Sword's 'the feel of SmartDesign' is a key element of Warner Lambert's ethos: 'we're making the world feel better'.

Things you didn't know about
Wilkinson Sword

Henry Nock, the company's founder, was England's leading gun maker in the 1770's. He produced many types of guns, including sporting guns and rifles, pistols, military weapons and the unique and renowned seven barrelled shotgun.

In the 1880s a letter appeared on the front page of The Times stating that British soldiers were losing their lives in the Sudan as a result of being armed with inferior swords supplied by foreign companies. The letter went on to say that if our loyal British lads were supplied with Wilkinson Swords, this would never have happened.

At the turn of the 20th century, Wilkinson diversified into a number of non shaving related areas such as typewriters, bicycles, motor cars and motor cycles. The common factor was that each was the very best quality and design available at the time.

Many of the ideas incorporated in the design of the Series 5 Touring Motor Cycle were so advanced that they were only generally accepted many years later. Innovative ideas on the motor cycle included rear springing, a water cooled engine, shaft drive and internally expanding brakes. Customers had the choice of handlebars or a steering wheel!

Wilkinson Sword produced 2.5 million bayonets during the First World War.

Today, the company is one of the 100 oldest in the UK.

The company continues to produce ceremonial swords for use by military ranks, worldwide.

The fastest barber on record is Dannie Rowe who shaved 1,994 men in just one hour using a Wilkinson Sword Retractor razor in 1988. This record remains unbeaten.

The Market

"Where is the wisdom we have lost in knowledge? Where is the knowledge we have lost in information?"
T.S Eliot, The Rock

If there is a theme to the twentieth century, it is information. From the secrets of DNA to the infinite breadth of the Internet, it is information that challenges, changes and shapes our lives. And as information becomes ever more available, it is vital to distil it to a useful form.

Pub and restaurant guides, share price information, train times, cinema guides, houses for sale, company reports, tourist information, sports results, lonely hearts columns - if there is something you need to know, you can guarantee that someone, somewhere is compiling it. It is in this context that YELLOW PAGES operates as both a provider and distiller of information.

In the age of new media, YELLOW PAGES is developing new ways of disseminating information, but the brand is best known as the leading provider of directories in the UK. The directories business was recently estimated to be worth around £800 million and its dynamic growth reflects the increased use of the telephone as a medium for sales and customer service in the 1990s.

Achievements

From its national launch in 1966, YELLOW PAGES has grown to be the leading directory brand in the UK. Some 28,000,000 directories are distributed to homes and businesses across the country. UK households receive a new YELLOW PAGES directory every year.

With such a high level of penetration, YELLOW PAGES represents a crucial source of new business for companies nationwide. More than 350,000 advertisers place over 650,000 advertisements in YELLOW PAGES to promote their goods and services (Source: YELLOW PAGES Sales Data). And because all companies with a business telephone line are eligible for a discretionary free 'line' entry, there are about 2.5 million entries nationwide.

Over 50% of adults refer to YELLOW PAGES every month which means that the directory is used over 100 million times in any given month. (Sources: TGI and Taylor Nelson 1996/97).

History

Although directories are closely associated with telephone usage, they actually pre-date Alexander Graham Bell's invention by a couple of centuries. The first directories can be traced back to Elizabethan times when street directories were published detailing the names and addresses of residential and business addresses in a given area. By the 1840s, Kelly's London Post Office directories began to emerge.

The arrival of the telecommunications era offered further potential for the publishers of directories. In 1966, the General Post Office, which was the controller of most UK telephony at the time, introduced and developed YELLOW PAGES as a national business. Its first YELLOW PAGES was launched in Brighton. In the early years it was bound into the standard telephone directories.

By the mid 1970s, YELLOW PAGES had attained almost 100% coverage nationwide and existed as a stand alone product in its own right. YELLOW PAGES became a registered trademark in the UK in 1979.

The Product

YELLOW PAGES is the UK's most comprehensive business information directory. It is designed to give consumers easy access to a supplier capable of meeting their needs. There are 74 directories covering virtually every geographical area in the UK and they give over 1,800,000 businesses access to 28,000,000 homes and commercial premises nationwide.

In keeping with its advertising message that YELLOW PAGES is "not just for the nasty things in life", only a small proportion of advertisers are 'emergency' businesses such as plumbers and glaziers. Advertisers have the option to buy advertising space in any of the YELLOW PAGES directories and to place ads in a range of sizes in any of the 2,500 classifications available. So, from abattoirs to zoos, YELLOW PAGES has the capability to meet most advertisers' needs, no matter how unusual.

As well as the classified section, each YELLOW PAGES also contains preface information with a local focus, such as town centre maps. Product innovation of this type will continue to play a major part in the future development of the directories. The 'Inside Guides,' which can now be found in a number of the London YELLOW PAGES and other cities which provide ideas for things to do in the area are part of a move to make YELLOW PAGES more than just a directory.

Central to the success of YELLOW PAGES is the fact that the more people use YELLOW PAGES, the more shops and businesses buy advertising space and this in turn increases the value of the directory to users.

Recent Developments

By being sensitive to developments in technology and changing customer needs, YELLOW PAGES has continued to refine and improve its core directory product and extend into new areas.

Recent brand extensions include: Business Pages, a specialist directory covering businesses that supply goods and services to other businesses; Talking Pages - a 24 hour freephone line providing up to date details on businesses, shops and services

throughout the UK; and Yell, the YELLOW PAGES Web site. Yell is made up of three key services - the UK Yellow Web which summarises nearly 3,000 UK Web sites, Film Finder detailing what's on and when, at over 400 UK cinemas and Electronic YELLOW PAGES.

http://www.yell.co.uk

All these brand extensions are intended to maintain YELLOW PAGES' status as a leading information provider well into the next century.

Promotion

YELLOW PAGES has always recognised the importance of building the brand through strong advertising campaigns. The 'Let Your Fingers Do The Walking' campaign, which ran for 13 years through the 1970s and early 1980s, put YELLOW PAGES on the map.

But by 1983, YELLOW PAGES had reached a crucial stage in its development. A review of the brand highlighted that although consumers had heard of YELLOW PAGES, they had a very limited perception of the brand. It was seen as a product largely associated with unpleasant tasks such as finding a plumber or electrician in an emergency.

As a result, consumers found it difficult to attach many positive brand values to YELLOW PAGES. It was seen as a product 'best forgotten' rather than a brand 'best remembered'. The opportunity for growth lay in positioning YELLOW PAGES as something consumers turn to for all their information needs. A fundamental redesign of the product was undertaken in 1983 which included the introduction of a more consistent and striking cover design.

The 'Not just for the nasty things in life' TV campaign began with a simple premise. A man called JR Hartley uses YELLOW PAGES to find a book that he had written in his younger days. This particular execution became the starting point for one of the UK's longest running and most famous ad campaigns. A series of commercials was developed around this idea - the boy needing a French polisher to repair his parents' coffee table damaged during a riotous party, the gardener who was bought a motorised lawn mower by his employers, the ex-England football managers buying Terry Venables a cake to wish him good luck in his new job.

An indication of the popularity of the campaign was the number of comedy spin offs that it spawned. Jasper Carrot, Hale & Pace, Fry & Laurie and Spitting Image are just some of the artists who have helped shape popular perceptions of YELLOW PAGES through send-ups of the ads.

The most recent TV commercial, called 'Life', gives the brand a more youthful appeal.

It portrays momentous events in the life of a slightly nerdish hero, set to a Ramones cover version of Phil Spector's hit song 'Baby I Love You'.

This contemporary style has been extended to Yellow Pages' outdoor poster activity which includes colourful, modern images juxtaposed with Yellow Pages classifications. The campaign has also been adapted to innovative 'alternative' media including an entire branded London tube train on the Circle line.

Since 1983, YELLOW PAGES usage has increased by two-thirds. But the success of the YELLOW PAGES brand is not only reflected in usage growth. In recent tracking research, over 40% of those interviewed considered YELLOW PAGES to be 'quite a good friend' - a considerable achievement for a simple telephone directory.

Brand Values

As the UK's leading directory, YELLOW PAGES bridges the gap between buyers and suppliers. The brand plays a crucial role in people's lives - both at home and in the workplace. It is a life line to a number of businesses, which can advertise their wares and services to the large numbers of consumers who use YELLOW PAGES.

With an eye on the future, the company is now positioning itself at the cutting edge of new technology, taking advantage of new media to disseminate information.

® Registered trademark of British Telecommunications plc in the UK.

Things you didn't know about
Yellow Pages

Some 28 million YELLOW PAGES directories are distributed to homes and businesses across the country.

The book 'Fly Fishing' by JR Hartley was not written until 1991 - eight years after the commercial was first aired. It became a Christmas best-seller.

More than 350,000 advertisers place over 650,000 advertisements in YELLOW PAGES every year.

YELLOW PAGES is most often used to help people find information about the automotive, restaurant and construction sectors.

By laying a year's worth of YELLOW PAGES directories end to end, a yellow path could be built stretching from London to Beijing.

On average nearly 50 people use YELLOW PAGES every second of every day in the UK.

Directory

Abbey National
Abbey National Plc
Abbey House
201 Grafton Gate East
Milton Keynes
MK9 1AN

adidas
adidas (UK) Ltd
The Adidas Centre
PO Box 39
Pepper Road
Hazel Grove
Stockport
SK7 5SD

adidas (Ireland) Ltd
Elm House
Unit 4
Leopardstown Business Park
Sandyford Industrial Estate
Dublin 18

American Express
American Express Europe Ltd
Portland House
Stag Place
London
SW1E 5BZ

Andrex
Kimberly-Clark Ltd
1 Tower View
Kings Hill
West Malling
Kent
ME19 4HA

Audi
Audi UK
Yeomans Drive
Blakelands
Milton Keynes
MK14 5AN

Avis
Avis Rent-A-Car Ltd
Trident House
Station Road
Hayes
Middlesex
UB3 4DJ

BBC
BBC
Broadcasting House
Portland Place
London
W1A 1AA

Bell's
United Distillers and Vintners
Templefields House
River Way
Harlow
Essex
CM20 2EA

BMW
BMW (GB) Limited
Ellesfield Avenue
Bracknell
Berkshire
RG12 8TA

Boddingtons
Whitbread Beer Company
Porter Tun House
500 Capability Green
Luton
Bedfordshire
LU1 3LS

BT
BT Centre
81 Newgate Street
London
EC1A 7AJ

Budweiser
Anheuser-Busch European Trade Ltd
8 Devonshire Square
Cutlers Gardens
London
EC2M 4LP

Carlsberg
Carlsberg-Tetley Brewing Limited
107 Station Street
Burton-on-Trent
Staffordshire
DE14 1BZ

Club Med
Club Med
106 Brompton Road
London
SW3 1JJ

Coca-Cola
Coca-Cola Great Britain
Charter Place
Vine Street
Uxbridge
Middlesex
UB8 1ST

DHL
DHL International (UK) Ltd
Orbital Park
178-188 Great South West Road
Hounslow
Middlesex
TW4 6JS

Direct Line
Direct Line Group Ltd
Direct Line House
3 Edridge Road
Croydon
Surrey
CR9 1AG

First Direct
First Direct
Millshaw Park Lane
Leeds
West Yorkshire
LS98 1FD

Foster's
Scottish Courage Ltd
Fountain House
160 Dundee Street
Edinburgh
EH11 1DQ

Gillette
Gillette UK Ltd
Great West Road
Isleworth
Middlesex
TW7 5NP

Gordon's
United Distillers and Vintners
Templefields House
River Way
Harlow
Essex
CM20 2EA

Häagen-Dazs
Pillsbury UK Ltd
Harman House
1 George Street
Uxbridge
Middlesex
UB8 1QQ

Halifax
Halifax Building Society
Trinity Road
Halifax
West Yorkshire
HX1 2RG

Hamleys
Hamleys
188-196 Regent Street
London
W1R 6BT

Heineken
Whitbread Beer Company
Porter Tun House
500 Capability Green
Luton
Bedfordshire
LU1 3LS

Heinz
H J Heinz Company Ltd
Hayes Park
Hayes
Middlesex
UB4 8AL

Interflora
Interflora (British Unit) Ltd
Interflora House
Sleaford
Lincolnshire
NG34 7TB

Johnson's Baby
Johnson & Johnson UK Ltd
Foundation Park
Roxborough Way
Maidenhead
Berkshire
SL6 3UG

Kit Kat
Nestlé UK Ltd
York
YO1 1XY

Lucozade
SmithKline Beecham plc
SB House
Great West Road
Brentford
Middlesex
TW8 9BD

Macleans
SmithKline Beecham plc
SB House
Great West Road
Brentford
Middlesex
TW8 9BD

Manchester United
Manchester United Football Club
Old Trafford
Manchester
M16 0RA

McDonald's
McDonald's Restaurants Ltd
11-59 High Road
East Finchley
London
N2 8AW

McVitie's
McVitie's
The Watermans Business Park
The Causeway
Staines
Middlesex
TW18 3BA

Michelin
Michelin Tyre plc
The Edward Hyde Building
38 Clarendon Street
Watford
Herts
WD1 1SX

Mini
Rover Group Ltd
International Headquarters
Warwick Technology Park
Warwick
CV34 6RG

Moët & Chandon
Möet Hennessy UK Ltd
13 Grosvenor Crescent
London
SW1X 7EE

Mothercare
Mothercare UK Limited
Cherry Tree Road
Watford
Hertfordshire
WD2 5SH

Nikon
Nikon UK Ltd
Nikon House
380 Richmond Road
Kingston-upon-Thames
Surrey
KT2 5PR

Perrier
Perrier Vittel (UK) Limited
Trinity Court
Church Street
Rickmansworth
Hertfordshire
WD3 1LD

Persil
Lever Brothers Ltd
3 St James's Road
Kingston-Upon-Thames
Surrey
KT1 2BA

PG Tips
Van den Bergh Foods
Brooke House
Manor Royal
Crawley
West Sussex
RH10 2RQ

Philishave
Philips DAP
The Philips Centre
420-430 London Road
Croydon
CR9 3QR

Pirelli
Pirelli Tyres Limited
Derby Road
Burton-On-Trent
Staffordshire
DE13 0BH

Polo
Nestlé UK Ltd
York
YO1 1XY

Reebok
Reebok UK Ltd
Moor Lane Mill
Lancaster
Lancashire
LA1 1GF

Samsonite
Samsonite Europe N.V.
Westerring 17
B-9700
Oudenaarde
Belgium

Save the Children
The Save the Children Fund
17 Grove Lane
London
SE5 8RD

Sellotape
Sellotape GB Ltd
The Woodside Estate
Dunstable
Bedfordshire
LU5 4TP

Smarties
Nestlé UK Ltd
York
YO1 1XY

Sony
Sony Consumer Products Group
The Heights
Brooklands
Weybridge
Surrey
KT13 0XW

St Michael
Marks & Spencer Plc
Michael House
147-167 Baker Street
London
W1A 1DN

Stella Artois
Whitbread Beer Company
Porter Tun House
500 Capability Green
Luton
Bedfordshire
LU1 3LS

Tampax
Procter & Gamble Ltd
St Nicholas Avenue
Gosforth
Newcastle-upon-Tyne
Tyne and Wear
NE99 1EE

Tesco
Tesco Stores Plc
Tesco House
Delamare Road
Cheshunt
Waltham Cross
Hertfordshire
EN8 9SL

The National Lottery
Camelot Plc
Tolpits Lane
Watford
Hertfordshire
WD1 8RN

The Sun
News International Newspapers Ltd
PO Box 481
London
E1 9BD

Thomas Cook
Thomas Cook Group Ltd
Worldwide Headquarters
45 Berkeley Street
Piccadilly
London
W1A 1EB

Virgin
Virgin Group
120 Campden Hill Road
London
W8 7AR

Virgin Atlantic
Virgin Atlantic Airways Ltd
Crawley Business Quarter
Manor Royal
Crawley
West Sussex
RH10 2NU

Visa
Visa International
PO Box 253
London
W8 5TE

Walkers
Walkers Snack Foods Ltd
1600 Arlington Business Park
Theale
Reading
Berkshire
RG7 4SA

Wedgwood
Waterford Wedgwood
Barlaston
Stoke-on-Trent
ST12 9ES

Wilkinson Sword
Wilkinson Sword Ltd
Sword House
Totteridge Road
High Wycombe
Buckinghamshire
HP13 6EJ

Yellow Pages
BT Yellow Pages
Queens Walk
Reading
Berkshire
RG1 7PT